8S   3M   35-
                    0. New
$ D1036638

EVENT-CITIES 4

MIT Press books may be purchased at special quantity discounts for business or sales promotional use. For information, please email special_sales@mitpress.mit.edu or write to Special Sales Department, The MIT Press, 55 Hayward Street, Cambridge, MA 02142.

Event-Cities, published in 1994 on the occasion of Bernard Tschumi's exhibition at The Museum of Modern Art in New York, is an expanded version of *Praxis Villes-Evenements* (Le Fresnoy and Massimo Riposati, Editeurs, Paris). *Event-Cities 2* includes work from 1994 to 1999, and also features the 1982 Parc de la Villette. *Event-Cities 3* includes work from 1999 to 2004. *Event-Cities 4* gathers together projects developed by Bernard Tschumi from 2004 to 2009, as well as the 2002 Alésia MuseoParc.

Book design and production: Bernard Tschumi and Grace Robinson-Leo, with Paula Tomisaki, Nefeli Chatzimina, Kate Scott, Colin Spoelman, and Alexa Tsien-Shiang
Copy editor: Lisa Palmer
Printer: Massimo Riposati, Edizioni Carte Segrete, Rome - Italy

Library of Congress Cataloging-in-Publication Data

Tschumi, Bernard, 1944–
        Event-cities 4 : concept-form / Bernard Tschumi.
        640 p.   23 x 16,5 cm.
        Includes bibliographical references.
        ISBN 978-0-262-51241-1 (pbk. : alk. paper)
        1. Tschumi, Bernard, 1944– 2. Architecture, Modern—21st century.
        3. Architecture—Philosophy.
        I. Title. II. Title: Event-cities four : concept-form.
        NA1353.T78A35 2010
        724'.7—dc22   2010011628

Printed and bound in Italy - Grafica Ripoli for Edizioni Carte Segrete, Rome
riposati@cartesegrete.com

BERNARD TSCHUMI

EVENT-CITIES 4
Concept-Form

The MIT Press
Cambridge, Massachusetts
London, England

Acknowledgements

I wish to thank our teams at the New York and Paris offices of Bernard Tschumi Architects for the intensity of their commitment to the projects presented in this book, particularly Kim Starr and Joel Rutten with Christopher Lee, Rémy Cointet, and Kate Scott in New York and Véronique Descharrières with Jean-Jacques Hubert, Antoine Santiard, Vincent Prunier, Rémy Cointet, and Alice Dufourmantelle in Paris. The following individuals also deserve special thanks: in New York: Nefeli Chatzimina, W.Y. Frank Chen, Irene Cheng, Angela Co, Adam Dayem, William Feuerman, Phu Hoang, Matthew Hufft, Jane Kim, Dominic Leong, Athanasios Manis, V. Mitch McEwen, Ciro Miguel, Paula Tomisaki, and Francoise Akinosho, Sara Arfaian, Piyush Bajpai, Taylor Burgess, Stephanie Chaltiel, Mathieu Crabouillet, Casey Crawmer, Adrien Durrmeyer, John Eastridge, Ben Edelberg, Rychiee Espinosa, Melissa Goldman, Shai Gross, Gary He, Paul-Arthur Heller, Julien Jacquot, Sae-Hyun Kim, Alan Kusov, Sara Kwon, Adam Marcus, Kyungjune Min, Shaikha Al Mubaraki, Thad Nobuhara, Micah Roufa, Laurence Sarrazin, Matthew Stofen, Loren Supp, Danh Thai, Alexa Tsien-Shiang, Guillaume Vallotton, Amy Yang, Yang Yang, and Micheal Young. In Paris: Anais LeBrun, Joseph Battistelli, Eric Boyer, Dror Brill, Yann Le Drogo, Sarah Gould, Adrien Del Grande, and Valérie Mascunan. A special role has been that of Colin Spoelman, who has maintained the media overview of our work for the last few years, taking on an important narrative role in many of our project submissions and presentations. I also thank David Benjamin, who helped with several earlier publications.

Among consultants and associate architects, particular thanks is due to Hugh Dutton, whose remarkable talent and professional knowledge enriched the projects he participated in, especially at La Roche-sur-Yon, as well as Luca Merlini and Emmanuel Ventura for our Lausanne M2 project. We also direct thanks to Buro Happold, Carter-Burgess (Jacobs), CFSA Lausanne, SLCE New York, Jacqueline Osty Associates and Bernard Hemery, CPG Consultants, Lekker Design, and Yves Dessuant (PROGRAMME).

Among clients who invented new programs and hence were at the origin of important architectural projects, Gaetan Bucher, Pierre Keller, and Pierre Nussbaumer deserve particular mention. I am deeply appreciative of the support and confidence of Peter Trimp in The Hague and Angelo Cosentini and John Carson in New York.

Event-Cities 4 benefited from the careful overview of Grace Robinson-Leo, who took charge of the editing, graphic design, and overall production work. I especially wish to thank Roger Conover of the MIT Press, who from the very beginning encouraged the development of what could be called a "project discourse" in the form of the *Event-Cities* series. Credit is also due to my colleagues and students at Columbia University in New York, with whom my conversations on concept-forms, vectors and envelopes, and topo-types originated.

Last but not least, I wish to thank Kate Linker, without whom many of these projects would not be what they are, and whose critical outlook constantly reminds all of us that architecture is as much about culture as it is about building.

Contents

concept-form

Introduction

Like earlier books in the series, *Event-Cities 4* documents architectural works of our time, exploring how contemporary practice can inform us about the definition of architecture today.

In each project presented, constraints—whether functional, economic, or site-related—are the starting point of the work. They provide the necessary conditions for developing an idea or a concept. Such external constraints are highly specific. In no case is the site or program generic (e.g.: "a house") or self-invented. Requirements are given by clients or by public institutions. They take the form of dozens of meticulously detailed prescriptions that the architects and their team of engineering and other consultants must generally follow to the letter. Many of the projects were done for building competitions, hence requiring an ability to evolve from design to actual construction. Eventually, these constraints must engage the art of architecture in our time.

The *Event-Cities* series is not about promoting one esthetic over others. Instead, it aims to develop a project discourse through the reality of architectural practice. In this fourth volume we address one particular aspect of the question of form in the making of architecture, but it is not about visual concerns. Readers looking for elaborate formal or "iconic" investigations will not find them, since this is not the purpose of the architectural work. In other words, this book is not about the "wow" factor, but rather about the "what" and the "how."

The first *Event-Cities* (1994) proposed concepts of "crossprogramming" and "disprogramming" in architectural urbanism and urban architecture, arguing that all architecture is as much about the events that take place in spaces as about the architectural spaces themselves.

Event-Cities 2 (2000) suggested that all architecture is made out of vectors and envelopes, announcing an envelope discourse that would become prevalent some ten years later. Concerned with strategies and devices, it also included a comprehensive documentation of the Parc de la Villette (1982-98).

Event-Cities 3 (2005) opposed concepts, contexts, and contents, demonstrating how these notions were simultaneously separate and interdependent, whereby strategies of indifference, reciprocity, and conflict among them could inform architectural theory and practice. It also introduced color notation into the project documentation for the first time. (The earlier volumes are in black and white.)

This volume, *Event-Cities 4*, enters a different realm, which does not replace but instead complements the earlier research.

Concept-Form

During the period of work covered by the first three volumes of *Event-Cities*, one word was almost never used, except in order to attack it: "form." Form did not need to be discussed because it was always seen as the result of an architectural strategy, never as a starting point. Yet in the past few years, in the course of developing a number of projects worldwide, the notion of "concept-form" began to emerge. It first came out as we embarked on exotic projects at a considerable distance from our New York and Paris bases.

As architects, we were increasingly asked to leave a global mark by intervening in areas we knew little about. We wanted to be locally responsible and did not want to impose standard recipes in the way several centuries of colonization first, and globalization later, had left their marks on cultures little prepared for extensive urbanization.

We proposed an alternative, described here as a "concept-form." (In French: *"forme-concept"*) What is a concept-form? Let's say you have to plan a city somewhere from scratch. The concept-form is an abstract configuration that can be implemented in a particular place or culture, while nonetheless accepting and accommodating its cultural and situational idiosyncrasies. It is a concept that generates a form, or a form that generates a concept, in such a way that one reinforces the other. The concept may be programmatic, technological, social, and so on. But the form must be relatively abstract, since many aspects of the program are indeterminate, the technology economically uncertain, and the social fabric possibly in constant mutation. The form hence may be singular or multiple, regular or irregular, among other differences. There are many concept-forms ready to be selected from the existing catalogue of architectural ideas, while others are still to be invented. As we show with our Elliptic City project, concept-forms are not arbitrary: they must be appropriate to a particular site, program, and socio-economic culture while accommodating or even accelerating evolution. Even so, the concept-form represented a major shift from our earlier projects. Suddenly form would be a starting point of sorts, whereas it had seemed an end result before.

Precedents

As we developed these "concept-form" projects in faraway places, we began to realize that we had unsuspectingly already been engaged in comparable strategies elsewhere and earlier. For example:

1.   At the Parc de la Villette in Paris (*Event-Cities 2*), our programmatic concept was expressed through an abstract system of superimposed points, lines, and surfaces, whereby the points of intensity were small and arranged in a regular grid while the lines were movement vectors.

2.   For Chartres (*Event-Cities*), our concept took the form of the superimposition of a dozen autonomous layers of infrastructure, landscape, and activities.

3.   In Lausanne (*Event-Cities*), on a site located in a former industrial valley, we counterbalanced the city's existing topography with the typology of five inhabited bridges, each of them acting as a generator of new urban development.

4.   In Beijing (*Event-Cities 3*), when confronted by the threatened demolition of a cultural and historical quarter, we advocated for its conservation by building the requested residential neighborhood 20 meters in the air instead of on the ground. Our concept was a lattice configuration adaptable to any of the existing ground constraints.

5.   In Dubai, for a site located on an artificial island destined to house an opera house, theaters, and a museum, our concept involved a three-dimensional band planning strategy responding to the climate and to evolving programmatic possibilities. A similar concept had already been tested for our Tokyo Opera House project (*Event-Cities*).

Concept-Form and Program

In each of the above cases, an abstract device had been developed to act as the generator of an architectural scheme. While it was a programmatic strategy turned into a concept, it had to assume the configuration of a form—a concept-form—in order to exist. The process always started with a program (there can be no architecture without program), but programs are never neutral or innocent. For example, if the requirement is that no space in a room can be further than 20 feet, or seven meters, away from a window in order to provide direct daylight and facilitate a view, your housing block will obviously not be a 100-meter-deep uninterrupted mass. Hence, the concept and its form are always a function of one or several program characteristics. Programmatic imagination has done much to qualify architecture in the last hundred years, from the Constructivists' social condensers to contemporary libraries (e.g. OMA's Seattle Library). Just as the program of a prison once led to the type of the panopticon, programs and forms constantly intersect, whether in a relationship of reciprocity, conflict, or indifference. (Forget "Form follows function" and "Function follows form.")

Concept-Form vs. Type

But if the panopticon was clearly a type, our exploration of concept-forms suggested something different. A concept-form differs from a type in that it is not bound by history or historical context. Traditionally, typological analysis has been attentive not only to form and configuration, but also to the symbolic identification of types. In this sense, a concept-form has no a priori meaning attached to it. The concept-form of a circular building is not necessarily meant to refer to or recall Roman amphitheaters or panopticon types, even if they all share certain geometrical characteristics. Hence, analogies between typological forms and concept-forms are not necessarily relevant. One cannot construct a theory of concept-forms based on linguistic analogies in the way structuralism looked at types, because concept-forms do not originate in history.

Most typological studies suggest that architecture depends on constants, and that all architecture develops out of prior architecture. However, concept-forms are diagrams without history, even if inevitable parallels will be established. For example, a solid hovering over a base is nothing but what it is: a solid hovering over a base. One can, of course, make parallels with temples located on top of plinths or with statues on their pedestals. Yet we suggest that this is irrelevant, since a concept-form is never symbolical. It is certainly autonomous, but autonomous from history only. Like any other abstraction, a concept-form loses its autonomy as soon as it is populated by reality. There is no architecture without something that happens in it. Once an abstract concept-form is built, it is confronted with its contents and therefore is no longer abstract. It now assumes an unstable and changing role, far from the permanence of its original diagram.

Autonomy

As discussed and argued in *Event-Cities 3*, concept, context, and content can be separated analytically, but any built architecture inevitably merges these three terms, making any fixed meaning impossible. Similarly, a concept-form begins as an abstraction, but immediately assumes a social, political or, alternatively, sensuous experiential character as soon as it is built. A concept-form has no a priori authority based on function, material, or precedent, and because of this, it has ultimate authority, for it cannot be challenged on functional, material, or historical grounds. Concept-forms are outside the history of the discipline of architecture and yet inevitably intersect with it. Why? For example, let's again take the daylight requirement in a building. It will determine the maximum distance between the building's outer envelope and its inner core, so that daylight still penetrates to the core. This depth is a constant of sorts, since it makes it easy to differentiate housing from shopping malls as seen from the air. Such required building depth is an inevitable constraint. Other such constraints include gravity or human size. These constraints have a major effect on architecture, yet they are not "architectural" per se.

The concept-form is generally autonomous, since it is not always derived from these functional requirements but must be selected from among other concept-forms as capable of accommodating functional or programmatic requirements. Trying to differentiate the intrinsic qualities of a work vs. its extrinsic characteristics may apply to a work of art but can never apply to architecture. (A program is always extrinsic, a vault is generally intrinsic, and yet they inevitably intersect.) A concept-form is never arbitrary or subjective. It is always a "project," in the sense that it is there to project itself toward some future content or context. It must be performative, because it must eventually allow the building to perform according to programmatic or even symbolic criteria, but it is not in itself programmatic or symbolical. The point-grid of the Parc de la Villette in Paris does not refer to anything in particular, yet it is a conceptual and organizational device that allows the assemblage of activities in the park.

Of course, Le Corbusier's Plan Voisin also used a point-grid for another Parisian project, but it is the many potentials of the point-grid that count, not its anecdotal or historical uses. A point-grid can also be a system of coordinates or a decorative motif, a dot screen or a bed of nails, and can ultimately become the focus of an amicable debate among architectural colleagues (Le Corbusier's Venice Hospital, a London Admiralty map used in our London Joyce's Garden, Eisenman's Cannaregio project for Venice, our Parc de la Villette in Paris, etc.).

In a way, a concept-form is always a device or an empty form that awaits fulfillment. Hence it is abstract and figurative at the same time, for as soon as one fills the abstract form with the necessities of content, it inevitably becomes figurative. In other words, a concept-form is an abstract figure that precedes figuration. A concept-form begins as a dematerialized or immaterial form, but it cannot escape its subsequent or event-ual materialization.

It is not a face, or a mask, or a surface. One concept-form may take many different faces. For example, let's take the concept-form that informs Manhattan. Each block is similar in principle but has the potential to appear entirely different. Manhattan's gridded logic is a concept-form at the scale of the city, an event-city by the time it gets built.

Concept-Form: Between Diagram and Type
One definition of architecture is that architecture is the materialization of a concept, of an idea. But it is difficult to go directly from thought to material without some mediating device. Materialization presupposes perception and experience; it encompasses cultural, social, political, and technical dimensions. Eventually it needs to take a material form. As a mediating device, the diagram is the first of a number of steps or shortcuts between a thought (a *"cosa mentale"*) and an architectural work. The most precise architectural diagrams have nothing to do with forms or with words. They precede form and word; they are the graphic translation of thought. Diagrams can be understood in many ways,

for example, as a transformational sequence (if they correspond to a method of work) or more classically, as a simplified version of a *parti*. Other diagrams show movement vectors or arrows. Such diagrams are about notating the movement of a body in space. The arrows can be "solidified" and turned into architectural ramps, hallways, or elevators, but they can also be located in the middle of a large expanse of open space, and therefore have no visible physical presence at all. Hence diagrams may often have little to do with physical form. (Think also of relational diagrams or genealogical trees.)

Concept-forms, however, are situated between diagrams and types, since a diagram can be purely conceptual and have nothing to do with form, while a type is always represented by a form. While a concept-form can describe a geometrical scheme, there are discontinuous point-like schemes that have little to do with geometry. (See, for example, the Ile Seguin scheme in this book.) They are concept-forms insofar as they are generated by an idea or concept that can only be expressed through a form. But they are not forms in and of themselves. Here, the form is not "formal," but rather the direct transposition of a concept. To cite an example: the notion of the concept-form links Yuendumu aboriginal floor paintings to art works by Richard Long. Even though they come from vastly different traditions and histories, both configurations of concentric circles illustrate a similar concept-form.

Concept-Form and Envelope
At the time of this writing, a prevalent area of discourse and research involves investigation into the nature of architectural envelopes. While a major part of the discourse on envelopes originated with the intention to eliminate the historical distinction between facade and roof (see *Event-Cities 2* and *3*), recent discussions tend to look at the envelope as the separation between the inside and the outside, focusing on the latter, with the argument that the interior of the building is increasingly dealt with by specialists in other disciplines rather than by architects. In some of the main building types of our time—shopping malls, cineplexes, libraries, and museums—where there is no cause-and-effect relation between the inside and the outside, the architect is now said to be "liberated" from representing the interior but committed to generating an unlimited number of interpretations or "affects" that contribute to the urban setting.

However, it is the contention of this book that the exacerbated separation between the inside and the outside is not a "natural" phenomenon of our times, but simply one architectural strategy among others. In other words, there are programs that require either transparent, translucent, or opaque envelopes, and to emphasize the envelope's singleness is a conceptual decision (rather than an inevitable historical or technical condition).

Concept-Form vs. Composition
To suggest that today's external envelopes are largely done by architects while the internal arrangements of rooms are done by others excludes a major dimension of architecture: the general organization of masses that affects both the interior and exterior, the articulation of spaces between buildings, the sequences of movement within and between them, and so on. Classical architectural theory once distinguished "distribution" (the arrangements of rooms or interior partitions) from "disposition" (the relationship between the different parts of a building). Whether a building is organized in a linear, circular, or fragmented manner is part of "disposition," and an important component of concept-form. ("Disposition" is sometimes confused with "composition," but "disposi-

tion" suggests a conceptual economy of means as opposed to an esthetic arrangement.)

A concept-form is different from a composition or even a *parti*. (Remember: a composition is made up of a group of elements composed in such a way that removing one destroys the coherence or beauty of the whole; a *parti* is a generic composition, independent of programmatic considerations.) The additive set of *folies* at La Villette is not a composition, nor is it a *parti*. Series, juxtapositions, and superpositions are not compositional devices; they are inherently non-compositional.

From Typology to Topology

With the exception of a few projects presented in this volume, the concept-forms in *Event-Cities 4* are inherently "still." They arrest movement. They take all of the programmatic constraints and insert them into their tight geometries. However, "still" does not mean static. For example, in the pair of Biennale pavilions in the Abu Dhabi Sheikh Zayed National Museum project, one pavilion's typological "stillness" is merely the beginning of a topological transformation that leads to the fluid geometry of the second pavilion. The second pavilion's pliable form is then frozen temporally to become the end of a process that the concept-form of the first pavilion initiated. In the case of the Links-*Shabaka* Media Zone project, the original concept-form of "an object on a plinth" is relatively static; only the number and dimensions of the towers can change. Its fixed-point coordinate system is the starting point of dynamic processes that are defined in terms of directional vectors applied to the original concept-form. The buildings' outline becomes endlessly pliable, since it will be frozen only when it is turned or trans-formed into concrete, steel, or glass. Various parameters permit the linear original concept-form to respond dynamically to program, the movement of people, economics, sustainability, and/or site conditions. Yet, because at the time of writing actual "built" buildings and construction materials are still inherently static, the new concept-form needs to be tested in the light of the very constraints that provided the parametric basis for transformation into a different kind of social or programmatic envelope. Once again, the project's driving force is never an esthetic preoccupation.

Siting a Concept-Form

Unless a concept-form is site-specific (for example: Libera's house for Malaparte), it remains untested as long as it lacks a site. The introduction of a site requires that a concept-form be sufficiently flexible in its configuration to allow for adjustment. The constraints inherent to a site become part of the definition of a concept-form. Any given concept-form can have several volumetric iterations, depending on its site constraints. For example, a tightly confined site may imply a dense vertical cylindrical volume with a narrow inner court. A large open site can allow for a loose or fragmented horizontal cylindrical volume with a large inner court. Each of these volumetric iterations is part of the same concept-form.

Not Only What It Looks Like, but Also What It Does

A concept-form can be organized as a single unified volume or as the articulation of discrete volumes; as a collage or assemblage; in minimalist or picturesque modes; as a typology or a topology; as an "icon" or as "an invisible set of relations"; as a rigid framework or a matrix of movement vectors; as a repetitive regular grid or a distorted one; as Mies van der Rohe's rectangles or as Frank Lloyd Wright's hexagons; as a "duck" or as a decorated shed. It can use analogies with literary, mathematical, or biological structures. It can be a closed system as well as an open one, with the possibility of endless growth and change. It can even be generated through collisions or contaminations of varying geometries, and spliced into some recombinant organism. Ultimately, it can echo art practices that radically question the primacy of form, from Marcel Duchamp's readymades to Tino Seghal's "constructed situations." Once again, concept-forms are not about materiality or the visual. There is no particular reason to organize a building or set of buildings in a circle, a rectangle, a series of fragments, an ellipse, a mat or, volumetrically, as a sphere, a tetrahedron or simple cube, a slab, or a blob. There may even be no correlation between section and plan, or between plan and elevation. However, the concept-form requires coherence and consistency. Incoherent concepts are not viable concepts.

The form is as much about the concept as the concept is about the form. A concept-form takes its strength and justification from constraints and strives for an economy of means. It works with and against the program and never ignores it. It is characterized by the strength of the obvious (*"la force de l'évidence"*). WHAT REALLY COUNTS IS NOT ONLY WHAT IT LOOKS LIKE, BUT ALSO WHAT IT DOES.

Ideally, a concept-form is a generator of new conditions. It freely uses or invents forms to locate activities or to generate events. Yet there is no ideal concept-form. One concept-form may be more appropriate than another to a given program or a given site. Cities, new or old, are conceived as a juxtaposition and superimposition of a number of vastly different concept-forms. Ultimately, concept-forms are about events, since they must be both lived and worked in. Their mandate is about the lives of those who inhabit them, for better or for worse.

A concept-form is neither a method nor the only way to approach an architectural problem. Each problem has its own logic. Often it is how you read or formulate a problem that gives you several potential solutions, among which you then make a choice. Once again, the concept-form is not about the visual or the esthetic. The concept-form is a-formal; it is not hierarchical and does not reflect a rigid set of rules. It is rather a specific moment in a thought process when an architectural strategy becomes the generator for making buildings. The concept-form requires intent, since it is about designing conditions rather than conditioning designs.

EVENT-CITIES 4

The projects in *Event-Cities 4* explore the issue discussed above. In certain cases, the question of the concept-form is addressed directly, as in the Elliptic City project. In others, the issue is only peripheral to the project, which has other priorities. In most cases, however, the project encompasses several concept-forms conflated into a single building; the combination of superposition/sequence/single envelope is one such possible configuration, but it is documented under only one of these features in this book. In a few cases, the project has nothing to do with concept-forms. In other words, the concept-form is not intended to act as a universal architectural device.

Part A: Elliptical/Cylindrical

Part A begins with the idea of architecture, or a small city, made out of independent entities, each without an apparent relationship with the others. All of these entities are enclosed in an elliptical shape so as to preclude any compositional or directional readings among them. The Alésia MuseoParc project is constituted in part by two independent cylindrical volumes, one screened in wood, the other in stone. Both are based on the idea of a loop responding to the programmatic requirements of a museum visit. The site conditions for a bank in Athens deform the cylinder, while the site reinforces it in Rolle, Switzerland, turning the cylinder into a dome. At La Roche-sur-Yon, structural forces and weather protection requirements suggested a 70-meter-long horizontal tube that acts as a bridge.

In all of these cases, the concept-form is intimately connected to the program that it contains.

Part B: Banding/Striation
Expanding on a concept first proposed in 1986 for our Tokyo Opera House competition submission, the project for the Dubai Opera Island explores the juxtaposition of autonomous bands or strips, this time extending the programmatic articulation of a concert hall at the scale of a master plan.

Part C1: Superimposed and Part C2: Raised
Part C expands on a concept introduced with the Parc de la Villette and reinterpreted with our recent Acropolis Museum (*Event-Cities 3*): the superimposition of autonomous systems. Although only the two Abu Dhabi Media Zone projects and the scheme for EDF in Paris-Saclay employ explicit programmatic superimposition in the literal sense, the Busan Cinema Center and Sheik Zayed Museum projects both superimpose an enclosed and highly organized functional area on an open, public ground level.

Part D: Gridded Loop
Our project for Mediapolis in Singapore is located within a general district plan by Zaha Hadid Architects. Our plan turns the original grid into an urban strategy of rigorous street fronts and flexible rear yards.

Part E: Discontinuity/Repetition
Part E explores how a discontinuous concept-form can give the appearance of continuity. In the case of the Paris Ile Seguin project, the strategy makes use of a cinematic device in order to convey the illusion of a continuous urban envelope.

The design for an exhibition about new architectural projects in Paris takes small advertising billboards—an urban artifact familiar to all Parisians, called the *"sucette,"* or lollipop—and locates them at random throughout a large exhibition hall to create dynamic readings between the moving visitors and the exhibition panels.

Part F: Linear/Sequential/Continuous
Here, linearity is the theme. Determined by the program or by site conditions, the line is never arbitrary but instead engages specific conditions in a sequential form. Passageway, linear atrium, "great hall"—each archetype acts as a common denominator for all of the other programmatic elements.

Part G: Faceted/Folded/Angular
Each of the projects in Part G has in common a low-budget enclosure, together with specific volumetric particularities that result from program or zoning requirements. Simple faceted or folded envelopes respond to these constraints and are used to produce a dis-

tinct identity for each building. Our first folded envelope was designed and constructed at Le Fresnoy in 1991. (See *Event-Cities*.)

Part H: Filter Envelopes

The question of camouflage and envelopes has been already explored in *Event-Cities 3*. It takes on a new dimension in the renovation of the Zoo de Vincennes in Paris, since the buildings are required to serve as a near-invisible backdrop for the animals that are on display. Is this a concept-form or the ultimate dissolution of form? Formlessness as a concept-form?

Bernard Tschumi
March 2010

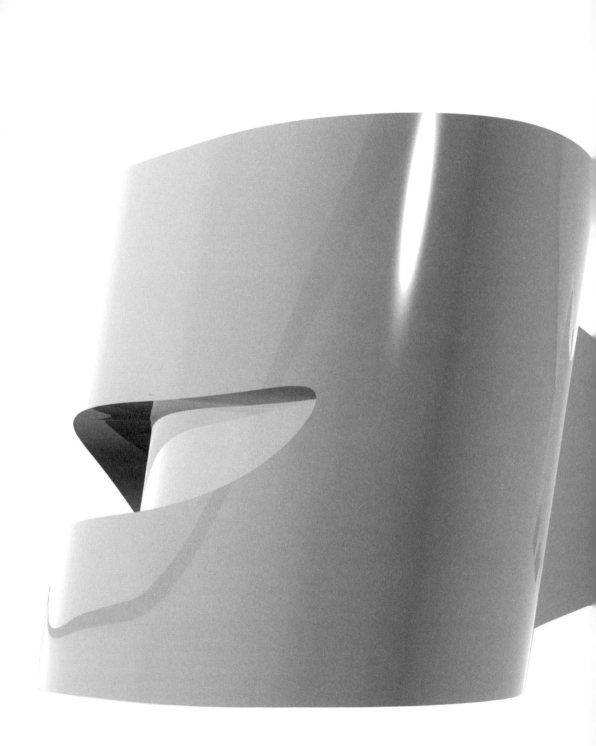

Prologue

In 2008 the University of Cincinnati organized an event to celebrate the influential former dean of its School of Architecture, Jay Chatterjee. A number of architects and designers were asked to propose individual pieces of furniture whose production would be sponsored by a major manufacturer and later sold at a benefit auction. Our project was inspired by our own contribution to University campus architecture, the Richard E. Lindner Athletics Center. (See *Event-Cities 3*.)

TypoLounger, 2008

ArchiFurniture

Concept-form and Programmatic Indeterminacy

Small projects sometimes provide opportunities to explore larger issues and to test their conceptual significance. Invited to design a piece of furniture, we examined the question of form in relation to program. The topic of our investigation was a question: How could a fixed form (a concept-form) be able to accommodate different programs? Freed from context—a piece of furniture can be located anywhere—and from the major technical constraints often required by large structures, the project explored the relationships among form, volume, orientation, and program.

Our Athletics Center plays against a primarily L-shaped object in a continuous game of architectural scales. "TypoLounger" is a solid form that consists of a continuous wrapped surface that circumscribes an inclined solid. The form accommodates four pockets, each of a different character and quality. This sculptural furniture can be placed on a ground plane in more than one way. TypoLounger can be rotated around its axis, giving each orientation a different quality in space; thus, the plan becomes the elevation and the section becomes the plan. Through changing positions, "TypoLounger" supports different types of use: as a chair that you sit on, a bed that you lie down on, a playful object that you can jump on, or any number of other programs.

The form was developed using computer modeling to bend, twist, pinch, and cut the originating shape of our Athletics Center "boomerang." The resultant object is clad in a smooth white skin made out of Formica Solid Element ARCTIC 102. The seamless and undulating surface further distorts the orientation of the piece and the ambiguity of its purpose.

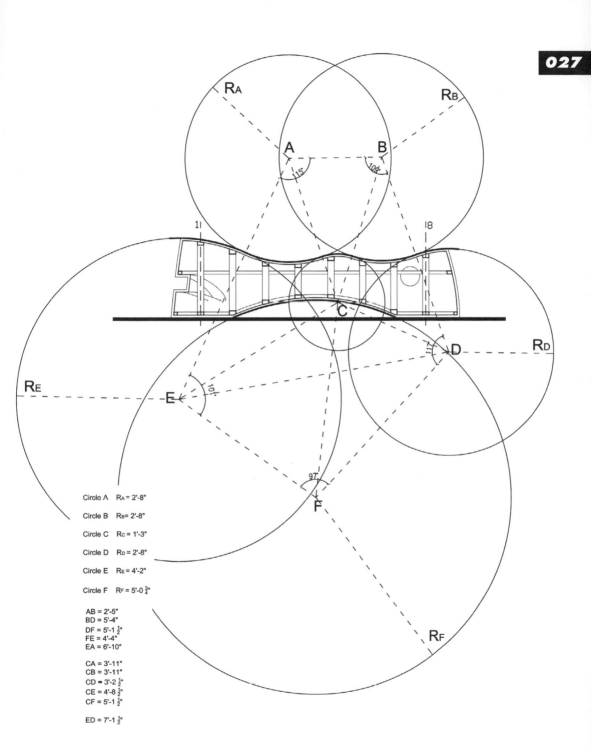

Circle A R_A = 2'-8"

Circle B R_B= 2'-8"

Circle C R_C = 1'-3"

Circle D R_D = 2'-8"

Circle E R_E = 4'-2"

Circle F R_F = 5'-0 $\frac{3}{4}$"

AB = 2'-5"
BD = 5'-4"
DF = 5'-1 $\frac{1}{2}$"
FE = 4'-4"
EA = 6'-10"

CA = 3'-11"
CB = 3'-11"
CD = 3'-2 $\frac{1}{2}$"
CE = 4'-8 $\frac{1}{2}$"
CF = 5'-1 $\frac{1}{2}$"

ED = 7'-1 $\frac{1}{2}$"

A diagram of the chair's form as a negative space

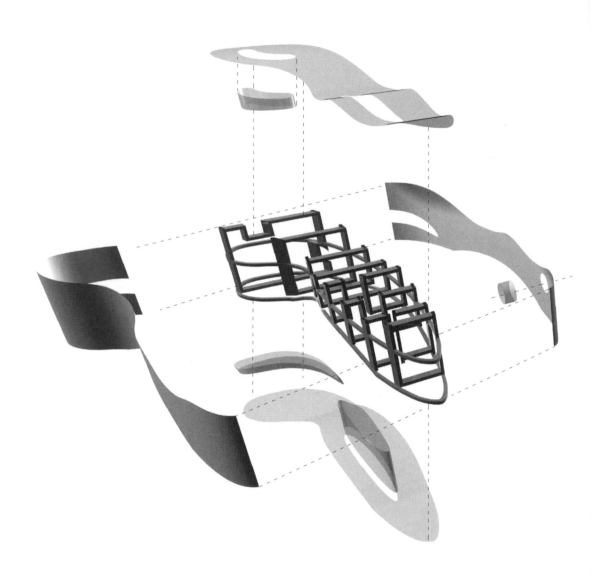

Exploded axonometric diagram

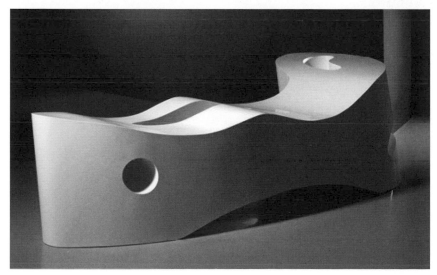

The Formica chair in the fabrication shop (top) and completed (bottom)

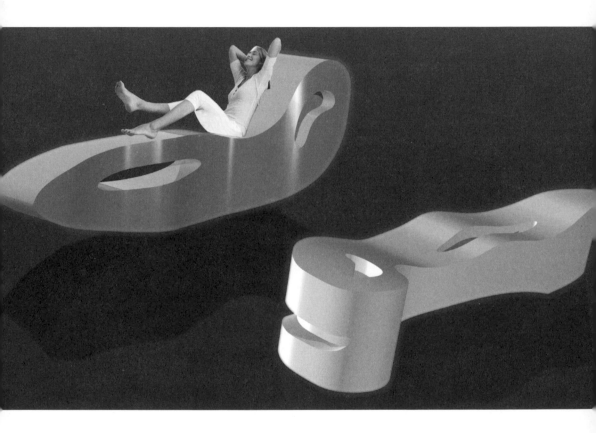

The sculptural form undulates, tilts, twists, and torques on all sides, so that the definitions "up," "down," "top," and "bottom" become ambiguous. Placed one way, it is a bed. Turned another, it is a seat or a desk. One more maneuver and it is a post to be leaned on. Openings and holes provide storage for a book, a pillow, or a glass of wine. The object's positioning defines its use.

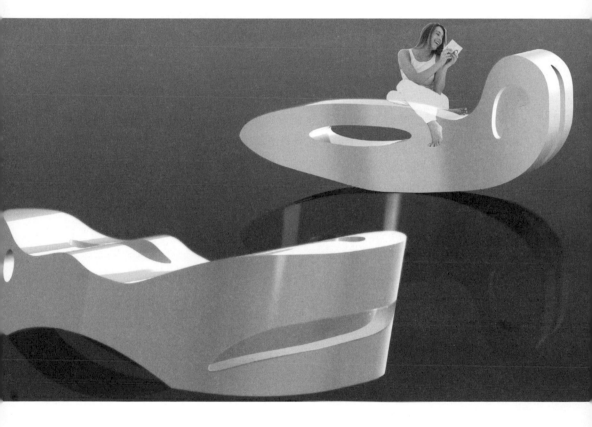

A concept-form is an abstract configuration that can be implemented in a particular place or culture, while nonetheless accepting and accommodating its cultural and situational idiosyncrasies. It is a concept that generates a form, or a form that generates a concept, in such a way that one reinforces the other. The concept may be programmatic, technological, social, and so on.

A. Elliptical/Cylindrical

Part A begins with the idea of architecture, or a small city, made out of independent entities, each without an apparent relationship with the others. All of these entities are enclosed in an elliptical shape so as to preclude any compositional or directional readings among them. The Alésia MuseoParc project is constituted in part by two independent cylindrical volumes, one screened in wood, the other in stone. Both are based on the idea of a loop responding to the programmatic requirements of a museum visit. The site conditions for a bank in Athens deform the cylinder, while the site reinforces it in Rolle, Switzerland, turning the cylinder into a dome. At La Roche-sur-Yon, structural forces and weather protection requirements suggest a 70-meter-long horizontal tube that acts as a pedestrian bridge.

In all of these cases, the concept-form is intimately connected to the program that it contains.

Dominican Republic, IFCA Master Plan, 2005-

Elliptic City

Small City Wanted

Imagine a large island somewhere in the Caribbean, with lush beaches, mountains, and dense forests. The island has a long history dating back to the time when Spanish ships discovered it on their way to the American mainland. The island is the size of Switzerland, and was once one of the largest growers of sugarcane in the west. Now its second largest city is, paradoxically, New York, where almost 500,000 of its nationals live and contribute to the island economy by sending home regular "remittances" to their families. Tourism and a number of free trade zones contribute to the economic equation that makes the island a growing force in the Americas. Today, it is caught between two worlds: one of poverty and the other of potential future riches, since international investment will one day act as a motor of its economic and social development.[1]

To approach this potential new world, a small "city" needs to be designed on the island for 12,000 people involved in all aspects of world finance in the most contemporary environment possible. Many will come from the sophisticated capital cities of Europe and North and South America; most will come from the island itself. Some parts of the project will require high security; others, an inviting atmosphere encompassing shops, hotels, and residences. The 30-square-kilometer site is ideally located by the ocean, not far from the capital city and its main airport. The site is *tabula rasa* for the most part, but also contains 8,000 squatters living in shanty barrios. How will the designers approach the challenge of its existing and potential diversity?

Global vs. Local

Today, globalization means that areas formerly only moderately touched by worldwide financial trends are subject to unprecedented economic acceleration. New infrastructures and cities seem to appear almost overnight, while international architects are asked to intervene, sometimes after three-week competitions, in areas and cultures they often know little about. While the incongruous insertion of architectural signatures into alien environments may rightfully be questioned, these interventions can also be considered an inevitable part of the import and export of cultures over the ages. How should world architects intervene in these worldwide cultures—by repeating an egotistical individual style or searching for an elusive communion, caught between pastiche and nostalgia, with mutating local cultures? Or is there another way? We searched for an alternative, described here through the means of a concept-form.

Challenge

We began work on this project, the Independent Financial Centre of the Americas and its affiliated buildings, in early 2006. In addition to the challenges posed by the site and its global initiative, the island posed an ecological challenge. Today, according to World Bank statistics, nationally protected land covers 52% of the island's territories, in contrast to the 10% "target" for most other nations. This fact provided a starting point for a landscape strategy based on the numerous landscape features—from agricultural grids to axially arranged gardens to topographical contours—that historically have paved the way for the planning coordinates of cities. We also wanted to keep nature and landscape flowing throughout the project.

---

1. The Island is the Dominican Republic, and the driving force of the project is the forthcoming Independent Financial Centre of the Americas. The IFCA aims to offer unprecedented links between global financial institutions and regional trading facilities.

Manhattan

Saint-Tropez

Kowloon: 45,000 people per km2

Los Llanos: 2,000 people = .26km2

Manhattan: 24,000 people per km2

Los Llanos: 12,000 people = .5km2

Wash. DC: 2,100 people per km2

Los Llanos: 12,000 people = 5.7km2

Salt Lake City: 640 people per km2

Los Llanos: 12,000 people = 20 km2

In order to conceptualize the size of such a large site, we compared it to the scale of other cities and imagined how much space would be used with different densities.

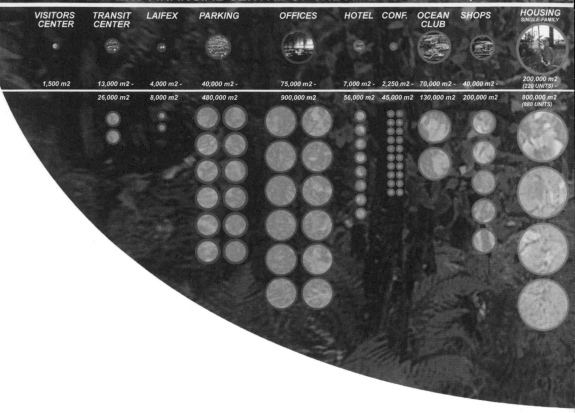

VISITORS CENTER	TRANSIT CENTER	LAIFEX	PARKING	OFFICES	HOTEL	CONF.	OCEAN CLUB	SHOPS	HOUSING SINGLE-FAMILY
									200,000 m2 (220 UNITS) -
1,500 m2	13,000 m2 -	4,000 m2 -	40,000 m2 -	75,000 m2 -	7,000 m2 -	2,250 m2 -	70,000 m2 -	40,000 m2 -	
	26,000 m2	8,000 m2	480,000 m2	900,000 m2	56,000 m2	45,000 m2	130,000 m2	200,000 m2	800,000 m2 (880 UNITS)

A program and phasing in constant evolution made us explore a flexible strategy of "places of intensity," in which each place could be enlarged to cover surfaces of several dozen acres each, with existing nature maintained intact in between them. These places would be like programmatic clusters or islands, characterized by elliptical configurations of different potential sizes. In this project, our own places of intensity consist of a cluster of ellipses. The concept-form of the ellipse is, of course, first and foremost a geometrical and spatial figure. But it is not coincidental that an "ellipsis" is also a figure of speech, meaning a short-cut that joins together different elements.[2]

---

2. Definitions (Oxford English Dictionary):
Ellipse. 1. A plane closed curve in which the sum of the distance of any point from the two foci is a constant quantity. 2. Trans: an object or figure bounded by an ellipse.
Ellipsis. Pl. Ellipses. 1. = ELLIPSE 1, 2. now rare. 2. GRAM. The omission of one or more words in a sentence, which would be needed to express this sense completely.
Elliptic. 1. That has the form of an ellipse, pertaining to ellipses. 2. Gram: characterized by ellipsis (sense 2).
Other parallels: Art: A figure of construction omitting one or more elements in a statement, without altering its meaning. Film: A cut between two film sequences that are not consecutive in time. A connection omitting whatever is not indispensable to the understanding of the story, so as to be brief.

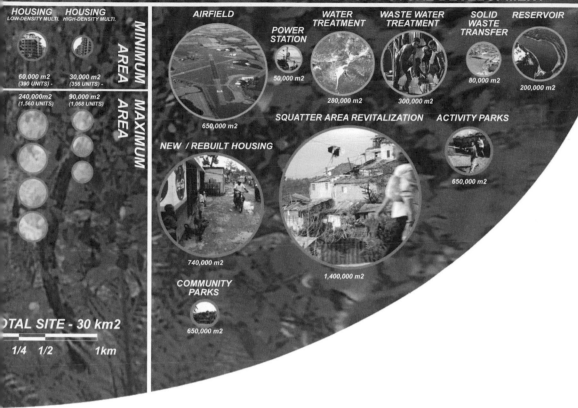

HOUSING LOW-DENSITY MULTI. HOUSING HIGH-DENSITY MULTI.

MINIMUM AREA

60,000 m2 (390 UNITS) -   30,000 m2 (356 UNITS) -

240,000m2 (1,560 UNITS)   90,000 m2 (1,068 UNITS)

MAXIMUM AREA

AIRFIELD

POWER STATION

WATER TREATMENT

WASTE WATER TREATMENT

SOLID WASTE TRANSFER

RESERVOIR

50,000 m2

80,000 m2

200,000 m2

280,000 m2

300,000 m2

650,000 m2

SQUATTER AREA REVITALIZATION   ACTIVITY PARKS

NEW / REBUILT HOUSING

650,000 m2

740,000 m2

1,400,000 m2

COMMUNITY PARKS

650,000 m2

TOTAL SITE - 30 km2

1/4   1/2   1km

Anarchipelago

Each individual ellipse is like an island; our "city" works as a literal archipelago. (We call it an "anarchipelago" so as to distinguish it from urban studies that use the word archipelago in a metaphorical sense, by which the "ocean" is often made out of an existing anonymous city fabric, while the "islands" include architectural monuments.)

In Elliptic City, buildings or streets are not read as connective tissue; the natural site is maintained in its original state between them. Nature can, if necessary, be cultivated so that it appears as if natural, undesigned, or untouched.[3]

3. In 1977 a striking urban scenario was proposed by O.M. Ungers, Rem Koolhaas, and Hans Kollhoff on the occasion of a seminar at the Berlin Summer Academy. On the assumption that Berlin was likely to continue shrinking, its reduction could be organized selectively by preserving and developing specific existing enclaves, while simply erasing or diminishing the density of other, less relevant parts through the creation of free space, city parks, public gardens, etc. By analogy, this scenario could be compared to a potential urban island situated in a green lagoon, hence a "green archipelago." In his 2005 Ph.D. thesis at the Berlage Institute, Pier Vittorio Aureli took the analysis an important step further, expanding on the metaphorical "archipelago" as a possible direction for the relationship between architecture and cities today.

Tabula Rasa

Elliptic City presupposes a *tabula rasa*; namely, an untouched landscape ready to be transformed or a clean slate achieved by removing what already exists from the site, so as to start from scratch. Elliptic City is not a city that exists on top of the residues of existing cities or urban areas. Similarly, it does not take its reference points from architectural history, nor does it refer to notions of center or periphery. The ellipse is an abstract architectural entity that refers only to other ellipses, but not necessarily to the interval area in which it sits.

The Ellipses

Each individual ellipse acts as a place of intensity, namely, a determinate territorial field ready to accommodate a particular program or combination of programs. Each ellipse is assigned a program.

Programs can be described in multiple ways:
A. Functional (i.e. offices, housing, corporate facilities, hotels, shopping areas). Each function corresponds to a separate island or ellipse. Alternatively, each could be combined with others so that each function is represented in part in each island in such a way that each island is a microcosm of all programs combined together.
B. Social, political, or economic, whereby each island represents a particular group.
C. Thematic. Each island can be "themed" according to a variety of lifestyles.
D. Densities, by which each island can be distinguished according to the number of people using it (for example, by high-rise or low-rise density).
E. Public/private. Some islands can be intensely private; some islands are nothing but public space. Some can negotiate a balance between public and private aspects.
F. Stylistic. In this case, each island is built according to a specific individual vocabulary. In visualizing Elliptic City, we have re-appropriated and transformed the long-vilified "bubble diagrams" of mid-20th century urban planners.[4]

Orbits and Meshes

Each ellipse is located in a larger orbit that is itself an elliptical tract of land that has been dedicated for construction. Located inside the ellipses are the buildings (which may themselves be elliptical, through a *mise-en-abîme* or "Russian dolls" strategy). The orbits are situated in a broad mesh or loose grid that has been devised to facilitate the location of the orbits within the existing topography.

Frames: Inside/Out

The ellipses function as individual frames that exist among other frames. Although they participate in the whole, they nevertheless retain their independence. These frames contribute to a significant particularity of Elliptic City—its inversion of certain basic relationships common to the traditional city. In general, what is inside traditional city walls reflects local culture and indigenous characteristics, while the territory outside is alien and extra-territorial.

---

4. Often attacked for oversimplifying the intricacies of urban life, "bubble diagrams," as originally used by planners, displayed the weakness of being functional diagrams only. The bubble diagram's carefully identified and separate zones of activities were never able to take advantage of their discrete and autonomous identities. Arrows extending from bubble to bubble were insufficient to establish links.

POWER LINES

RIDGE

NETWORK OF CAVES,
DEPRESSIONS
& UNDERGROUND WATER

MINI-RIDGES

OPERATING
QUARRY

POPULATION OF
8,000 SQUATTERS AT
LOS GUAYACANES

AUTO PISTA

TO CASA DE CAMPO

TO SANTO DOMINGO
AND AIRPORT

30-SQUARE-KILOMETER SITE

0   1/2   1   2km

WITH LOWER MANHATTAN
AT THE SAME SCALE

In Elliptic City, the opposite happens. What is inside the walls belongs to the global economy of world finance and international politics. What is outside reflects the local culture, with its regional inflections and particularities. In this sense, Elliptic City is a traditional city in reverse, or inside-out: the global is inside, while the local is outside. What is within the frame belongs to the world, while the outside belongs to the neighborhood.

The function and appearance of frames or boundaries are therefore important components of Elliptic City. Frames can be welcoming, luxurious, tantalizing, and porous, or forbidding and defensive—the equivalent of barbed wire and sirens.

Identifiers

In addition to the frames or boundaries that delineate the ellipses by specific architectural or landscape qualities, the roofs of the new city are important identifiers.

The hot and humid climate, punctuated by torrential rains, plays an important role in island life, transforming both its landscape and its ways of life. Therefore, in order to provide protection from weather, the design of the project incorporates large flat roofs located high above the ground as a particular architectural feature that differentiates the city from all other cities and villages around it. These roofs act as umbrellas that filter out the sun and protect from the rain. Some are made of metal, others of wood, while still others are formed out of canvas or polycarbonate. Some roofs cantilever over extraordinarily long spans, while thin columns or cables stabilize others. (The island is located in a hurricane region.) Under the spectacular roofs, the shape of the offices could assume many different configurations.

Offices

The Financial Operations ellipse is located in the large orbit. Inside the ellipse are individual elements—operations and banking centers, a visitor center, a VIP center, and so forth. One of the first structures to be built on the site, the LAIFEX building is its only tall presence, characterized by a horizontal, two-story deck accommodating general facilities and a vertical beacon that provides views over the complex and the ocean.

Straddling the boundary of the ellipse is a transit center with two adjoining car-park structures that acts as a link between the business area and the outside. Providing information and security clearance, its mode of operation can be compared to a well-conceived airport check-in area.

Four-Star Business Hotel/Convention Center/Ocean Club/Shopping/Power Plants/Water Treatment Plants

Large programs have their own orbits and ellipses. In keeping with other programs, they are interchangeable from orbit to orbit.

Anything-Goes Orbit (Mix-City)

One orbit intentionally contradicts the strategy of specialization common to the other orbits, combining in one place all the activities that are possible or conceivable in a city—for example, apartments located above shops, fitness centers above restaurants, garages below offices, museums above light manufacturing. Traditional streets with sidewalks and squares provide public spaces within the overall ellipse.

Guayacanes

Guayacanes is an area where 8,000 squatters currently live in impoverished barrios. We rejected the proposal of relocating them elsewhere; since they were part of the site, we thought that they should be given the option of being part of the game that organizes it. In one reading, the residents belong to the "ground" and the public buildings that we envision—for instance, a baseball stadium, a town hall, and new schools—are ellipses or "figures" on that ground. In another reading, the residents join in and a semi-elliptical boundary protects their individual areas, which include newly designed housing, from others.

The Making of a Landscape

We remembered that city plans have often followed the grids of agriculture, the axes of gardens, and the contours of coastlines. Landscapes and gardens have often paved the way for cities.

As we learned about the site and the program, we realized that we were not designing a zone or a town. Instead, we were designing a landscape. However, landscapes are natural and Elliptic city is man-made. And yet, somehow, landscapes are whatever you decide a landscape is. A landscape can cover the whole site, or only certain parts of the site. Different parts of the site can have different landscapes, which can be connected following different schemes.

Butterfly: main road flanked by islands

Leaf: parallel roadways with program islands

Cheetah: islands of islands

Leaf: reduced coverage

Connection schemes

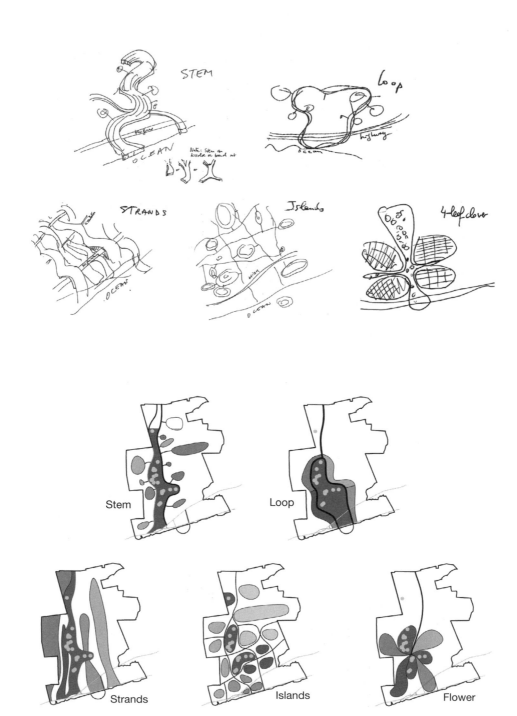

Five scenarios were analyzed for their functional potential.

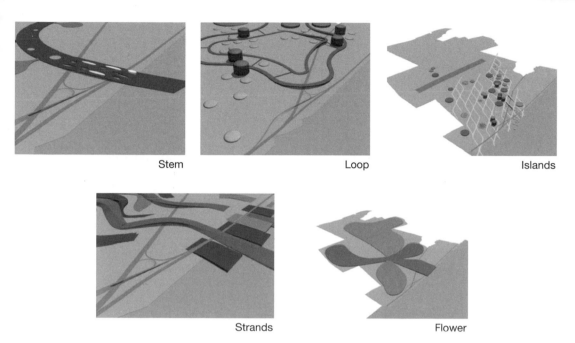

Stem

Loop

Islands

Strands

Flower

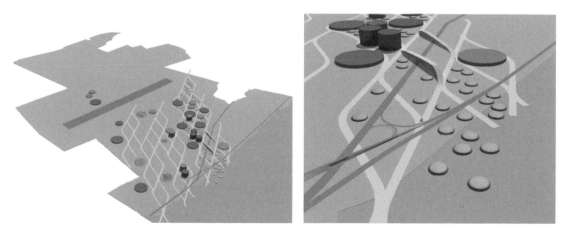

The "islands" concept proved to be the most feasible, as seen in these aerial perspectives.

Clusters: FSZ in the East

Lifestyles, FSZ (Financial Service Zone), and greenery/parks develop as clusters of individual islands, with Lifestyles in the West and the FSZ in the East. A loose web of roads connects the islands together.

Clusters: FSZ in the West

Lifestyles, FSZ, and greenery/parks develop as clusters of individual islands, with Lifestyles in the East and the FSZ in the West. A loose web of roads connects the islands together.

Branch: FSZ in the West

Lifestyles, FSZ, and greenery/parks develop as individual islands that branch off of two centrally located stems. Lifestyles are in the East, and the FSZ is in the West.

Option: Stem

Circulation is organized with a main stem and secondary stems, which branch off of and connect to separate programmatic "islands."

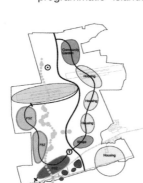

Option: Loop

Circulation is organized with a main road that branches into two loops: one west of the caves for the FSZ, and one east of the caves for housing. The two loops meet back together to cross the highway.

The islands strategy is both programmatically flexible and the least intrusive option for the site. Connecting the islands could be achieved via large loops or from a main stem.

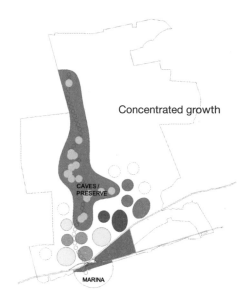

Concentrated growth

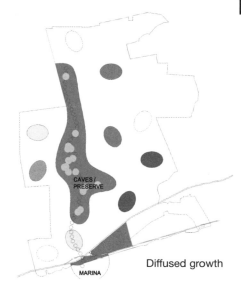

Diffused growth

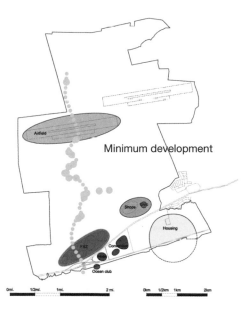

Minimum development

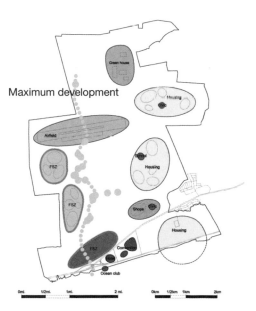

Maximum development

The islands can also grow in different directions to accommodate phasing.
For example, we can imagine a minimum and a maximum site development.

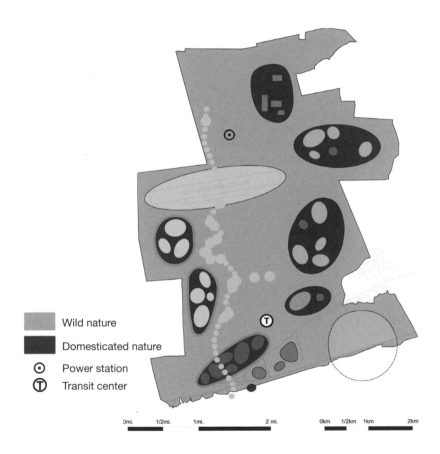

Wild nature

Domesticated nature

⊙ Power station

Ⓣ Transit center

0mi.   1/2mi.   1mi.   2 mi.   0km   1/2km   1km   2km

Our master plan responds to the Dominican Republic's attitude toward its natural resources: the Dominican Republic has an annual deforestation rate of zero.

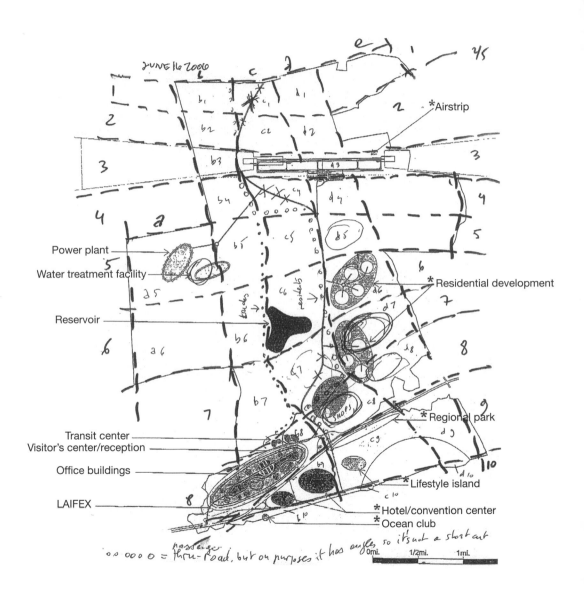

Power plant
Water treatment facility

Reservoir

Transit center
Visitor's center/reception

Office buildings

LAIFEX

*Airstrip

*Residential development

*Regional park

*Lifestyle island

*Hotel/convention center
*Ocean club

JUNE 16 2000

o o ooo o = thru-road, but on purposes it has angles, so it's not a short-cut

0mi.   1/2mi.   1mi.

Sketch including a possible roadway, which undulates so as not to be a short-cut

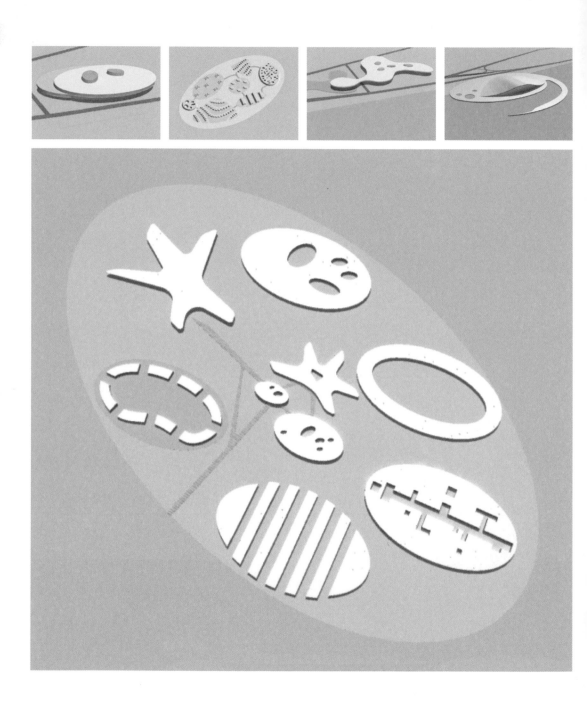

Each island could contain many different office types in the shape of similar islands. Our islands concept can be extended to other parts of the program to create shopping islands, housing islands, a convention-center island, or an ocean-club island, to cite a few examples.

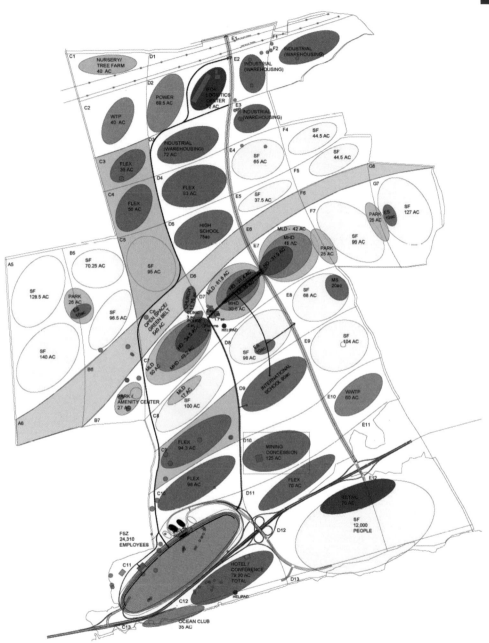

Several circulation systems linking the islands are possible.
The road system could be the equivalent of landscaped parkways.

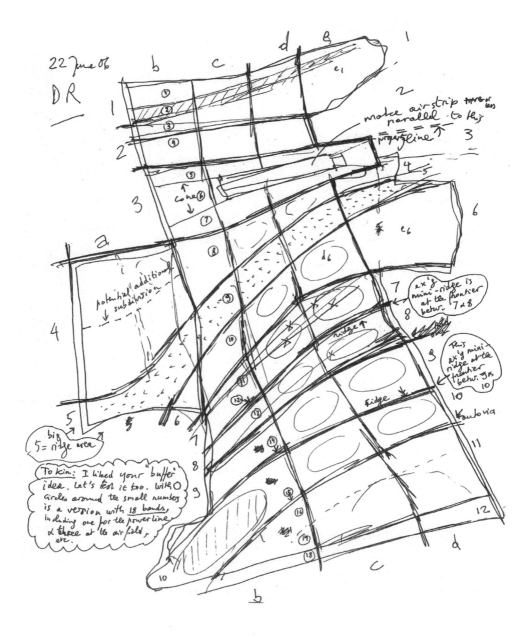

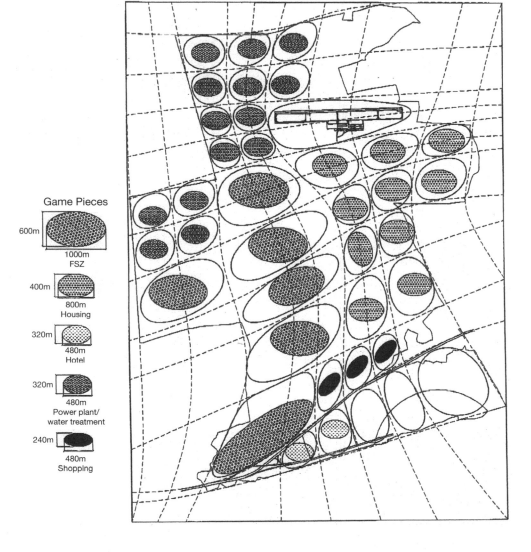

Game Pieces

600m — 1000m FSZ

400m — 800m Housing

320m — 480m Hotel

320m — 480m Power plant/ water treatment

240m — 480m Shopping

The concept of the game is introduced.

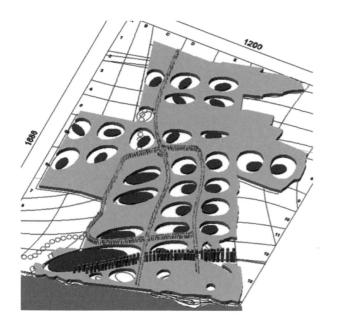

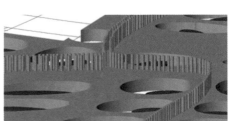

Main roads are seen as parkways amid the existing vegetation.

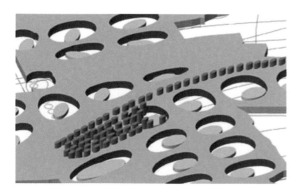

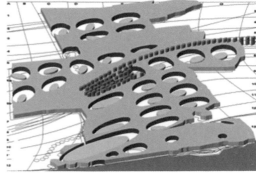

Super-hydrophile vegetation provides protection against erosion.

Connective Tissue

Between the "islands," we needed a connective tissue. We suggest keeping nature natural. Within the islands' controlled environment, we suggested having domesticated nature. Within this domestication, we still wanted to maintain the spontaneous character of the connective tissue. So we asked: How can the character of the connective tissue change according to the natural topography? Is it possible to keep the in-between "wild"? What is the balance between control and spontaneity?

The process of clearing vegetation can follow the idea of a shape (such as an ellipse), or the local specificities of the site (such as natural tree groupings, topography, and micro-environments). Can the edge of the clearing negotiate both the abstract and the local?

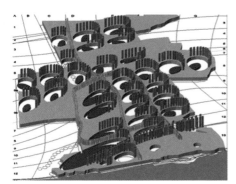
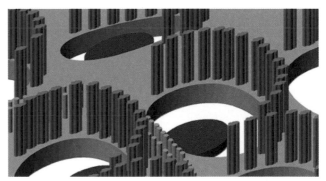

Orienting the islands in the same direction allows for protection of vegetation from wind.

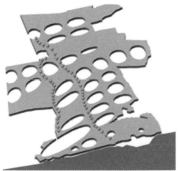
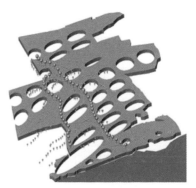

Robust vegetation takes advantage of the slight slope to purify waste.

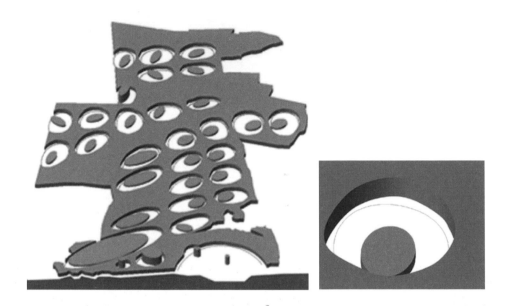

Clearings constitute the orbits. Built areas constitute the ellipses.

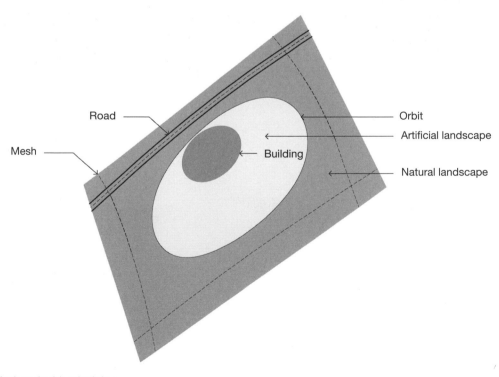

Road

Mesh

Orbit

Artificial landscape

Building

Natural landscape

Mesh and orbit principles

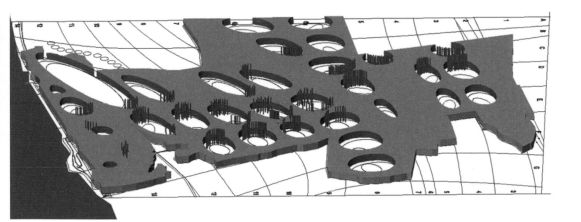

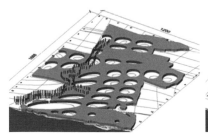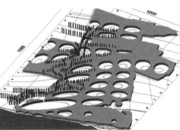

The use of vegetation reinforces the master-plan concept. Super-hydrophile vegetation flourishes alongside the network of caves and underground water, creating a lush landscape while also providing protection against erosion.

The Game (See also pages 90-95.)
The site and project in the IFCA are analogous to a game. The site, mesh, and orbits make up the game board, since they constitute the ground. The ellipses and buildings then become the pieces or figures. The game is ready to be played. Master planning is about the game and its strategy: what you design is a matrix that allows for multiple moves.

The Site: Given

The Mesh: A supple grid following the topography and defining coordinate axes to facilitate the location of major activities on the site. "Squares" are an average of 147 acres each.

The Roads: Mesh coordinates where main roads are generally located

The In-between: The existing landscape environment

The Orbits: Clearings within the existing landscape environment ready to accommodate the activity ellipses

The Ellipses: Carefully organized by landscaped areas ready to accommodate the future buildings. Planted and/or secure boundaries characterize the ellipses.

The Buildings: As required, according to need. Large cantilevered roofs act as common denominators.

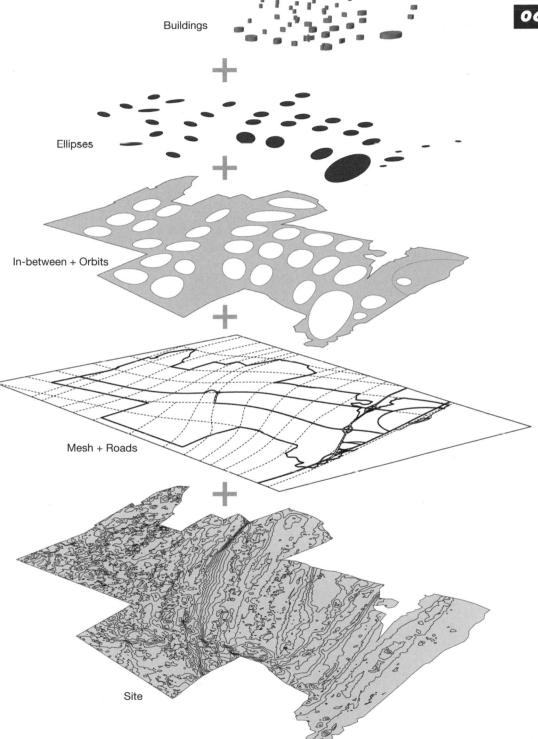

Buildings

+

Ellipses

+

In-between + Orbits

+

Mesh + Roads

+

Site

We suggested a mesh-like grid to indicate potential divisions between tracts of develop-
able land, creating 53 lots in total, with an average lot size of 147 acres. (The relationships
can be adjusted according to need.)

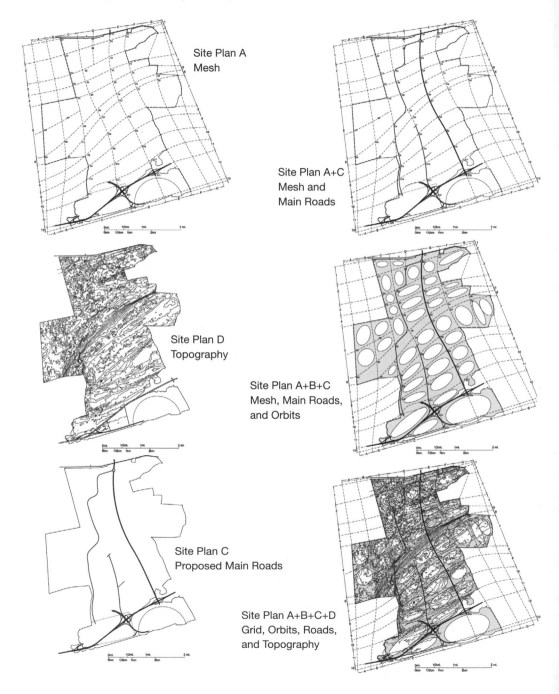

Site Plan A
Mesh

Site Plan A+C
Mesh and
Main Roads

Site Plan D
Topography

Site Plan A+B+C
Mesh, Main Roads,
and Orbits

Site Plan C
Proposed Main Roads

Site Plan A+B+C+D
Grid, Orbits, Roads,
and Topography

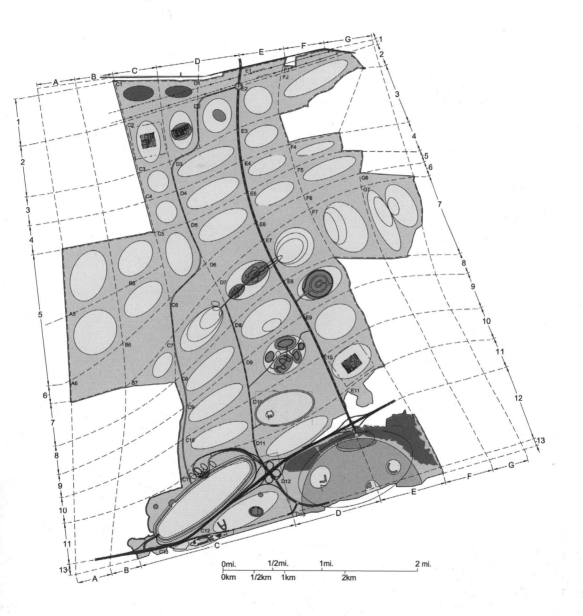

Master plan with Mesh and Orbits

Design Vocabulary

In visualizing the forms of the islands, we first looked for common denominators. The function and appearance of frames or boundaries are important components of the master plan. In addition to the frames or boundaries that delineate the ellipses through specific architectural or landscape qualities, the flat, umbrella-like roofs of the new city buildings are important identifiers.

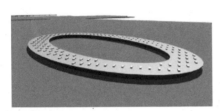

Ring + canopy

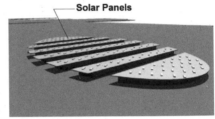

Solar Panels

Strips + canopies

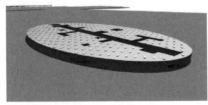

Linear courtyard + canopy

Archipelago of different office types

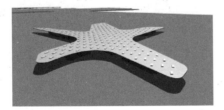

Star cluster + shared canopy

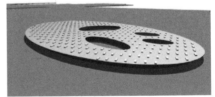

Courtyards + canopy

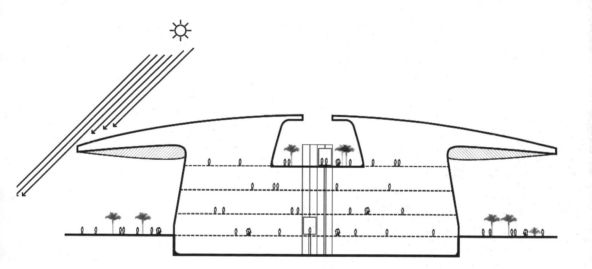

Hypothetical Office Section
Each building has a large awning. The roofs are equipped with solar panels.

Tight or Loose? Inclusive or Exclusive?

Boundaries always exist in architecture—boundaries between hot and cold, safe and unsafe, light and dark, wet and dry. Boundaries can divide or connect, act as a wall or as a threshold. They can be welcoming or forbidding. In Elliptic City, we proposed an array of boundaries of different types and uses, from the most porous and playful to the most hermetic and defensible.

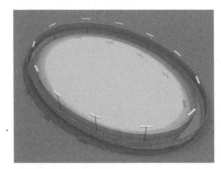

Security fence: Fortress

Wall: Medieval city

Hedge: Garden maze

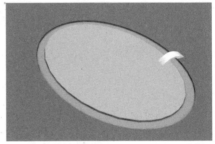

Water: Moat/lap pool

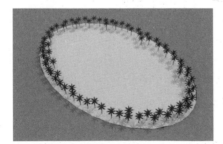

Palm trees: Oasis

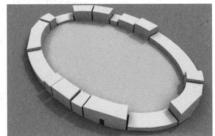

Buildings: Plaza

Each island is defined by a specific type of boundary, depending on its requirements.

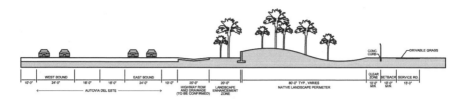

At highway

At adjoining property line

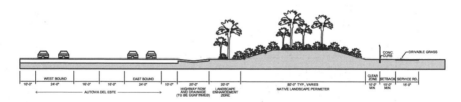

At highway

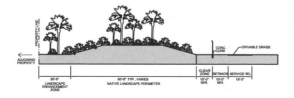

At adjoining property line

Wall-and-buffer zone (top) and berm-and-buffer zone (bottom)

Office Option: Mercury
1,480,000 square feet
(8 buildings, 5 floors, large, medium, and small plates)

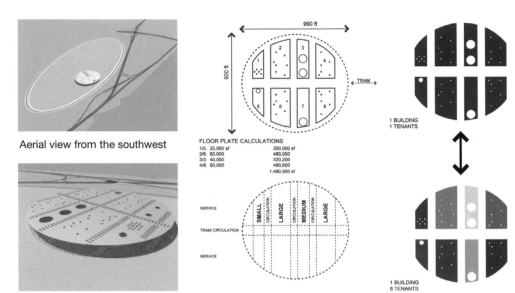

Aerial view from the southwest

Aerial perspective from the north

FLOOR PLATE CALCULATIONS

1/5.	25,000 sf	200,000 sf
2/6.	60,000	480,000
3/3.	40,000	320,200
4/8.	60,000	480,800
		1,480,000 sf

990 ft
900 ft
TRAM

SERVICE
TRAM/ CIRCULATION
SERVICE

SMALL CIRCULATION · LARGE CIRCULATION · MEDIUM CIRCULATION · LARGE

1 BUILDING
1 TENANTS

1 BUILDING
8 TENANTS

Office Option: Star
780,000 square feet
(5 buildings, 5 floors, 100-foot common depth)

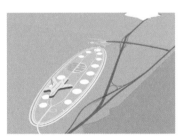

Aerial view from the southwest

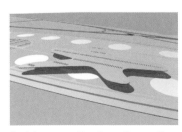

Aerial perspective from the north

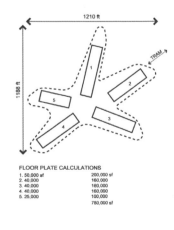

1210 ft
1188 ft
TRAM

FLOOR PLATE CALCULATIONS

1.	50,000 sf	200,000 sf
2.	40,000	160,000
3.	40,000	160,000
4.	40,000	160,000
5.	25,000	100,000
		780,000 sf

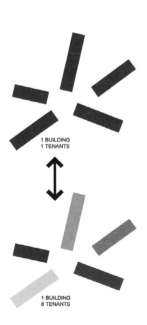

1 BUILDING
1 TENANTS

1 BUILDING
8 TENANTS

Office Option: Venus

747,200 square feet
(8 buildings, 5 floors, 100-foot common depth)

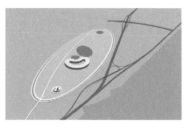

Aerial view from the southwest

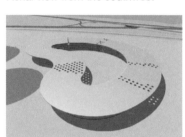

Aerial perspective from the north

975 ft

975 ft

FLOOR PLATE CALCULATIONS

1. 44,500 sf	178,000 sf
2. 15,400	61,600
3. 25,600	102,400
4. 16,500	66,000
5. 25,600	102,400
6. 16,400	65,600
7. 23,000	92,000
8. 18,800	79,200
	747,200 sf

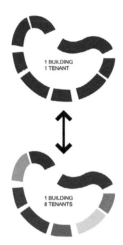

1 BUILDING
1 TENANT

1 BUILDING
8 TENANTS

Office Option: Neptune

732,000 square feet
(3 buildings, 5 floors)

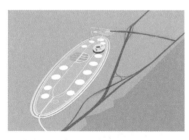

Aerial view from the southwest

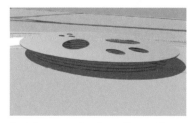

Aerial perspective from the north

550 ft

890 ft

TRAM

FLOOR PLATE CALCULATIONS

1. 51,750 sf	207,000 sf
2. 63,800	255,200
3. 67,500	270,000
	732,200 sf

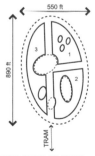

CIRCULATION/ SERVICE

TRAM

1 BUILDING
1 TENANTS

1 BUILDING
3 TENANTS

Offices

We have located the Financial Operations ellipse in the large orbit. Inside the ellipse are individual elements (operations and banking centers, a visitor center, a VIP center, and so forth). Straddling the boundary of the ellipse is a transit center, with two carpark structures adjoining it.

LAIFEX

One of the first structures to be built on the Financial Services Zone (FSZ) site, the LAIFEX building is the only tall presence in the FSZ. It is simultaneously a VIP visitors' center, an information and press center, a radio and TV station, and a lookout tower, with dining room facilities and a great view over the complex and the ocean.

LAIFEX is characterized by a large horizontal two-story deck accommodating general facilities, and a tall vertical beacon that provides views and acts as a lighthouse for the project.

LAIFEX
44,330 square feet
(base = 38,420 square feet, 2 floors;
tower = 5,900 square feet, 2 floors, 120 feet tall)

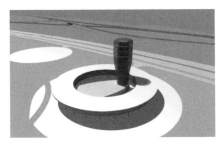
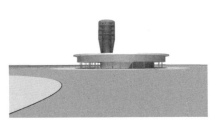

Aerial perspective and view from the FSZ facing southwest

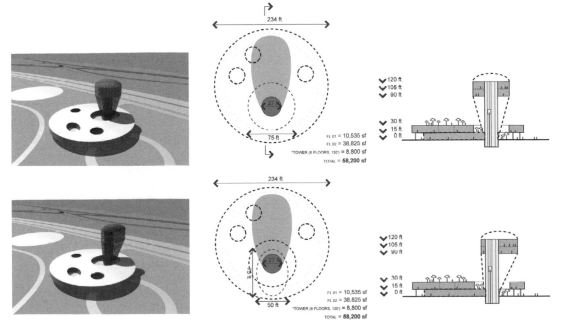

Options 1 and 2: perspective, plan, and section

Office Option: Jupiter

3,000,000 square feet
(7 buildings, 18 floors)

Aerial view from the southwest

Aerial perspective from the FSZ

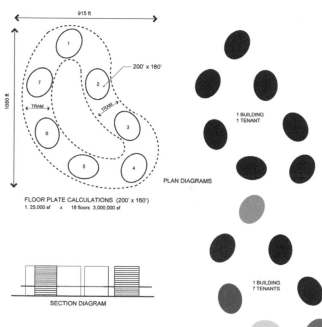

915 ft

1080 ft

200' x 160'

TRAM

TRAM

PLAN DIAGRAMS

FLOOR PLATE CALCULATIONS (200' x 160')
1. 25,000 sf   x   18 floors 3,000,000 sf

SECTION DIAGRAM

1 BUILDING
1 TENANT

1 BUILDING
7 TENANTS

Office Option: Saturn

1,500,000 square feet
(2 buildings, 5/15 floors, 120 feet w

Aerial view from the southwest

Aerial perspective from the FSZ

635 ft

520 ft

220' dia.

1

2

PLAN DIAGRAMS

FLOOR PLATE CALCULATIONS
1. 170,000 sf x 5 floors   625,000 sf
2. 38,000   18 floors   850,000

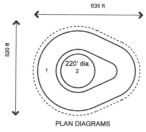

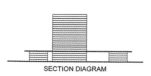

SECTION DIAGRAM

1 BUILDING
1 TENANTS

1 BUILDING
2 TENANTS

Office Option: Mars

1,500,000 square feet
(8 buildings, 5/15 floors, 100-foot common depth)

Aerial view from the southwest

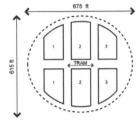

675 ft

615 ft

TRAM

FLOOR PLATE CALCULATIONS
1. 23,000 sf x 10 floors   230,000 x 2 = 460,000sf
2. 29,000   x 10 floors   290,000 x 2 = 580,000
3. 23,000   x 10 floors   230,000 x 2 = 460,000

1 BUILDING
1 TENANTS

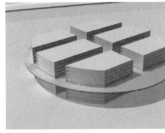

Aerial perspective from the FSZ

SECTION DIAGRAM

1 BUILDING
6 TENANTS

Office Option: Uranus

1,500,000 square feet
(8 buildings, 5 floors, 100-foot common depth)

Aerial view from the southwest

Aerial perspective from the FSZ

915 ft

120'

1080 ft

TRAM

TRAM

FLOOR PLATE CALCULATIONS (200' x 160')
1-7. 25,000 sf x 10 floors   1,750,000 sf
8.   356,000   x   5 floors   1,780,000

SECTION DIAGRAM

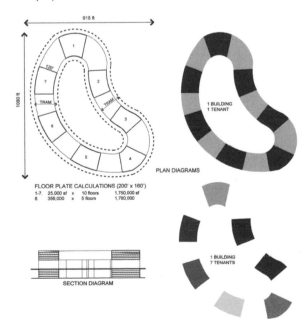

PLAN DIAGRAMS

1 BUILDING
1 TENANT

1 BUILDING
7 TENANTS

Housing

A residential orbit can accommodate several housing ellipses or islands. Each housing ellipse can hold a different type of residence, including one-family bungalows, urban villas, and four-story multiple residences, among others. The boundaries between the islands are planted with the lush vegetation characteristic of the Caribbean Islands.

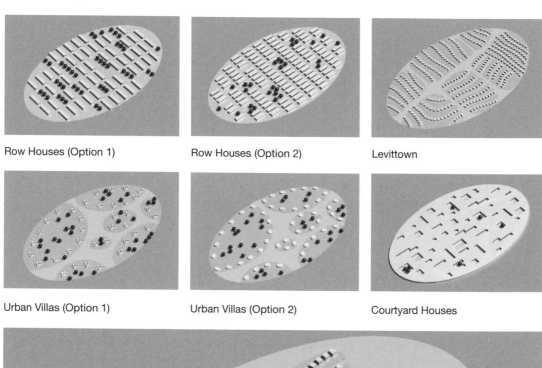

Row Houses (Option 1)

Row Houses (Option 2)

Levittown

Urban Villas (Option 1)

Urban Villas (Option 2)

Courtyard Houses

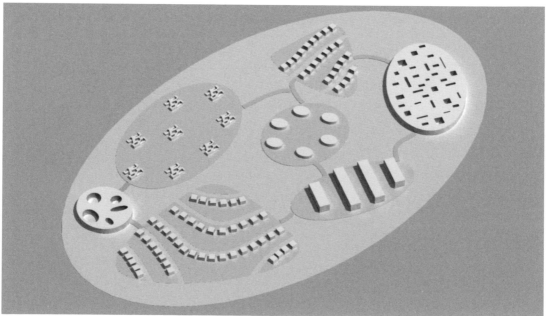

If each island were a different type of housing, the islands could be combined to create an archipelago with a mixture of lifestyles. In this case, each island would have a single type of housing and would be connected to other islands via a main circulation stem.

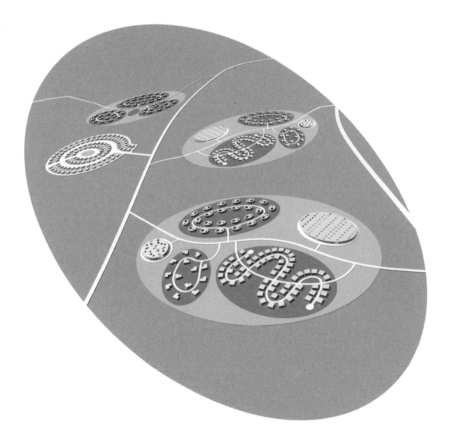

Archipelago of different housing types

The island has a total area of 212,000 square meters or 2.4 million square feet. We tested various housing schemes and densities. If an individual needs 100 square meters per person, the island can be home to 2,120 people. If an individual needs only 50 square meters, the population jumps to 4,240 people.

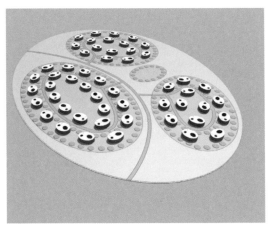 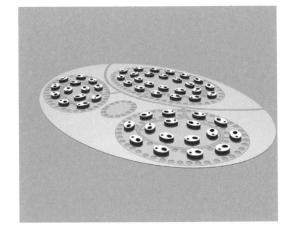

Single Family
4.5 units per acre (1,000 sq. meters per unit)
Total = 53 units

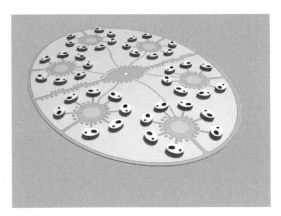 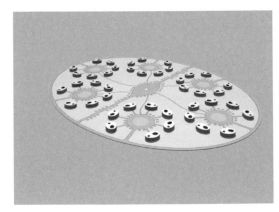

Single Family (Alternate Option)
4.5 units per acre (1,000 sq. meters per unit)
Total = 42 units

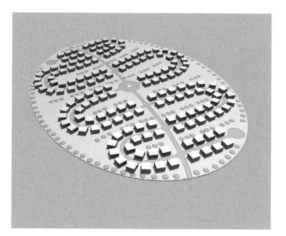

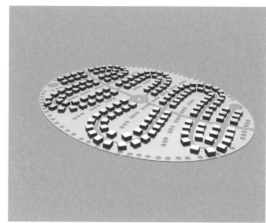

Town Home
15 units per acre (270 sq. meters per unit)
Total = 170 units

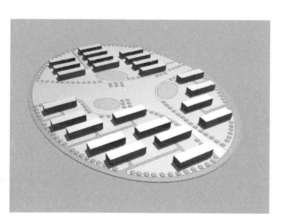

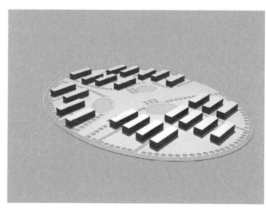

High-Density Row House
50 units per acre (80 sq. meters per unit)
Total = 576 units

Aerial view looking northeast

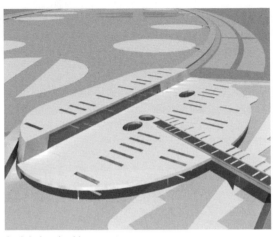

Aerial view looking west

View from the bridge to the carpark

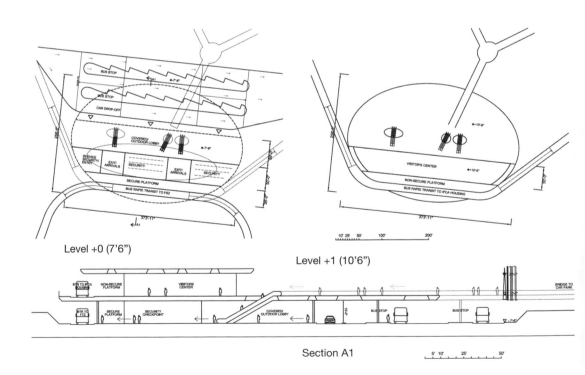

Level +0 (7'6")

Level +1 (10'6")

Section A1

Transit Center

The transit center is located over the edge of the FSZ. It provides information and security clearance.

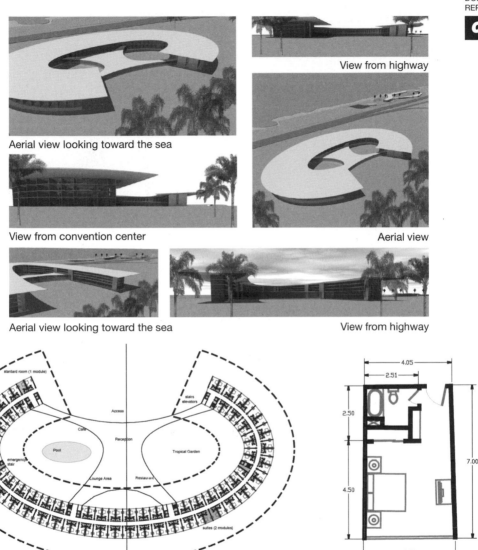

Aerial view looking toward the sea

View from highway

View from convention center

Aerial view

Aerial view looking toward the sea

View from highway

Hotel

A four- or five-star hotel with a central outdoor space will provide ocean views for most rooms.

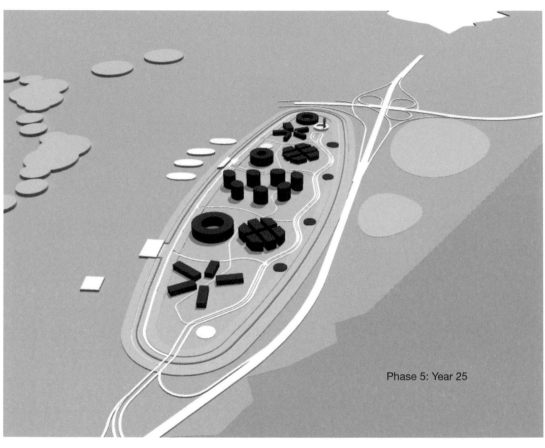

Phase 5: Year 25

Phase 1: Year 5

Phase 2: Year 10

Phase 3: Year 15

Phase 4: Year 20

Phases 1-5 Total Office Build-out:
9,000,000 gross square feet, including 5% carparks, a restaurant, and a wellness center

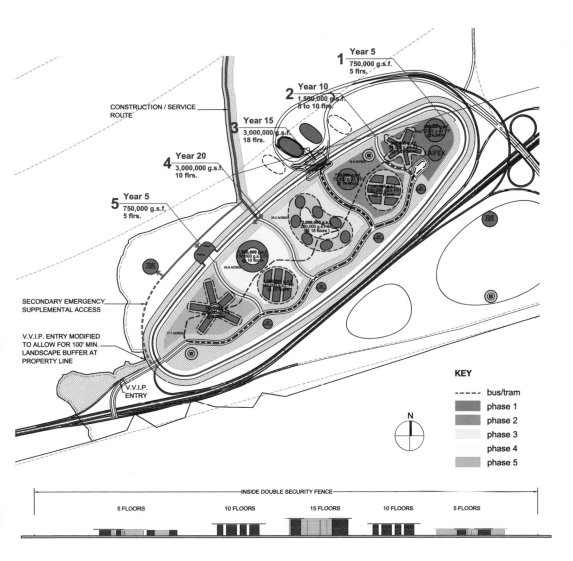

CONSTRUCTION / SERVICE
ROUTE

1 Year 5
750,000 g.s.f.
5 flrs.

2 Year 10
1,500,000 g.s.f.
5 to 10 flrs.

3 Year 15
3,000,000 g.s.f.
18 flrs.

4 Year 20
3,000,000 g.s.f.
10 flrs.

5 Year 5
750,000 g.s.f.
5 flrs.

AIFEX

SECONDARY EMERGENCY
SUPPLEMENTAL ACCESS

V.V.I.P. ENTRY MODIFIED
TO ALLOW FOR 100' MIN.
LANDSCAPE BUFFER AT
PROPERTY LINE

V.V.I.P.
ENTRY

KEY

- - - - - bus/tram
phase 1
phase 2
phase 3
phase 4
phase 5

N

INSIDE DOUBLE SECURITY FENCE

| 5 FLOORS | 10 FLOORS | 15 FLOORS | 10 FLOORS | 5 FLOORS |

200' 400' 600' 800' 1000'   1500'   2000'
100m 200m 300m 400m 500m 600m

Distribution option with base phasing

BEYOND THE GLOBAL ORDER · SCI-FI MEETS FINANCIAL TIMES · ...

TIME

THE NEXT FINANCIAL SERVICE ZONE

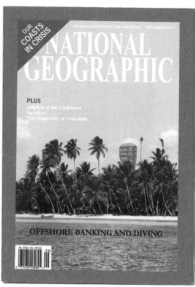

OUR COASTS IN CRISIS

NATIONAL GEOGRAPHIC

PLUS
Jellyfish of the Caribbean
Squatters
The Chemistry of Chocolate

OFFSHORE BANKING AND DIVING

THE DOMINICAN REPUBLIC IS THE HOT NEV

Us
WEEKLY

Brad and Angelina buy in the
DOMINICAN REPUBLIC!
ALL THE PICS of th
new oceanside property

BRAD ON

HER BEA

MS. UN

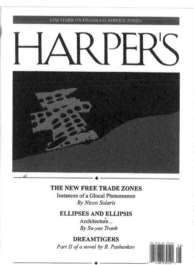

KIM STARR ON FINANCIAL SERVICE ZONES

HARPER'S

THE NEW FREE TRADE ZONES
Instances of a Glocal Phenomenon
By Nicco Solaris

ELLIPSES AND ELLIPSIS
Architecture...
By Su-yee Tranh

DREAMTIGERS
Part II of a novel by B. Pashenkov

PRICE $3.99   JULY 24, 2009

THE NEW YORKER

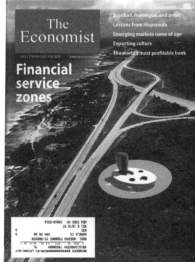

The Economist

Baseball, merengue, and pesos
Lessons from Hispaniola
Emerging markets come of age
Exporting culture
The world's most profitable bank

Financial service zones

We produced multiple magazine mock-ups for an exhibition at the 2006 Venice Biennale.

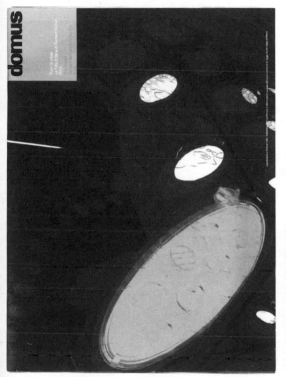

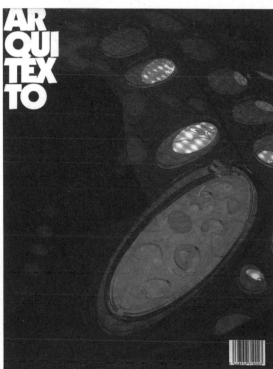

With the cover for the December 2006 *Arquitexto*, an imagined design became a reality.

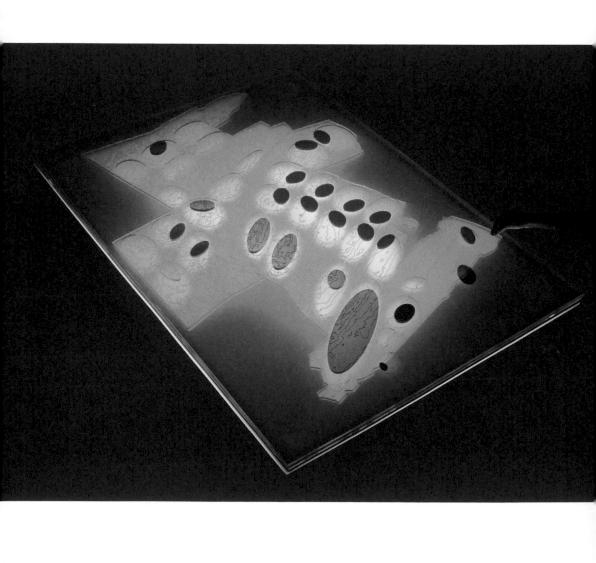

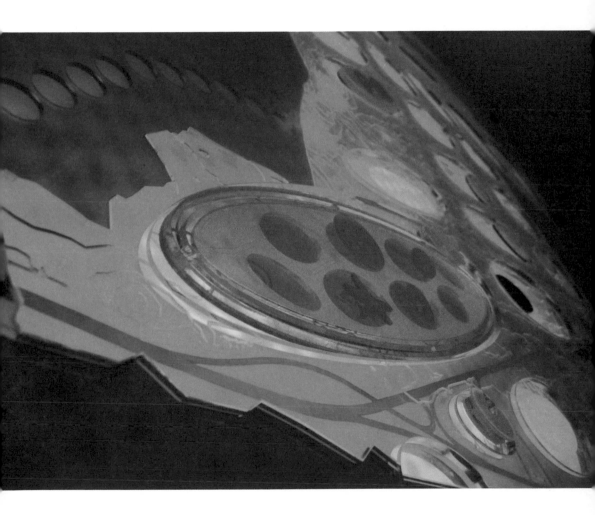

The model's movable pieces demonstrate the concept of the "game."

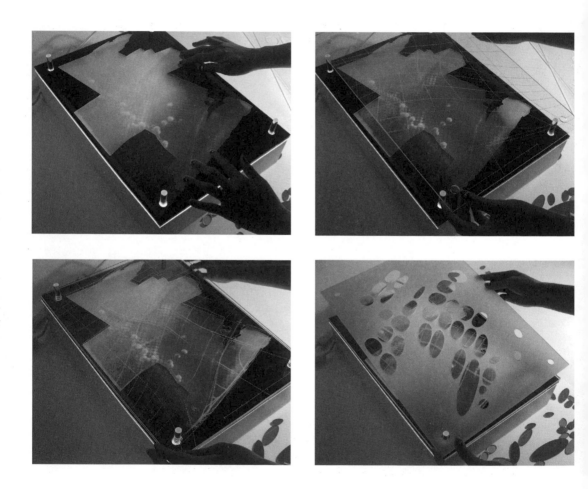

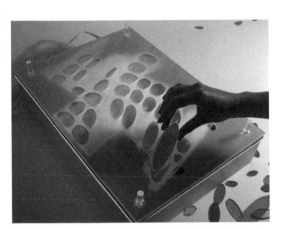

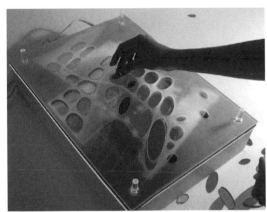

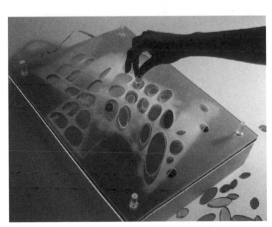

Playing the Master-Plan Game
A smaller version of the gameboard as presented at the 2006 Venice Biennale

Large programs
orbits and ellip
with other prog
interchangeab
orbit.

Alésia, France, MuseoParc, 2002-

Doubles

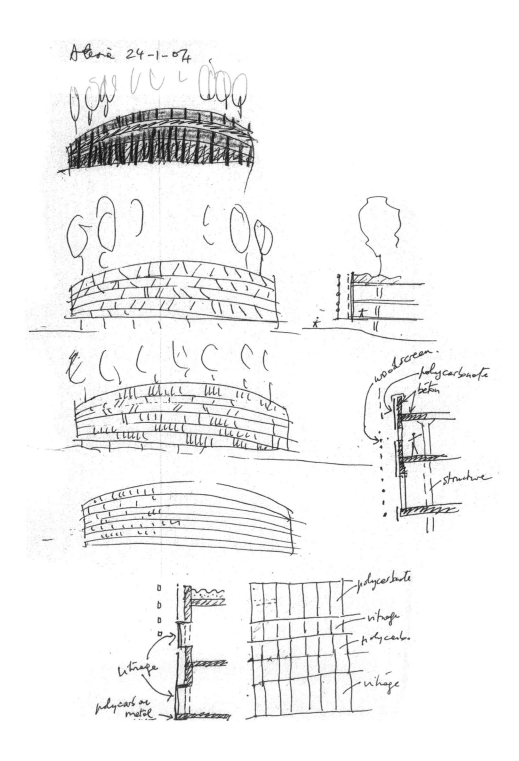

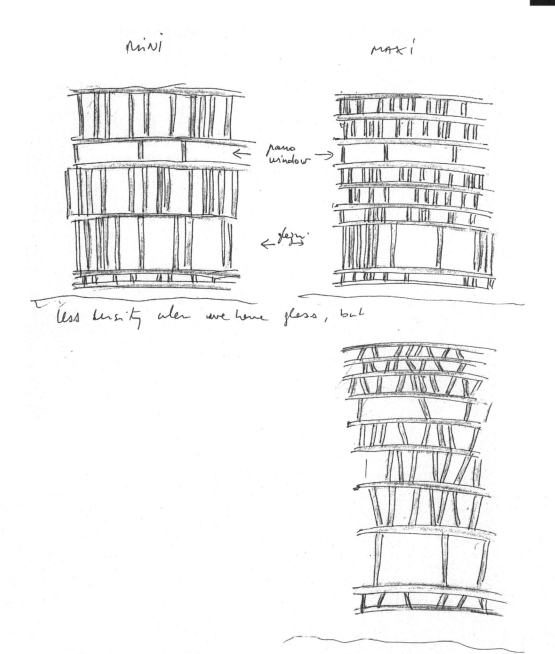

MINI

MAXI

pano
window →

← glazing

less density when we have glass, but

Sketches/diagrams: a concept-form with its potential envelope

The objective of this project is to celebrate, document, and explain a major event in French history: the battle of Alésia (52 BC), with its narrative of the resistance of Vercingétorix and the ultimate victory of Julius Caesar. The means to achieve this objective are two buildings (a museum and an interpretive center), a historical reproduction (a partial reconstitution of the battle fortifications), and several pedestrian paths in the historically preserved countryside.

Since the construction of the Bilbao Guggenheim, architecture has exerted an incontrovertible shift on the politics of museums and cultural institutions. We were tasked with both attracting the public and focusing attention on a historical event so as to give Alésia national and even international prominence. In other words, if the insertion of the architectural elements is local, their radiance is intended to be global.

To give maximum presence to historical events while showing the greatest possible sensitivity to the natural environment, to respond to the project's ambition while respecting the imperative of "modesty" required by the archeologists—in other words, to be simultaneously visible and invisible—is the paradox defining this project.

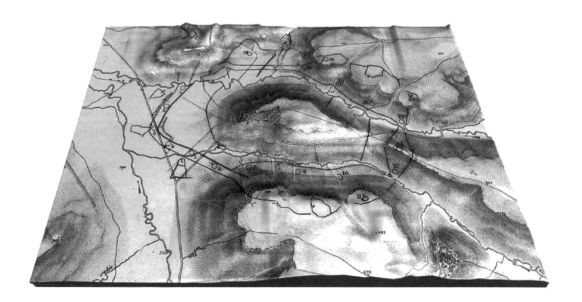

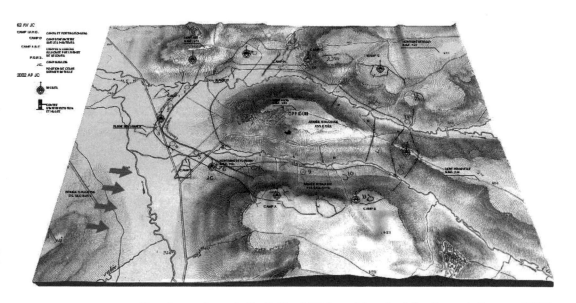

The site was home to the Battle of Alésia, a victory for Julius Caesar in the year 52 BC.

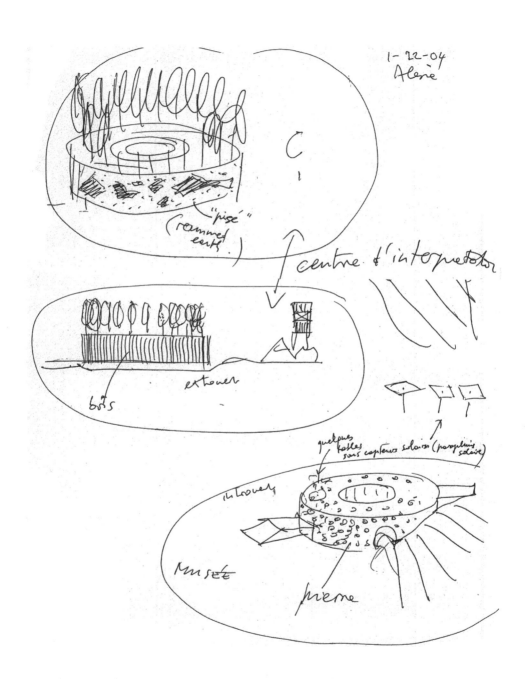

Both buildings follow the same concept-form, but their materials differ.

Alésia   1/28/04

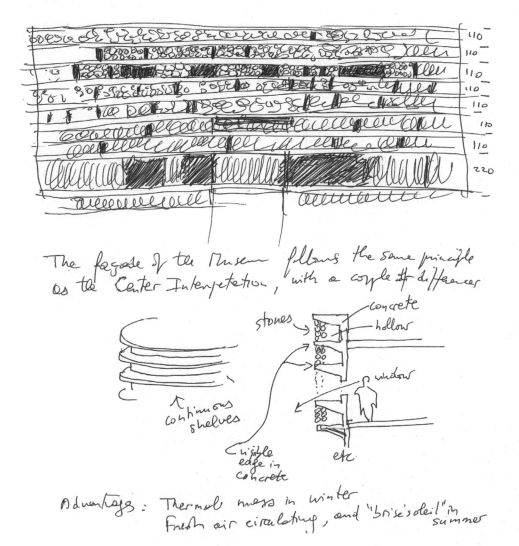

The façade of the Museum follows the same principle
as the Center Interpretation, with a couple of differences

continuous
shelves

stones

concrete
hollow

window

visible
edge in
concrete

etc.

Advantages : Thermal mass in winter
Fresh air circulating, and "brise'soleil" in
                                        summer

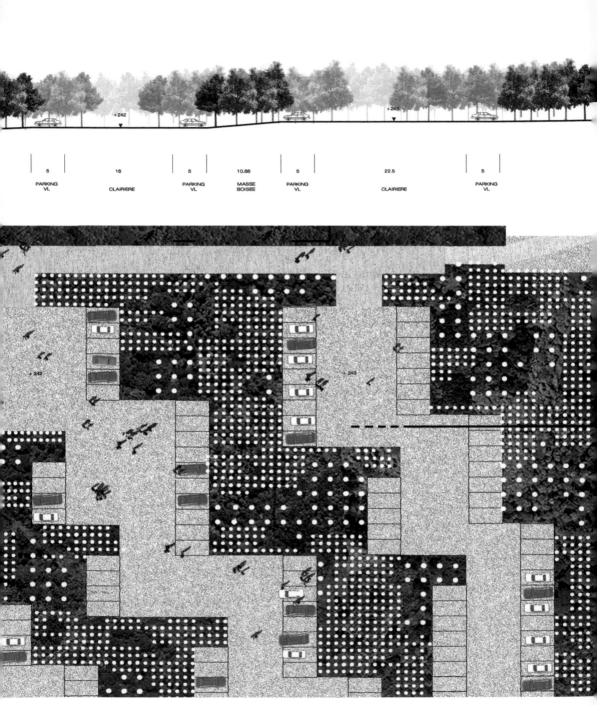

Interpretive center carpark (designed with landscaping by Michel Desvigne)

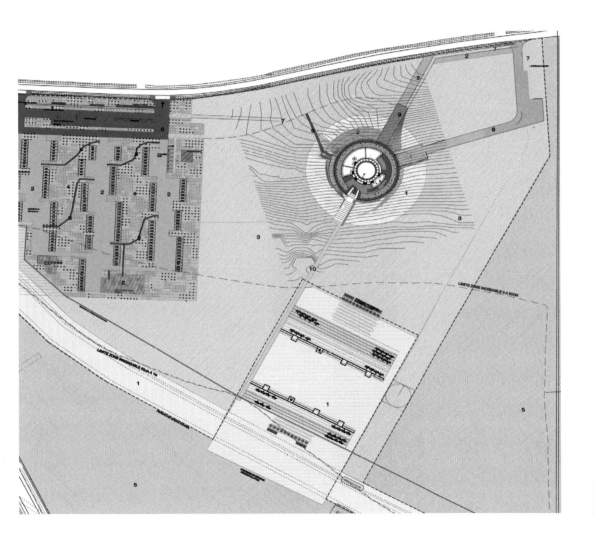

Interpretive center site plan

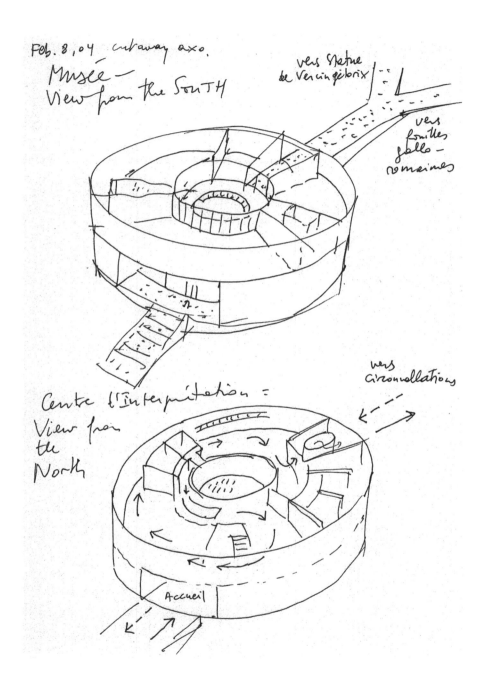

Circulation sketches for the museum (top) and interpretive center (bottom)

A concept-form differs from a type in that it is not bound by history or historical context. Traditionally, typological analysis has been attentive not only to form and configuration, but also to the symbolic identification of types. In this sense, a concept-form has no a priori meaning attached to it. The concept-form of a circular building is not necessarily meant to refer to or recall Roman amphitheaters or panopticon types, even if they all share certain geometrical characteristics.

The Interpretive Center: "Wood"

The interpretive center is situated at the border of the departmental row at a location called the "high meadow." Parking for visitors is hidden beneath the site, reinforcing the slope of the terrain while avoiding external visibility. In the case of overflow, two land-scaped parking areas (which utilize reinforced grass and landscaped screens) are also available.

The entrance is located on the ground floor, where the shop and the restaurant, as well as spaces for education, entertainment, and administration, are all easily accessible. Once inside, after ascending the ramp, visitors will find conference rooms tucked to one side, and, on the other, cinematic spaces that offer an almost 360-degree view over the site and neighboring landscapes (made possible by their elevated position on the second floor and the unfolding of the facade).

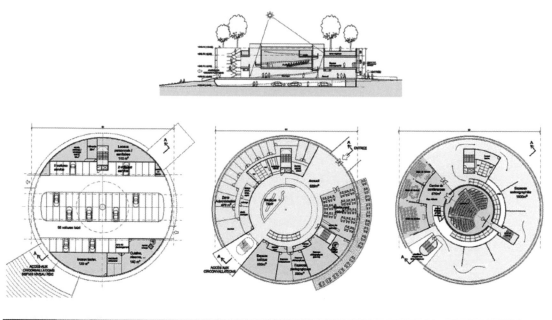

Section and L-1, L0, L+1 plans (competition stage)

Circulation flows in the interpretive center

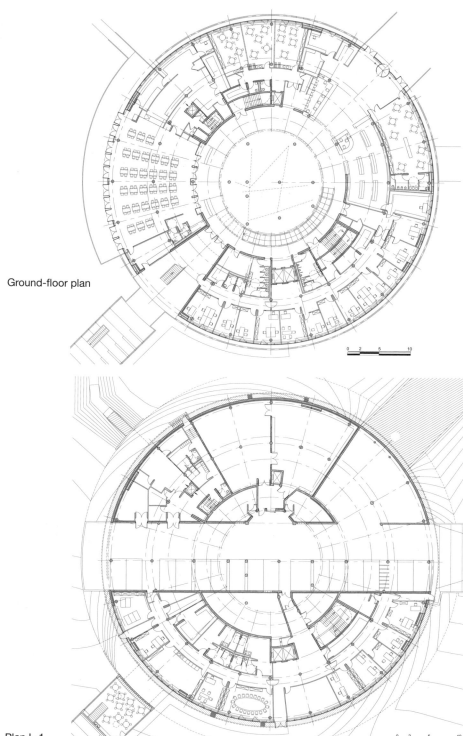

Ground-floor plan

Plan L-1

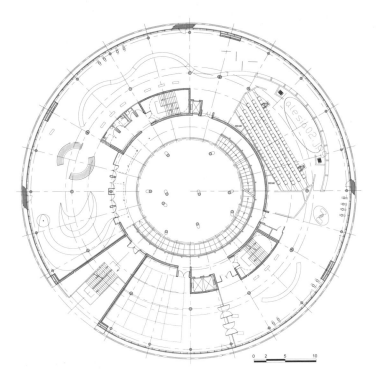

Plan L+1

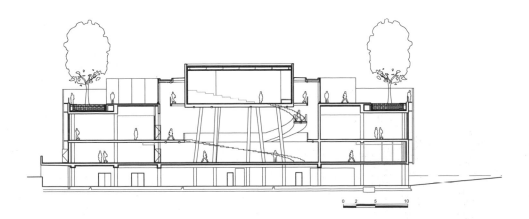

Plan R+1 and section

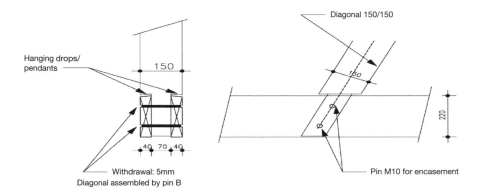

Hanging drops/
pendants

150

40 70 40

Withdrawal: 5mm
Diagonal assembled by pin B

Diagonal 150/150

150

220

Pin M10 for encasement

Detail: fixing of the diagonals and encasement (transverse section)

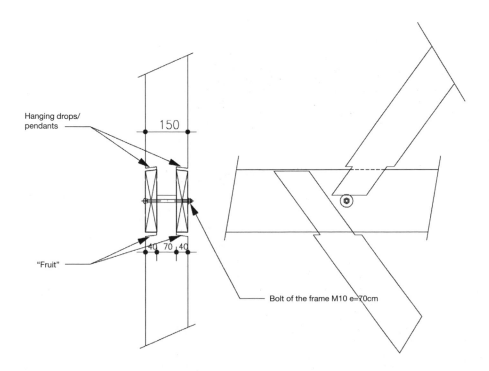

Hanging drops/
pendants

150

40 70 40

"Fruit"

Bolt of the frame M10 e=70cm

Detail: hooping the rings (transverse section)

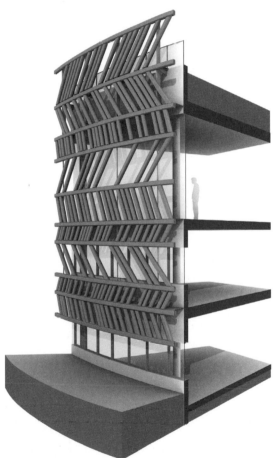

Mock-up of the wood envelope

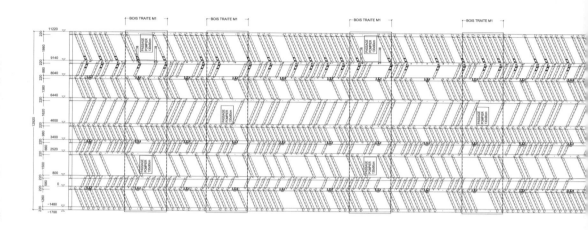

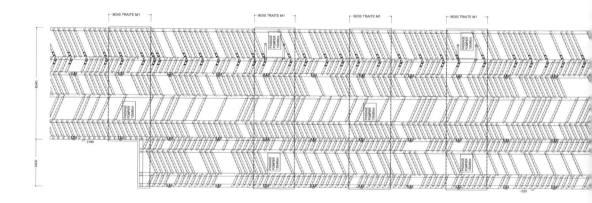

Interpretive center: unwrapped elevation

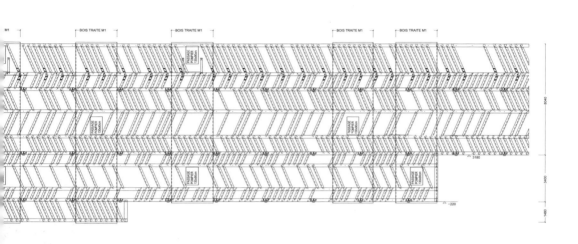

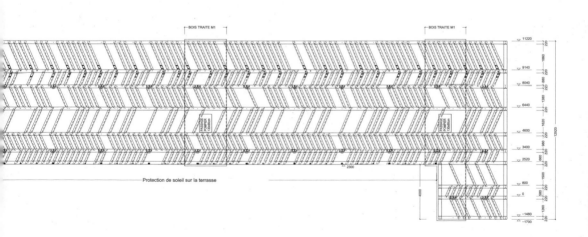

Protection de soleil sur la terrasse

The Museum: "Stone"

The building housing the museum is situated at the base of hilly terrain in the north of the village at a specific location, called "Curiot," that is characterized by a steep slope. The museum is both integrated into the surrounding neighborhood and visible from the main street of the village. Taking advantage of the steep incline, the bulk of the parking lot is inserted into the slope. Surrounding the sloped entry to the museum are a terraced café and a museum shop. A second part of the museum's collection is located along the same axis so as to be visible but not accessible to visitors. Administration areas are located on the same level.

At the top of the central staircase, the permanent exhibitions, temporary exhibition spaces, documentation center, and education spaces all hover above the glass located below. After visiting the galleries, visitors equipped with tickets can climb up to the Oppidum without descending, thanks to the slope of the landscape. The theatrical spaces look onto the village and over the plains where the Roman forces took up their positions centuries ago.

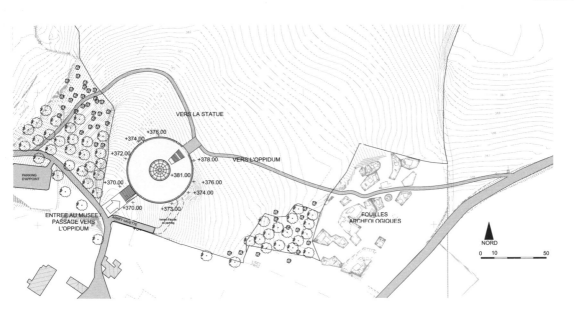

Site plan

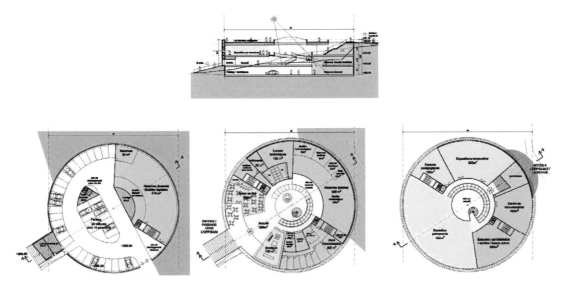

Section and L-1, L0, L+1 plans (competition stage)

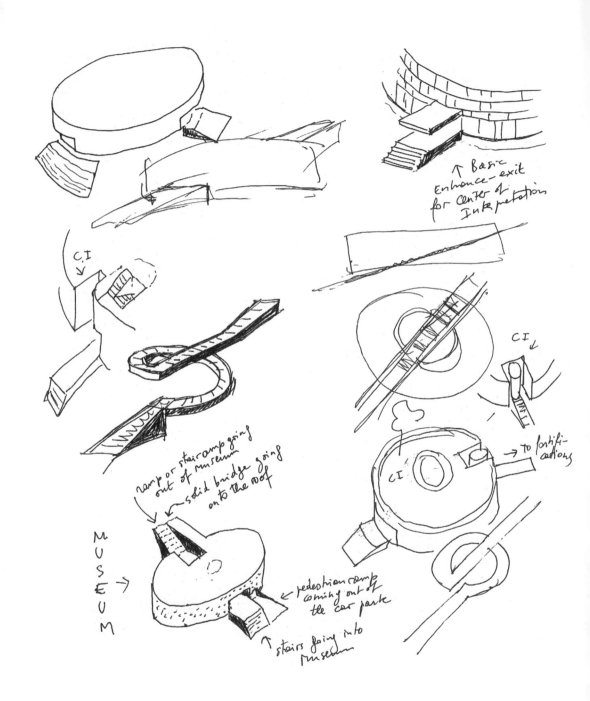

Sketches/diagrams: moving toward a concept-form for the museum

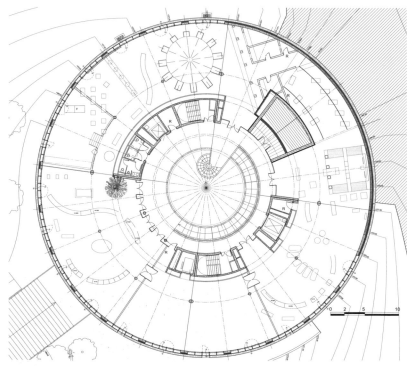

L+1 plan

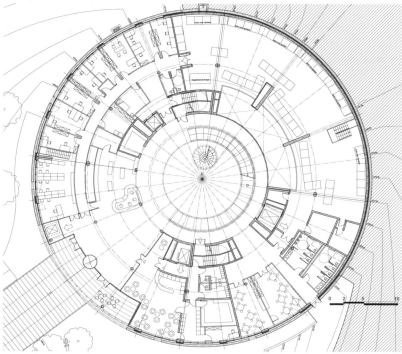

Ground-floor plan

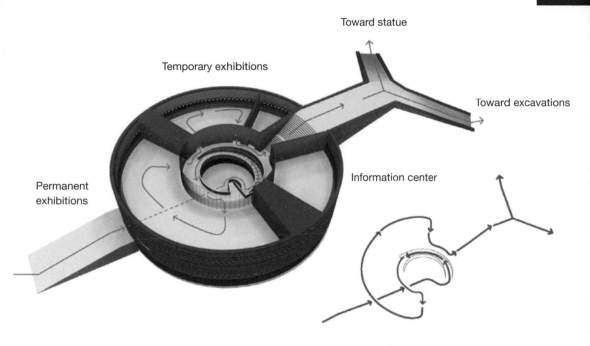

Toward statue

Temporary exhibitions

Toward excavations

Permanent
exhibitions

Information center

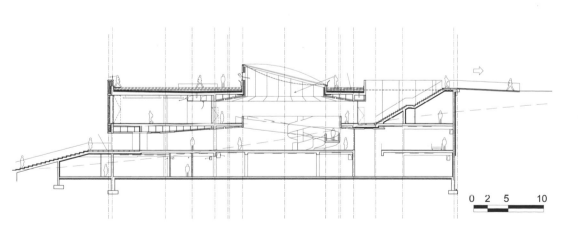

Circulation diagram and section of the museum

0 2 5   10

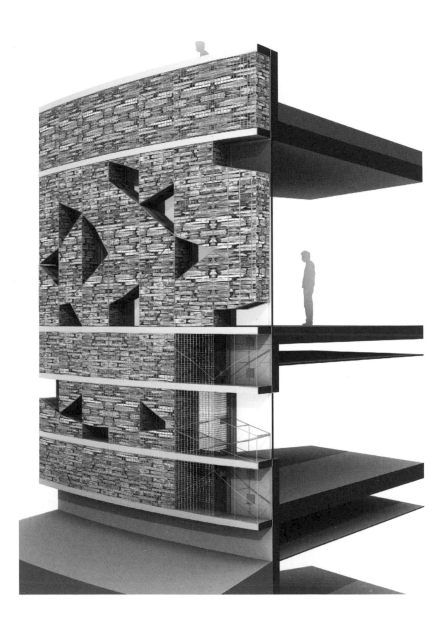

The museum: a stone envelope supported by concrete shelves

Mock-up of the stone envelope

	WOOD		EARTH
	STONE		GLASS
	CONCRETE		COPPER

1	Museum	Interpretive Center
Structure	TIMBER	TIMBER
Walls	STONE	EARTH
Windows	PUNCHED	PUNCHED
Roof	EARTH/GRASS	EARTH / GRASS

2	Museum	Interpretive Center
Structure	TIMBER	TIMBER
Walls	GLASS	EARTH
Windows	CURTAIN WALL	PUNCHED
Roof	GRASS / EARTH	GRASS / EARTH

4	Museum	Interpretive Center
Structure	CONCRETE OR STEEL	CONCRETE OR STEEL
Walls	GLASS	CONCRETE
Windows	CURTAIN WALL	PUNCHED
Roof	GRASS / EARTH	GRASS / EARTH

5	Museum	Interpretive Center
Structure	CONCRETE OR STEEL	TIMBER
Walls	EARTH	GLASS
Windows	PUNCHED	CURTAIN WALL
Roof	GRASS / EARTH	METAL (COPPER)

7	Museum	Interpretive Center
Structure	CONCRETE OR STEEL	TIMBER
Walls	STONE	COPPER
Windows	PUNCHED RIBBON	PUNCHED - RIBBON
Roof	GRASS / EARTH	COPPER

8	Museum	Interpretive Center
Structure	CONCRETE OR STEEL	CONCRETE OR STEEL
Walls	STONE	EARTH
Windows	PUNCHED - RIBBON	PUNCHED - RIBBON
Roof	GRASS / EARTH	GRASS / EARTH

10	Museum	Interpretive Center
Structure	CONCRETE OR STEEL	CONCRETE OR STEEL
Walls	CONCRETE	CONCRETE
Windows	PUNCHED	PUNCHED
Roof	GRASS / EARTH	WOOD OR COPPER

11	Museum	Interpretive Center
Structure	CONCRETE OR STEEL	CONCRETE OR STEEL
Walls	GLASS	GLASS
Windows	CURTAIN WALL	CURTAIN WALL
Roof	GRASS / EARTH	WOOD OR COPPER

Material envelope permutations (drawing by Kim Starr)

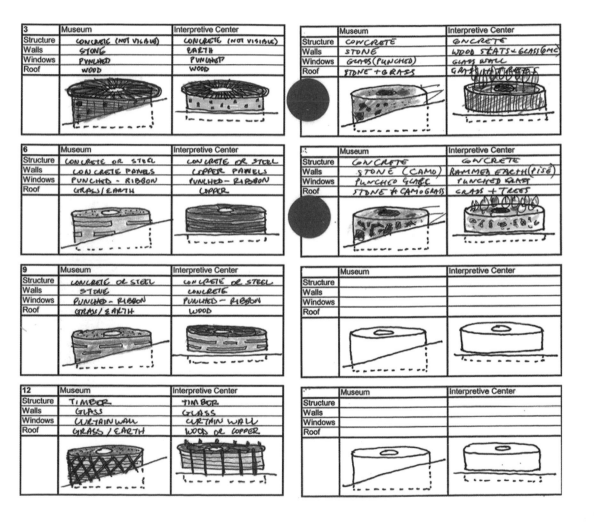

Any new architecture implies the idea of combination; all form is the result of combination.
("Although every creation is of necessity combinative, society, by virtue of the old romantic myth of 'inspiration,' cannot stand being told so." Roland Barthes, in *Sade/Fourier/Loyola*)

Athens, Bank, 2006

Plato's Academy

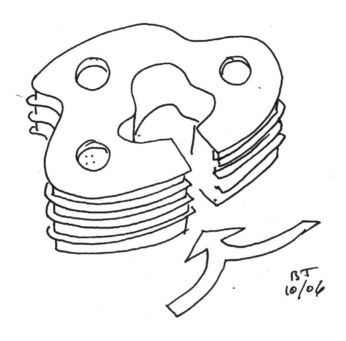

Curvilinear Outline

Image: How to design a bank in an era of electronic capital and invisible transactions?

Context: How to design a major building located in a newly developing business center at the edge of an important archeological park?

Technology: How to design a high-density office building while retaining flexibility and energy-efficiency in the hot Athens climate?

A hundred years ago, banks were designed to look like Greek temples; "real" banknotes were deposited or withdrawn; and the facades and central halls of financial institutions were represented as firm symbols of power. Today, money is part of a fluid, global net-work, and investment banking is about the flow of information above all else.

In this project for a bank located alongside Plato's Academy Park in Athens, we tried to express the new fluidity of information by using a curvilinear image. In keeping with its context, the building also reads as a pivot between the park and the surrounding office neighborhood. Finally, use of concrete and printed glass, among other features, allowed us to design an energy-efficient building. The project attempts to solve a challenging equation with simplicity, combining image, context, and technology in one precise state-ment.

Smooth lines define the outside of the building, with the edges of the floor plates acting as a shading device along the south facade. This is complemented on the east and west facades by glass fins. The floor-to-ceiling glazing is tinted a dark hue, while the glass fins have a white dotted screen comparable to the black dotted screen used for the Acropolis Museum.

The large floor plates are defined by smooth outlines, allowing for a variety of uses, from open space or individual offices of various sizes to meeting rooms, private dining rooms, and exhibition areas. Daylight penetrates not only from the perimeter but also from the center of the building, thanks to an inner outdoor courtyard. Additionally, the curvilinear geometry of the building optimizes energy conservation by yielding a nearly 10% reduc-tion in facade area when compared to a rectangular building configuration.

The entrance hall expands to the full height of the building's five floors and opens onto the inner court and its greenscape. On the top floor, three patios act as executive relaxation areas. Three circular nodes of stairs, elevators, and bathrooms service the entire building.

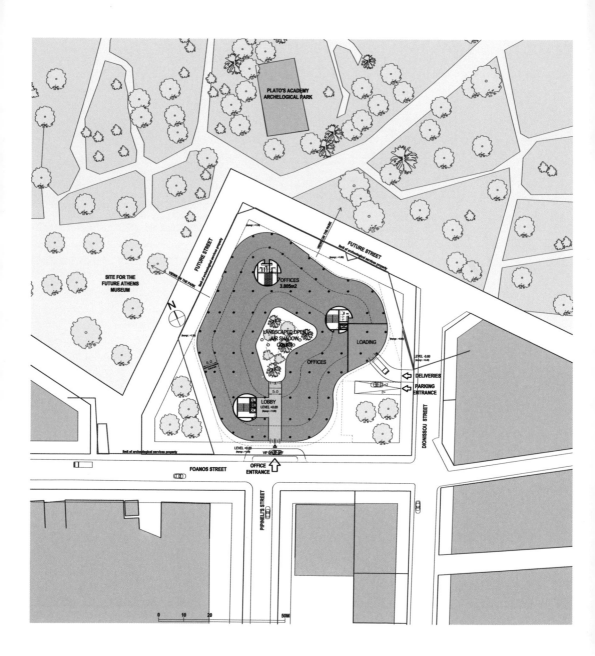

PLATO'S ACADEMY
ARCHELOGICAL PARK

FUTURE STREET

FUTURE STREET

SITE FOR THE
FUTURE ATHENS
MUSEUM

N

OFFICES
3.805m2

LANDSCAPED OPEN
AIR SHADOW

OFFICES

LOADING

DELIVERIES

PARKING
ENTRANCE

LEVEL -0.80

LOBBY
LEVEL +0.00

DIONISSOU STREET

LEVEL +0.00

VIP

OFFICE
ENTRANCE

FOANOS STREET

PIPINELI'S STREET

0   10   20   50M

Site plan

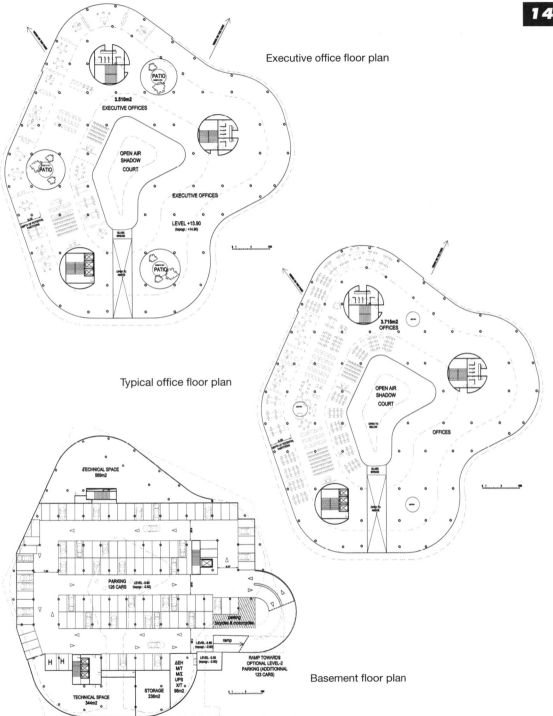

Executive office floor plan

3.510m2
EXECUTIVE OFFICES

PATIO

PATIO

OPEN AIR
SHADOW
COURT

EXECUTIVE OFFICES

LEVEL +13.90
(topogr.: +14.90)

GLASS
BRIDGE

OPEN TO
ABOVE

PATIO

Typical office floor plan

3.715m2
OFFICES

OPEN AIR
SHADOW
COURT

OPEN TO
BELOW

OFFICES

GLASS
BRIDGE

OPEN TO
ABOVE

TECHNICAL SPACE
569m2

PARKING
126 CARS   LEVEL -3.80
(topogr.: -2.80)

LEVEL -3.80
(topogr.: -2.80)

ramp

LEVEL -3.80
(topogr.: -2.80)

RAMP TOWARDS
OPTIONAL LEVEL-2
PARKING (ADDITIONNAL
123 CARS)

ΔΕΗ
M/T
M/Z
UPS
X/T
98m2

STORAGE
238m2

TECHNICAL SPACE
344m2

Basement floor plan

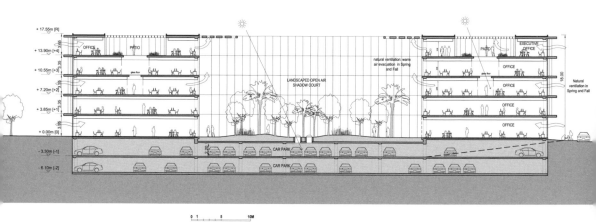

+ 17.55m [R]

+ 13.90m [+4]   OFFICE   PATIO   EXECUTIVE
                                                                                                                                                    OFFICE

+ 10.55m [+3]   glass floor   natural ventilation: warm   OFFICE
                                                                                        air evacuation in Spring
                                                            LANDSCAPED OPEN AIR   and Fall   Natural
+ 7.20m [+2]   SHADOW COURT   OFFICE   ventilation in
                                                                                                                                                           Spring and Fall

+ 3.85m [+1]   OFFICE

+ 0.00m [0]   OFFICE

- 3.30m [-1]   CAR PARK

- 6.10m [-2]   CAR PARK

0 1   5   10M

Section

Sustainability

The design integrates sustainability principles appropriate to the Greek climate and environment. The double glass body is tinted in a dark hue, ensuring a good U-value and shading coefficient. The slabs extend progressively beyond the facade. They are flush with the glass facade on the north side and gradually extend out to reach a maximum cantilever on the south side, optimizing the facade's protection from the high sun on the south. Glass fritted fins envelop the building, progressively changing depth in order to provide optimum protection from the low sun in the morning and evening. The fins are deepest on the east and west facades and become thinner toward the north and south sides. The roof slab also extends on the side of the court and is perforated, allowing it to protect the facade while providing light and shadow.

The gap between fins and facade is designed to allow the warm air to evacuate before reaching the interior facade layer. In summer, the slabs and fins cut the heat gain from the sun, while in winter the sun can penetrate the building and warm up the interior. In spring and fall the facade allows natural ventilation. The air can circulate thanks to a chimney effect provided by the court and the patios, which favor the evacuation of internal hot air.

The extension of the slabs also provides a surface that allows light to bounce onto the ceiling, which brings more indirect light into the center of the floor. A chilled ceiling system allows for more efficient air cooling, and the raised technical floor allows flexibility and ease of access to the ceiling.

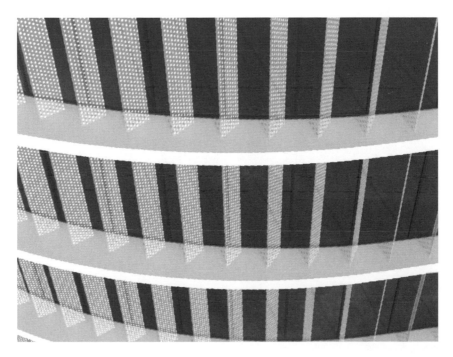

White-printed glass fins varying in depth according to orientation

Interior view of executive floor, offices, and patio

Rolle, Carnal Dome, 2009-

"Point d'orgue"

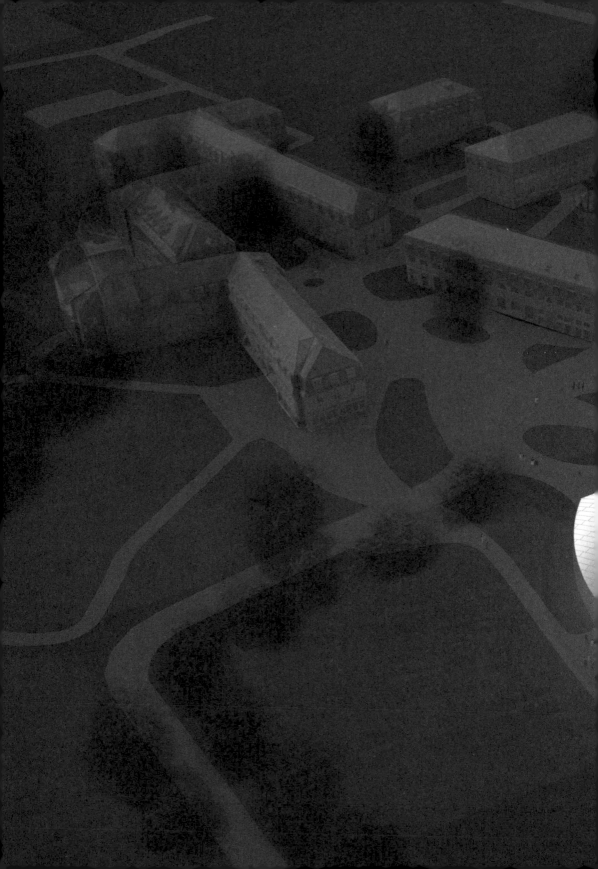

Multiprogrammatic Challenge

The campus architecture of Le Rosey, an international boarding school in Rolle, Switzerland, consists of a dozen buildings with a stately character. The top floors of these buildings are distinguished by mansard roofs, giving the campus homogeneity as well as a somewhat nostalgic identity that suggests a castle in the middle of a grove of trees. Within this context, the competition for a new arts center for the well-known school raised a series of questions:

How can a new structure infuse the campus with a contemporary architectural image while maintaining the qualities that have made the school a globally respected institution? How can the new arts center be integrated into the existing campus vernacular without imitating past buildings, but also without creating a disturbing break with them? How can architecture establish a complimentary relationship between the old and the new—a dialogue between tradition and modernity?

The program specified an 800-seat concert hall and several conference rooms, a learning center joined to a library, a teaching center, spaces for music and the arts, and several relaxation spaces to house a restaurant, a café, a student lounge, and other amenities.

A Common Denominator

Our strategy proposed a low, flat dome—a metal envelope that emerges from the landscape, shining in the sun by day and reflecting ambient campus light by night. This dome provides a common denominator for the various parts of the program. A place of meeting and interaction, it is situated at the base of the keystone-shaped area formed by the existing buildings.

From the air the dome appears as a distinctive object, but at ground level its gentle curvature fits into the landscape. In plan, its shape recalls a rose or rosette—a fitting allusion for Le Rosey. The reflective metal combines with the lush trees of the campus landscape to marry existing nature to the new facade, further complimenting the existing campus architecture.

A series of side openings articulates the periphery of the dome. A forecourt to the main entrance and the concert hall is located along the west facade. To the south, a terraced restaurant opens onto the main campus thoroughfare, which also serves as the primary access to Le Rosey's surrounding forest. A large planted terrace placed above the conference rooms offers views over Lake Geneva. To the north, the delivery area required for the installation of sets and for staging major performances is easily accessible, but discreet.

Interior: Clarity in Concept, Function, and Light

The dome's interior reads as a large space with a simple support system that allows for easy distribution of all programs. Natural light penetrates laterally to all areas that require an outside view. Wherever allowed by the program, the bulkheads are made out of transparent, translucent, or opaque glass in order to facilitate vision and transparency of the center's activities. Rooms that rest on the ground, including the conference rooms and performance areas, are made out of wood. Hence, the concept is realized through three main materials—metal, glass, and wood.

The distribution of activities is intended for legibility and clarity. Upon arrival, the visitor encounters the main concert or performance hall, the conference rooms, and the black-box theater. To the left are the ground-floor educational spaces. To the right is access to the learning center and the restaurant (which also has an independent entrance located near its terrace). Using a looping circulation concept, the center is designed as a journey. The visitor first passes the café and a store-kiosk located in the concert-hall foyer. From there, the path moves upward to an interstitial platform, revealing the library, followed by open spaces for discussion and group work with views toward the miniature arboretum. Visitors then reach a large staircase that accesses the mezzanine level, offering views over the black-box theater, the conference rooms and, finally, down to the library. Descending the staircase to take the route in reverse allows direct access to the conference rooms. The center takes its inspiration from the idea that art can be experienced as both a linear trajectory and a meeting of multiple disciplines. To this end, the center contains direct paths of movement as well as places designed for exchange and interaction. The looping logic of the path offers multiple modes of experience, since a user may visit the arts spaces, then the music portion, and finally enter a terrace without ever having to retrace his or her steps.

The building's compact shape (as determined by the dome) minimizes its external surface area, acting as a thermal shield. This provision drastically reduces energy consumption. The orientation of major traffic flows adds to compactness as well as visibility. The dome profile also minimizes the effect of prevailing winds. An entry on the southwest facade encourages fresh summer breezes while protecting against strong winter winds from the northeast.

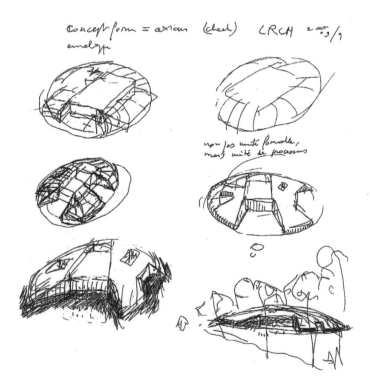

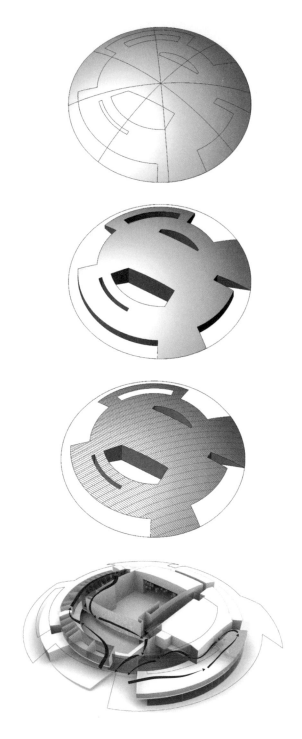

Movement vectors, volumes, and envelope

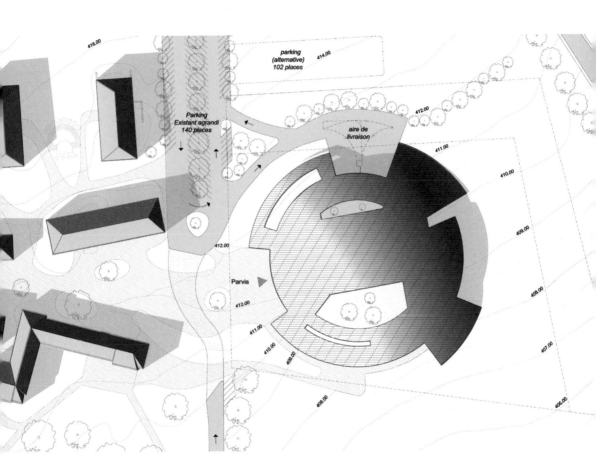

parking
(alternative)
102 places

416.00

414.00

412.00

411.00

410.00

409.00

408.00

407.00

406.00

Parking
Existant agrandi
140 places

aire de
livraison

412.00

Parvis

412.00

411.00

410.00

409.00

408.00

Site plan

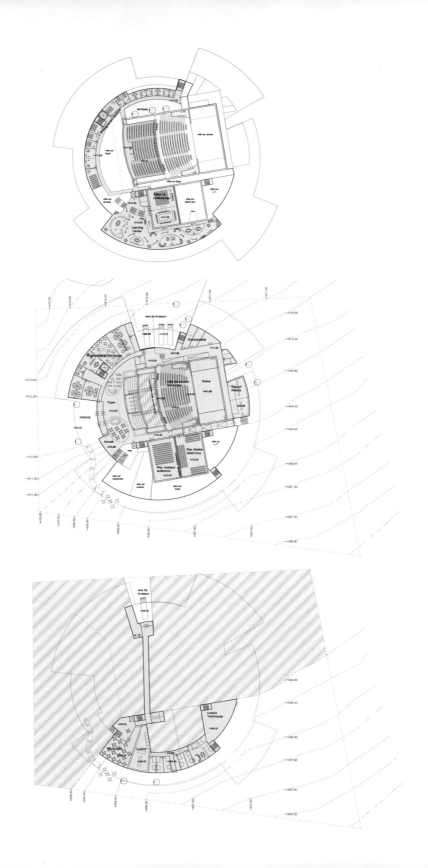

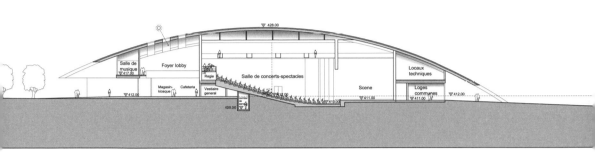

▽ 428.00

Salle de musique ▽417.00 · Foyer lobby · Régie · Salle de concerts-spectacles · Scène · Locaux techniques · Loges communes ▽411.00 ▽412.00

Magasin-kiosque · Cafeteria · Vestiaire general ▽412.00 ▽409.00 ▽410.00 ▽411.00

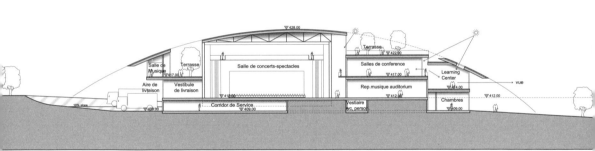

▽ 428.00

Salle de Musique · Terrasse · Terrasse ▽422.00 · Salles de conférence · Learning Center ▽414.00 · vue

Aire de livraison · Vestibule de livraison ▽417.00 · Salle de concerts-spectacles · Rep.musique auditorium ▽412.00 ▽412.00

10% slope ▽408.00 · Corridor de Service ▽409.00 · Vestiaire wc, person · Chambres ▽409.00

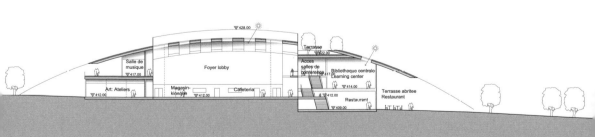

▽ 428.00

Salle de musique ▽417.00 · Foyer lobby · Terrasse ▽422.00 · Accès salles de conférence ▽417.00 · Bibliotheque controle Learning center ▽414.00

Art: Ateliers ▽412.00 · Magasin-kiosque ▽412.00 · Cafeteria · Restaurant ▽409.00 · Terrasse abritée Restaurant

Typical plans and sections

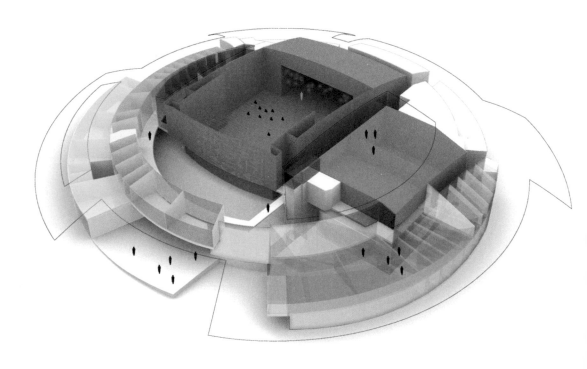

Concept-form as common denominator

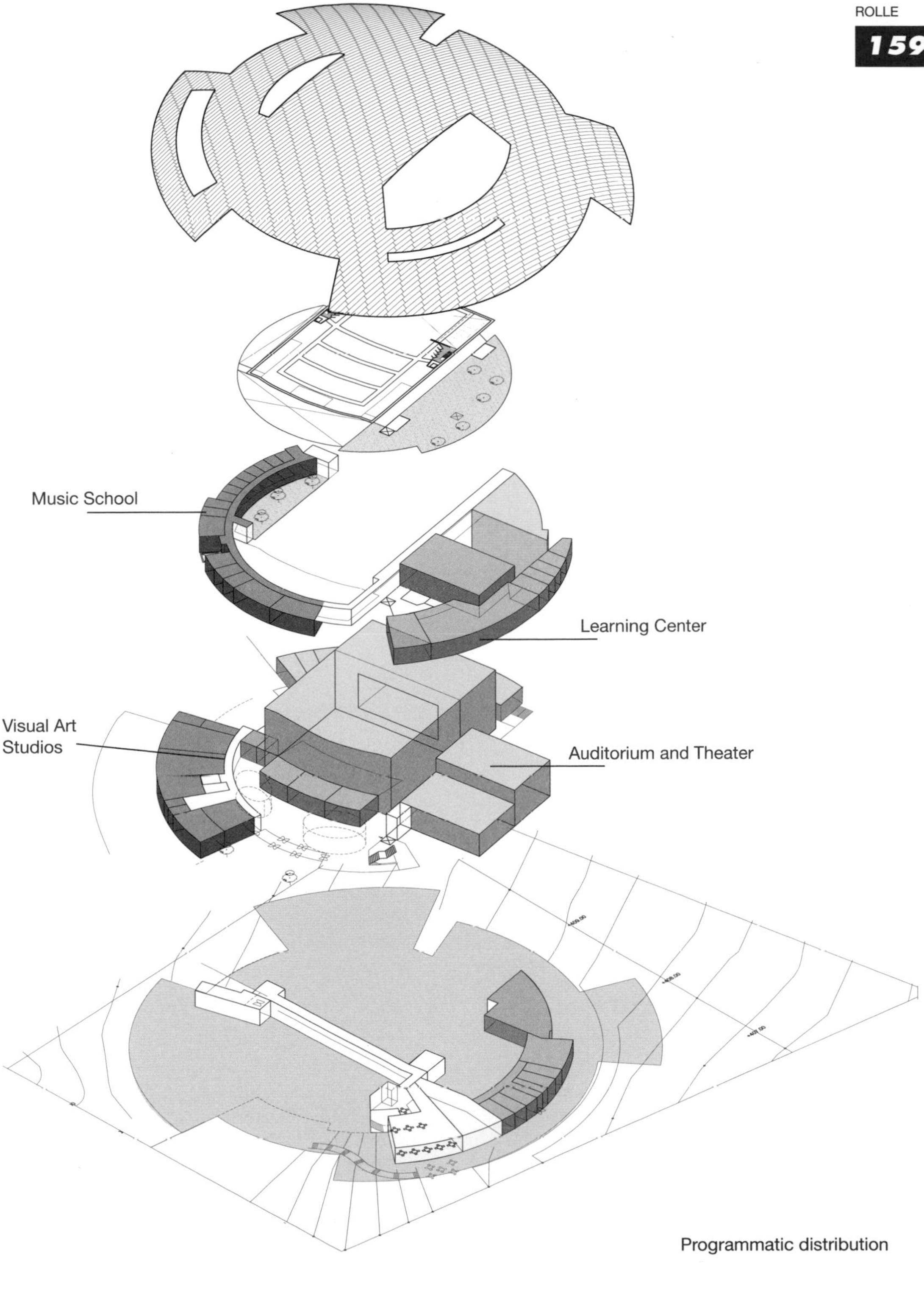

Music School

Learning Center

Visual Art
Studios

Auditorium and Theater

Programmatic distribution

View from the east

Entrance view

La Roche-sur-Yon, Pedestrian Bridge, 2007-09

(Bernard Tschumi/Hugh Dutton)

Architecture/Structure

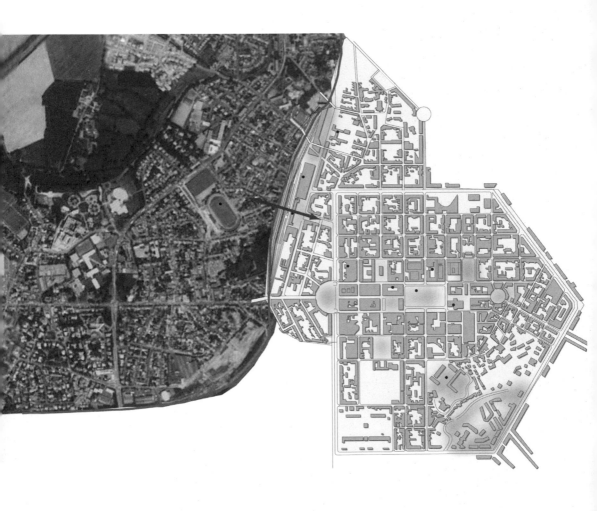

The bridge connects new districts to the historical city with both functional and symbolic links.

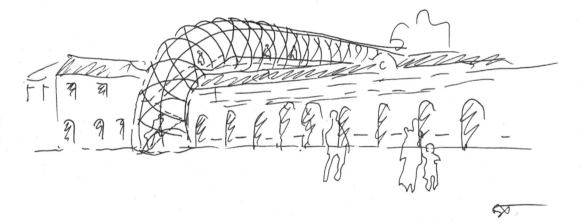

Urban Concept

The extension of the high-speed TGV train through La Roche-sur-Yon and nearby Atlantic border towns marks an important moment in the modernization of European and French train networks as well an occasion for cities to initiate well-considered transformations. The challenge of the new pedestrian bridge, which replaces an existing bridge that failed to meet the usage requirements of the TGV, was multiple. The bridge at La Roche-sur-Yon needed to be the public face of an efficient liaison between the city's western quarters and its center, an access point between two TGV arrival platforms, and a new point of entry into La Roche-sur-Yon that symbolizes the modernity suggested by the TGV.

Conceived through a joint collaboration between the fields of architecture and engineering, the bridge was designed by Bernard Tschumi and Hugh Dutton. The teams developed the design as both a utilitarian movement vector and a symbol of contemporary urban relations.

The bridge project is inscribed within a larger urban plan and long-term vision designed to re-link the historic city founded by Napoleon ("the Pentagon") with new neighborhoods located west of the city. From the beginning, the project was also intended to prepare for the arrival of the high-speed TGV train that would connect La Roche-sur-Yon to the largest railway stations in France. The passage under the electrified platforms had to be secure and user-friendly for a wide range of permissible users: travelers, neighborhood residents, the disabled, and cyclists, among others. The intention was to demonstrate the integration of an original structural system with a realized architectural concept, developed from urban-scale research on neighborhood identity and carried through into the expression of the smallest details of the built project.

It has been repeated in previous volumes of this series that there is no architecture without movement. A place of passage and movement, a pedestrian bridge is not a simple, static object but rather a dynamic vector in its use and perceptual effects. This dynamic is expressed as much through the structural system of this bridge as through its finishing materials, which include interlaced polycarbonate surfaces that protect passengers from weather and lighting that follows the rhythm of the structure. Even its bright orange-red color was chosen to emphasize the urban dynamic of the bridge as a pedestrian vector.

Structural Concept

An earlier bridge, contemporary with and inspired by the work of Gustave Eiffel, involved the use of lateral beams made out of a diagonal mesh of small plate strips, riveted together. The design of the new bridge uses the same diagonal-mesh language in tubular form to create a complete cylindrical volume through which the users pass. Footbridges over railways require side protection for the safety of the users as well as the trains below them. The complete volume provides a single structural solution that possesses the necessary inertia to span between the available support points as well as to provide support for the required protective screens and a canopy cover.

The bridge design is an homage to Robert Le Ricolais, a distinguished thinker and innovator in architectural and engineering design who was born in La Roche-sur-Yon. Le Ricolais is known for his research work in the development of spatial three-dimensional structures designed with the objective of "weightlessness and infinite span." His work extended beyond architecture and engineering into painting and poetry.

The triangulated mesh of the main La Roche-sur-Yon structural tube is articulated so as to distinguish between the tensile and compression forces by using simple tie rods for the tensile members. The ties have no compressive capacity and therefore express the tensile zones. The compressive members are in "T" or "H" sections that correspond to their magnitudes of force. The section sizes of the members vary as a function of the loading to optimize the steel mass and further express the forces in the system. Mid-span, the lower chords are tensile while the upper members are compressed. The inverse is true at the support points, where the bending moments are inverted. The shear forces in tubular truss are generally greater at the support points and tend more and more vertical approaching the supports. The pattern of triangulation of the truss follows this change in the direction of forces.

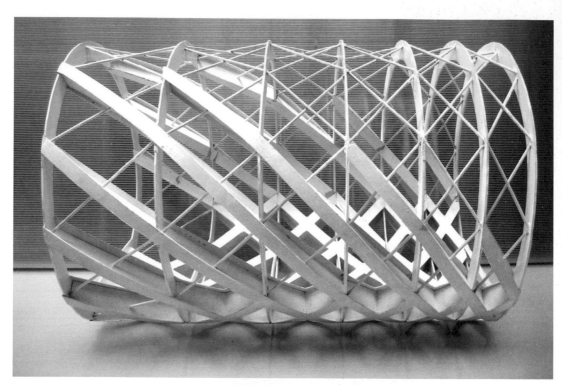

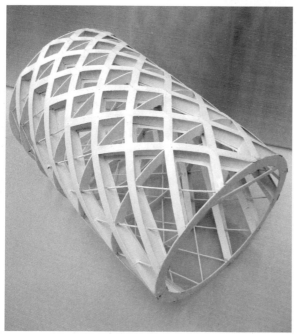

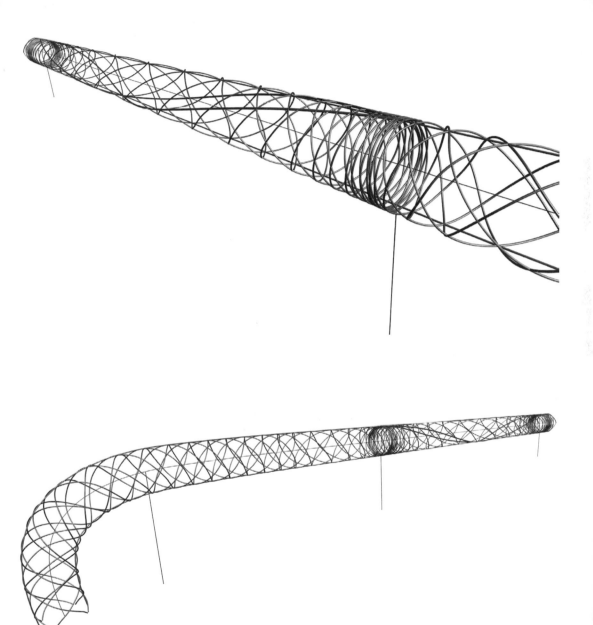

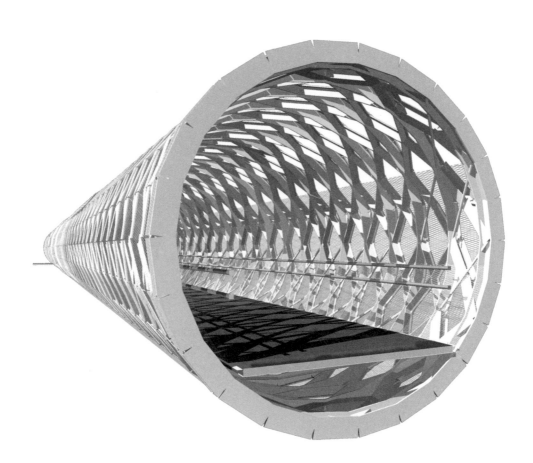

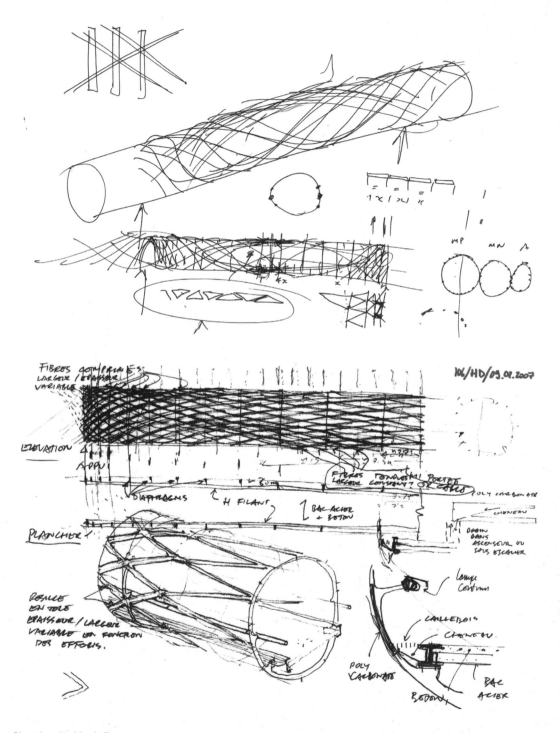

Sketches by Hugh Dutton

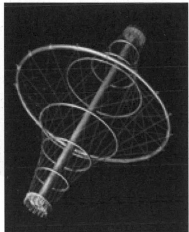

Robert Le Ricolais, to whom the bridge pays tribute

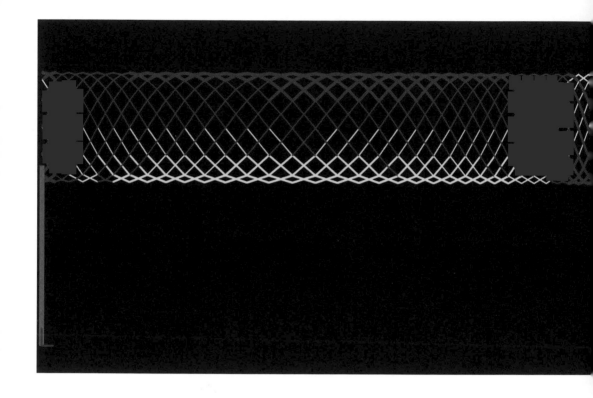

Structural studies by Hugh Dutton

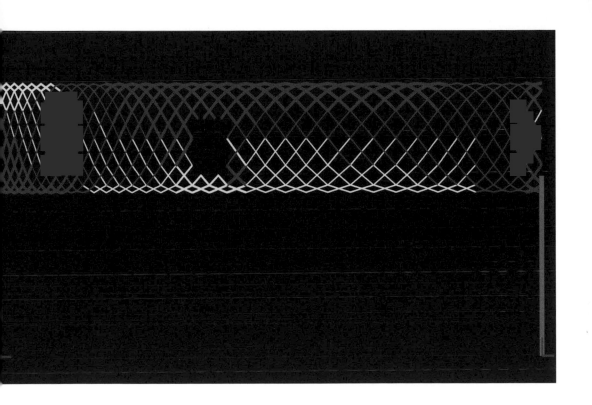

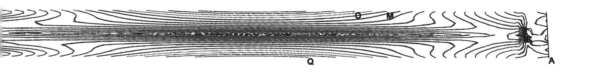

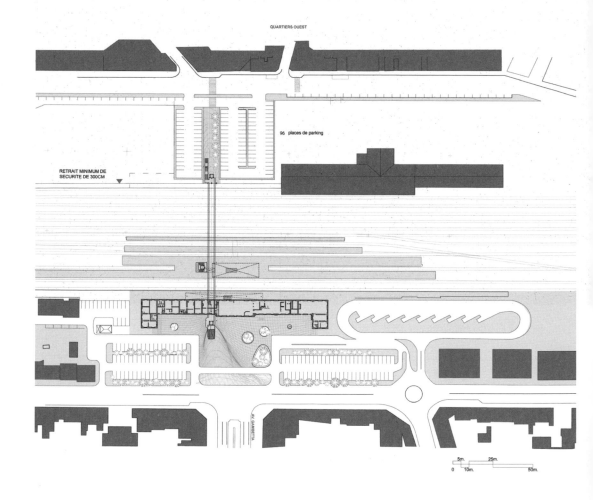

QUARTIERS OUEST

96 places de parking

RETRAIT MINIMUM DE
SECURITE DE 300CM

AV. GAMBETTA

5m.   25m.

0   10m.   50m.

Option 1: Although providing a shorter and more direct route, taking the bridge over the existing railway station was rejected by the city as too controversial.

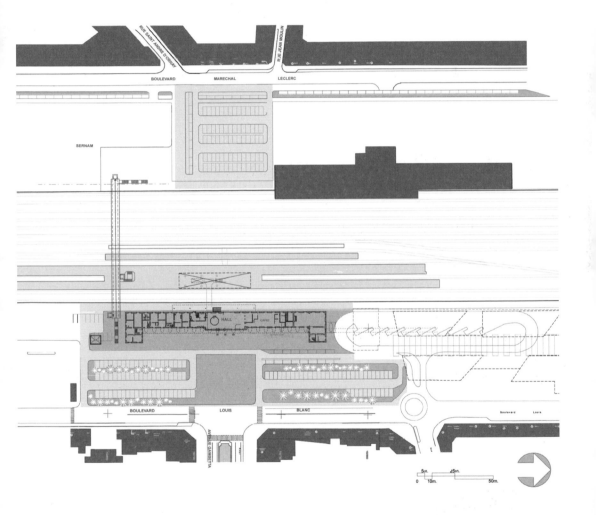

Option 2: the bridge as located to the side of the railway station

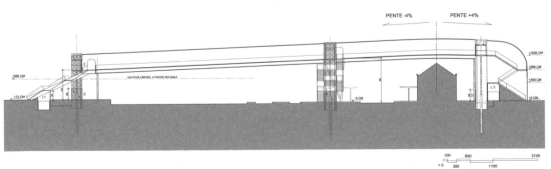

Option 1 (over the existing railway station): section of scheme

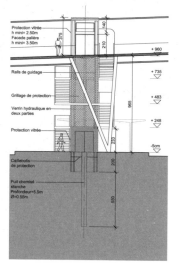

Protection vitrée
h mini= 2.50m
Facade palière
h mini= 3.50m

Rails de guidage

Grillage de protection

Verrin hydraulique en
deux parties

Protection vitrée

Caillebotis
de protection

Puit chemisé
étanche
Profondeur=5.5m
Ø=0.55m

+ 960
+ 735
+ 483
+ 248
-5cm

Section B

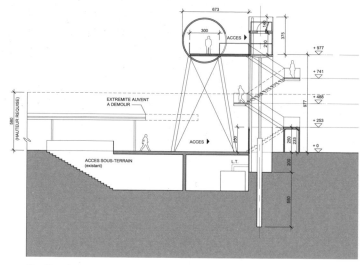

EXTREMITE AUVENT
A DEMOLIR

ACCES

ACCES

ACCES SOUS-TERRAIN
(existant)

L.T.

(HAUTEUR REQUISE)

+ 977
+ 741
+ 488
+ 253
+ 0

Section A

Access to the footbridge (platforms 2 and 3)

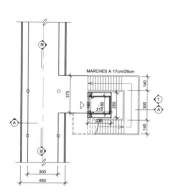

MARCHES A 17cm/26cm

Plan L+1 (footbridge level)

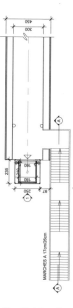

MARCHES A 17cm/26cm

Plan L+1 (footbridge level, from the south)

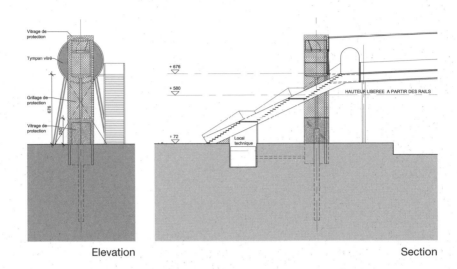

Vitrage de
protection

Tympan vitré

Grillage de
protection

Vitrage de
protection

+ 676

+ 580

+ 72

Local
technique

HAUTEUR LIBEREE A PARTIR DES RAILS

Elevation   Section

Access to the footbridge from the south

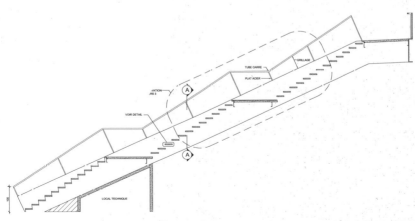

GRILLAGE

TUBE CARRE

PLAT ACIER

VOIR DETAIL

LOCAL TECHNIQUE

Detail of staircase: transversal section

B. Banding/Striation

Expanding on a concept first proposed in 1986 for our Tokyo Opera House competition submission, the project for the Dubai Opera Island explores the juxtaposition of autonomous bands or strips, this time extending the programmatic articulation of a concert hall at the scale of a master plan.

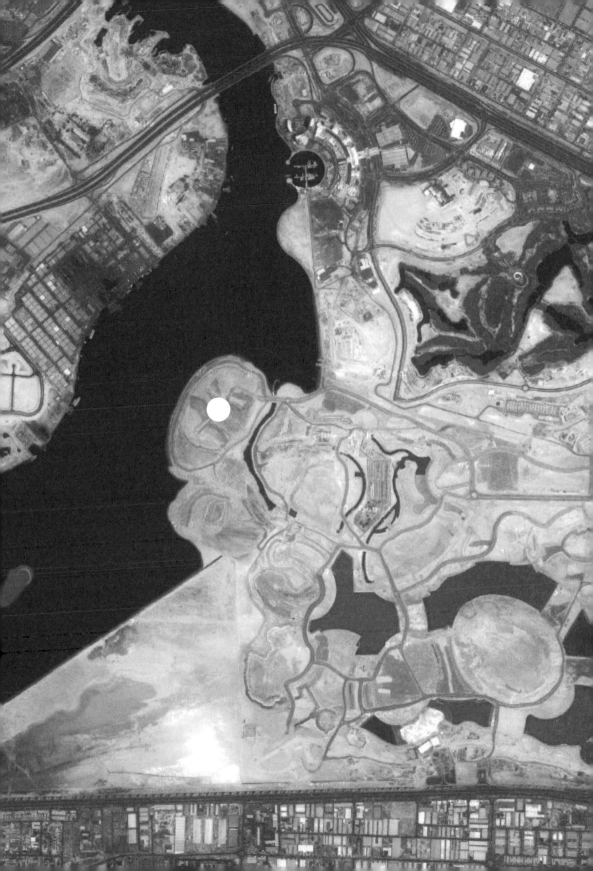

Dubai, Opera Island, 2005

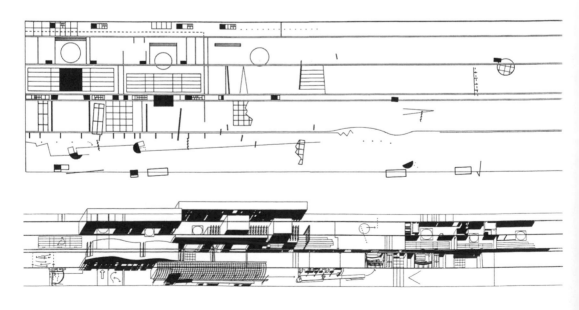

Diagram from Tokyo Opera House, 1986

Landscape Urbanism

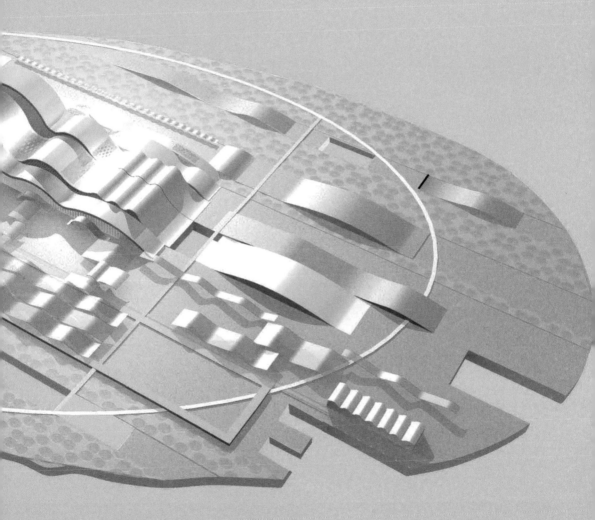

In a competition for a cultural center that included an opera, a theater, a music school, and a museum located on an artificial island in one of the most quickly developing economies in the world, we considered how to account for this speed of change so as to allow the project to evolve and contribute to the transforming culture. We also investigated how to make the harsh regional climate part of the architectural concept, turning it into a generator of form.

Landmark

The competition brief stated that the Cultural Center and Opera House should provide "a unique visual landmark of international significance for Dubai." We found the idea of a landscape preferable to the isolated "iconic" objects of the recent past, so we decided to address the island as a whole, allowing the landscape to become the building and the building to become a distinctive landscape. Together, they form a new landmark.

Strategy

We combined our experience in parallel programmatic bands with our research on double envelopes, since this combination could solve two major project requirements, organizational multiplicity and heat insulation. We aimed to turn these constraints into an image that blurred architecture and landscape.

Urban Notation

The parallel bands are analogous to varying sound waves or the lines of musical notation that can accept any kind of melody or rhythm. The bands expand into the landscape; in this manner, the building generates landscape and urbanistic potential at the scale of the island as a whole. Some interior bands are designed for meeting places, while others hold the exhibition and concert halls; still others are for backstages or offices. The exterior bands are designated for circulation and shaded outdoor theaters or sculpture gardens as well as pools. In contrast to the bands, an oval-shaped outdoor promenade allows for circulation across the island as well as access to and from the water.

Plan and Section

In plan, our parallel programmatic bands encourage efficiency and flexibility within each specialized strip and foster interaction from one strip to another. They also address the island site as a whole.

In section, our double-envelope concept allows us to address the building in the most energy-efficient way possible, by which the outer wave envelope covers climate and urbanistic issues while the inner envelope addresses specific functional or esthetic requirements. The space in between acts as a thermal buffer.

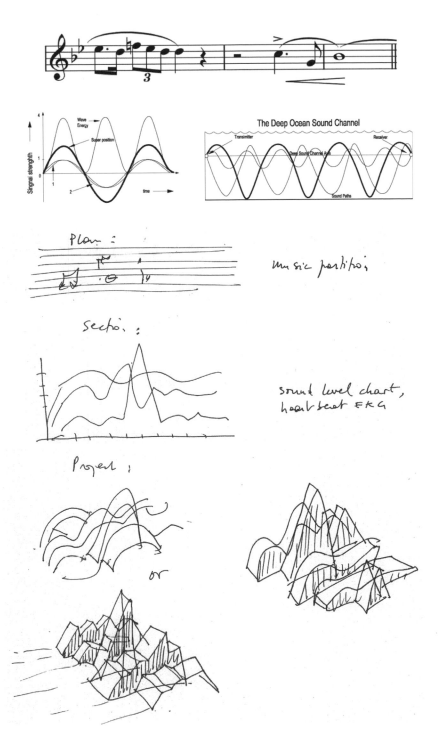

Plan :

music partition

sectio :

sound level chart,
heartbeat EKG

Project :

or

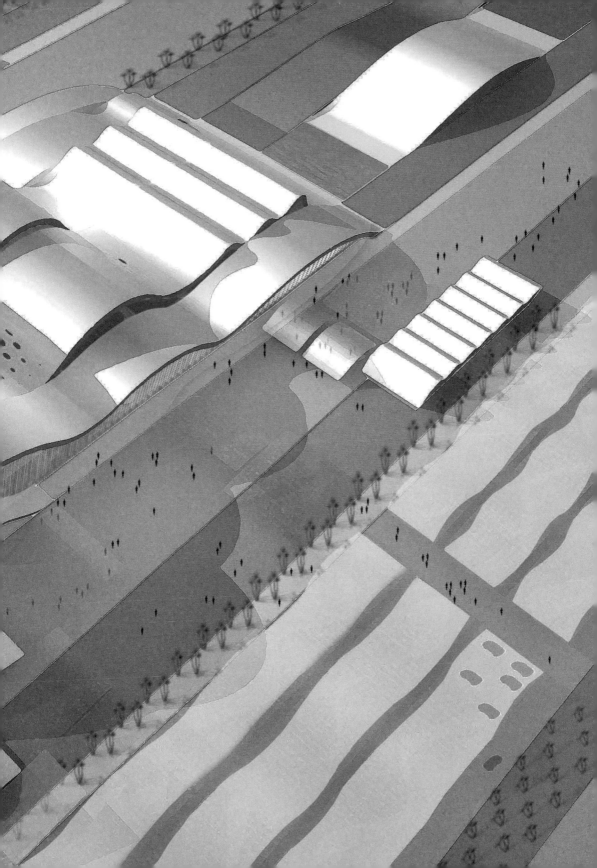

The Bands (See also page 212.)
A. The shaded outdoor pedestrian boulevard along the building provides direct access from the parking lot, taxis and buses, car park, helipad, and ferry boats. Several restaurants are located along the promenade that leads to the water.

B. The hall (and its mezzanines or theater lobbies) provides a vertical spectacle by means of translucent cylindrical stairs and elevators. The ground floor gathers together crowds from the box office, shops, bars, press office, reception and information areas, and possible temporary exhibition spaces. Several restaurants are distributed along the hall. The vertical foyers overlooking the hall can accommodate bars or buffets in addition to small party spaces.

C. The band with three auditoriums acts as an acoustically protected strip that accommodates audiences in volumes sized for sound quality as well as maximum visibility. It also contains the main museum galleries. This band, which includes VIP rooms and rest rooms, among other facilities, allows for potential expansion according to evolving programs at either end. It also includes patios or shaded courtyards that introduce natural light into the center of the complex and provide acoustical separation.

D. This band accommodates the main stages, side stages, and scenery assembly areas for the opera and the theater, as well as the main exhibition spaces. It is flanked by two central arteries that service the entire complex.

E. This band contains the backstage area and rehearsal spaces while allowing for shaded courtyards as visual relief, if desired.

F. The last band is allocated for artists and staff. It contains dressing rooms with related spaces as well as administrative offices for the opera, theater, general cultural center, and museum.

G, H, etc. Other bands can be created as needed.

A Hypercultural Landscape
Our approach offers a simple tool that can be used to address a variety of demands—a working instrument without a preconceived form, whose flexibility allows for the organization of the landscape as well as for viewing operas and more contemporary electronic spectacles. The organization of activities into parallel bands suggests a spatial model for art and culture as a parallel montage of attractions.

7 och" Seoul Air/M

It takes a lot longer to arrive at a concept
than to arrive at a form.

For the Dubai opera — we already have a concept
ready. (Tokyo opera). Let's turn it into a form.

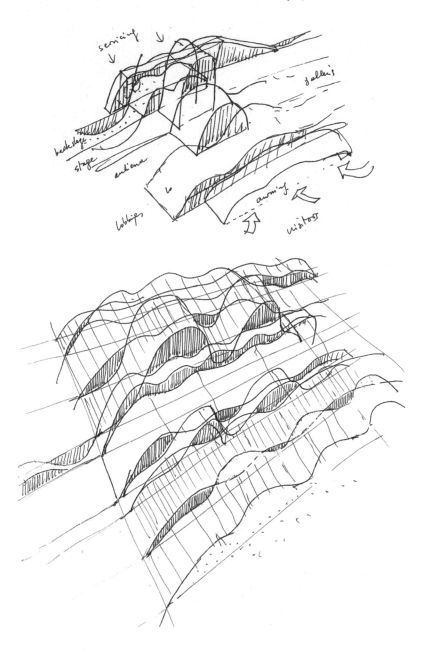

We wanted to open the main facade to the northwest in order to catch the last rays of the evening sun without too much exposure to heat. This choice determined the orientation of the parallel bands.

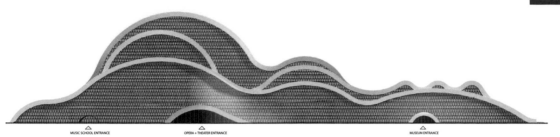

MUSIC SCHOOL ENTRANCE   OPERA + THEATER ENTRANCE   MUSEUM ENTRANCE

North elevation

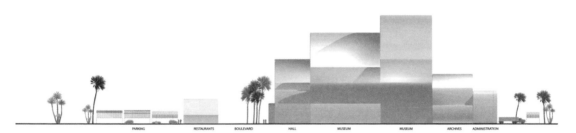

PARKING   RESTAURANTS   BOULEVARD   HALL   MUSEUM   MUSEUM   ARCHIVES   ADMINISTRATION

West elevation

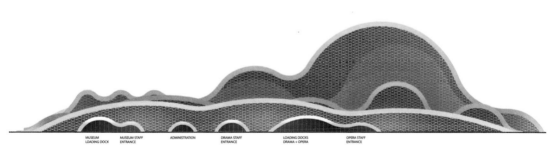

MUSEUM LOADING DOCK   MUSEUM STAFF ENTRANCE   ADMINISTRATION   DRAMA STAFF ENTRANCE   LOADING DOCKS DRAMA + OPERA   OPERA STAFF ENTRANCE

South elevation

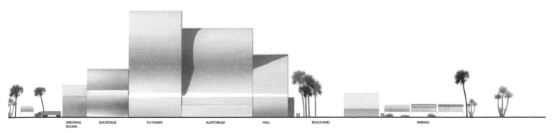

DRESSING ROOMS   BACKSTAGE   FLYTOWER   AUDITORIUM   HALL   BOULEVARD   PARKING

East elevation

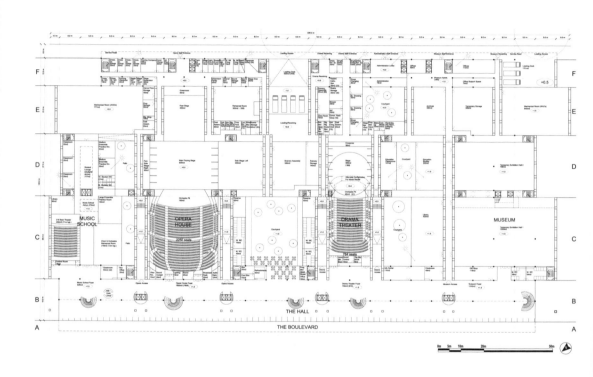

Main level (ground-floor plan)

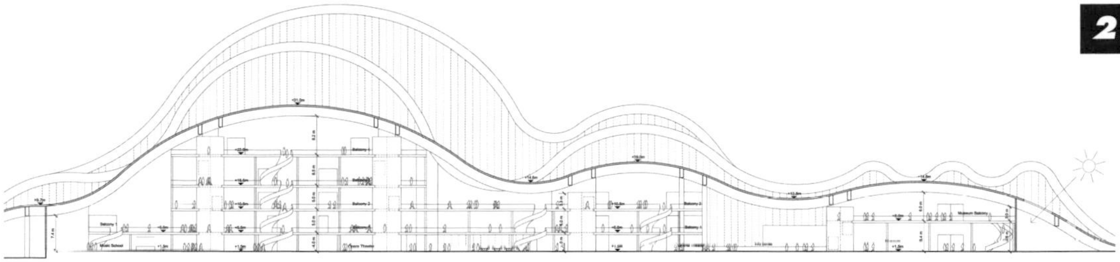

Long section through band B

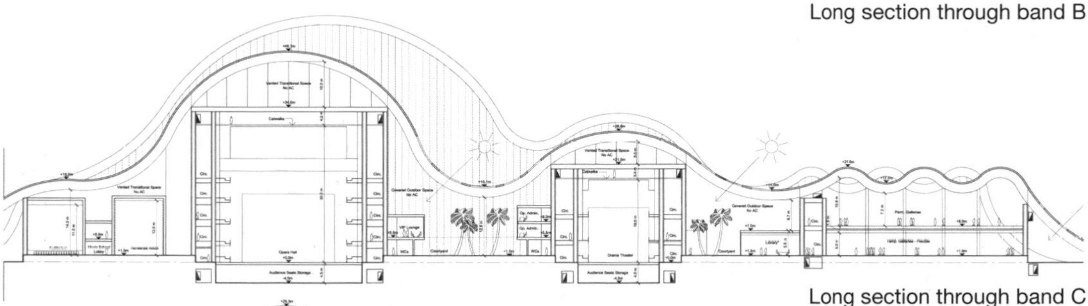

Long section through band C

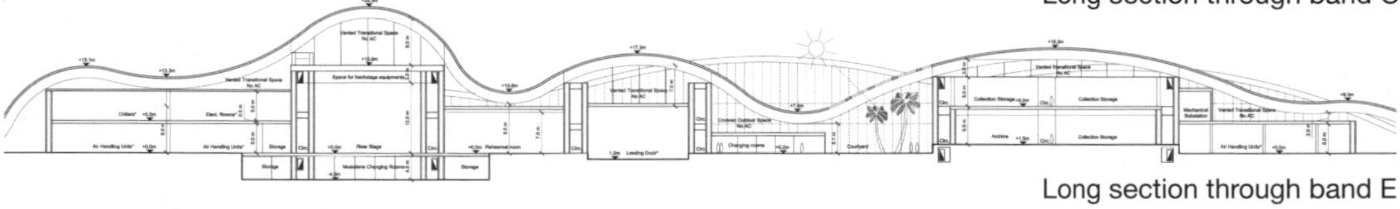

Long section through band E

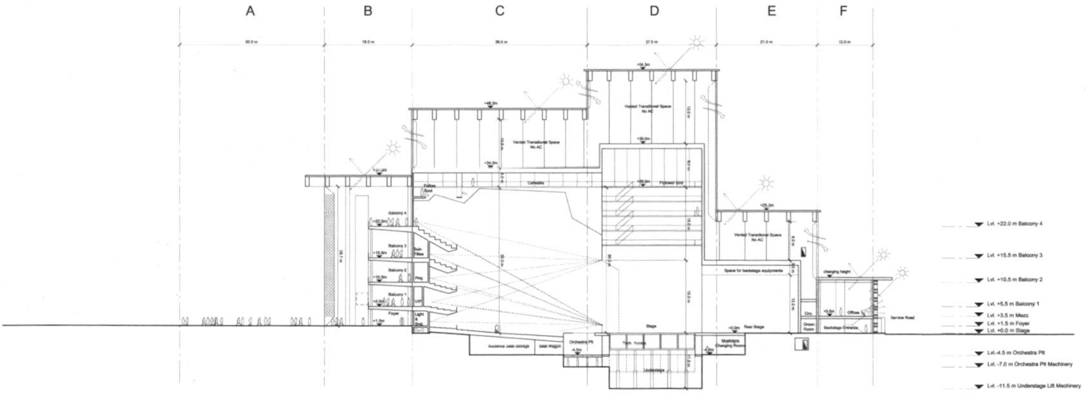

Cross-section through the opera theater

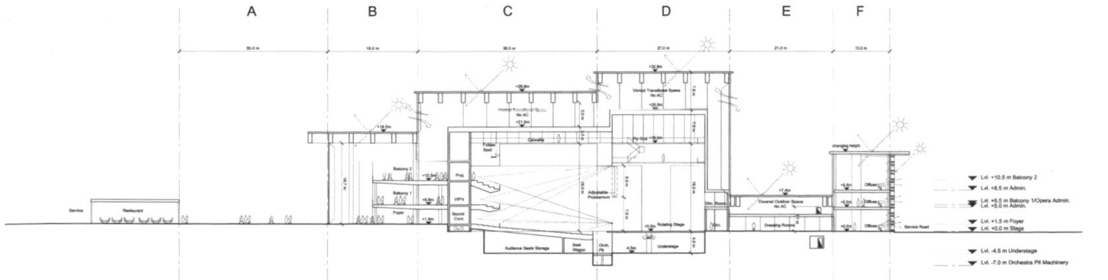

Cross-section through the drama theater

Interior view of concert hall

Lobby view

C1. Superimposed

Part C expands on a concept introduced with the Parc de la Villette and reinterpreted with our recent Acropolis Museum (*Event-Cities 3*): the superimposition of autonomous systems. Although only the two Abu Dhabi Media Zone projects and the scheme for EDF in Paris-Saclay employ explicit programmatic superimposition in the literal sense, the Busan Cinema Center and Sheik Zayed Museum projects both superimpose an enclosed and highly organized functional area on an open, public ground level.

Paris-Saclay, EDF, 2009

Suspended Garden

Future of Energy and Work Patterns

Located on a prominent plateau in a suburb known for concentrated educational facilities, research companies, and technology start-ups, the site is notable both for its prime location near creative industry and for its landscape. It lies on a high plain overlooking a river valley some 20 kilometers west of central Paris.

We had two design goals: First, to design a sustainable, low-energy-consumption building that would provide a visible symbol of the commitment of Europe's largest electrical company to the environment and to the future of energy. Second, to design a building prototype for workplace methodologies, emphasizing creativity, function and interaction, and spatial flexibility.

Program

The constraints consisted of 45,000 square meters of program, including directors' offices, workspaces, and sports and social facilities for the approximately 1,000 permanent and temporary workers who make up the eight core research departments, with an additional 15,000 square meters of future lab and research spaces allocated to varied departmental research needs. The program also included 7,000 square meters for restaurants, classrooms, and conference facilities intended for public access. All programs and services encircle a public forum designed as a central social space for the project.

Garden and Lofts

Our project expresses a new direction in the ideas of creative management: exchange and interaction spaces are now as important as production spaces. To achieve this goal, we examined several typologies, some new, some transformed through this project. Instead of building towers according to the urban form of a Manhattan, or structures situated on stilts above the "natural" environment as in the past, we combined the two typologies into a new model. Located on the ground floor are large, horizontal volumes ready for a range of potential uses, and above them is an extensive suspended garden. Finally, levitating above these levels is a series of "lofts" that are capable of accommodating the full variety of specified programs.

Restitution

Since the program dictated that we occupy just over one hectare on the Saclay plateau, our project restores this surface as a garden suspended seven meters above the ground. This suspended garden becomes the basis from which the project evolves. To the west, the garden provides an open area for food, lectures, and relaxation, while other sectors harbor industrial spaces. The garden suggests a natural landscape derived from the surrounding woods and fields through its use of native species, local flora, and a balanced ecology. Part of the excavated earth from the underground parking facilities is re-used for foothills on the eastern side of the site.

Garden

The project is intended to offer a new type of urban condition that retains the natural aspect and landscape of the Saclay plateau by fully integrating them into the project. The garden suspended above the roofs of the ground-level industrial spaces provides both a stage for interaction and a leisure landscape. The research offices and administrative spaces appear as if levitating above this large, natural environment.

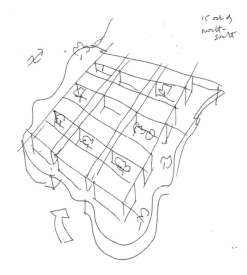

15 oct of
north-south

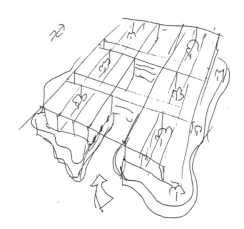

15 oct 09

East-
West

1 Jan of
flexible surface or
lifted surfaces
on facade?

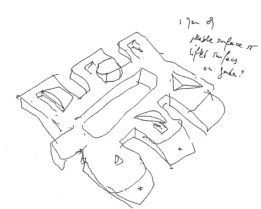

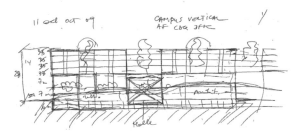

11 oct oct 09   CAMPUS VERTICAL
AF core 3FK

* Note: part of the excess earth material dug for
the car parks, is
reused for the hill
on the side

The Suspended Garden

The Hanging Gardens of Babylon were regarded as one of the Seven Wonders of the Ancient World. Our aim was not to recreate the Villandry gardens or the Parc Monceau (or even the Parc de La Villette), but rather to create an authentic garden for the contemporary workplace, a place of relaxation as well as encounter. The climbing greenery on the facades promotes thermal insulation, balances humidity, and affords acoustic comfort.

What we wanted to avoid:

Panopticon Penitentiary,
Statesville, Pennsylvania

Renault Technopole Guyancourt

Closed System Precedents

The Pentagon, Washington, DC.

Maison de la Radio, France

We asked: How can we conceptualize a contemporary green urban space while avoiding the closed
and self-contained designs of the past?

What we were interested in:

Superstudio: landscape
with people, the 1970s.
Think of the relationship
of the community with the
landscape.

The Uffizi, Florence,
Italy. A central public forum
flanked by identical buildings

Yona Friedman: The Spatial
City, 1958-59. A city raised
on pilotis

Open System Precedents

London, Adelphi Terrace. The arcades are as-
similated to a regular plinth scheme on the scale
of the city, which differentiates and characterizes
individual spaces.

A public park

Polystuchum aculeatum   Sesleria nitida   Ajuga retans   Anémone sylvestris

Dryopteris carthusianna   Sesleria autumnalis   Cytissus x praecox   Linum perenne

Anthyrium filix femina   Luzula nivea   Pachysandra terminalis   Thymus vulgaris

Local plant varieties to be used in landscaping

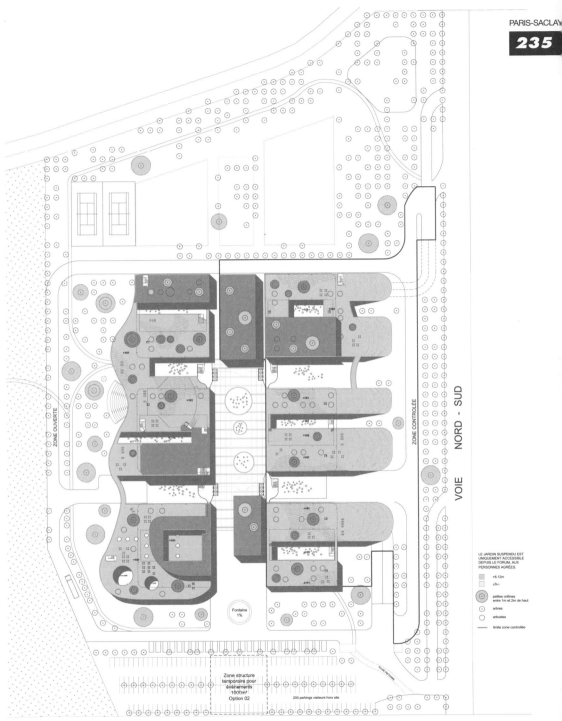

ZONE OUVERTE

ZONE CONTROLÉE

VOIE   NORD - SUD

Fontaine
1%

Zone structure
temporaire pour
évènements
1000m²
Option 02

200 parkings visiteurs hors site

ALLÉE PIÉTONNE

LE JARDIN SUSPENDU EST
UNIQUEMENT ACCESSIBLE
DEPUIS LE FORUM, AUX
PERSONNES AGRÉES.

+6,12m

±0,00

petites collines
entre 1m et 2m de haut

arbres

arbustes

limite zone contrôlée

EMPRISE   S.P.T.C.

The suspended-garden level

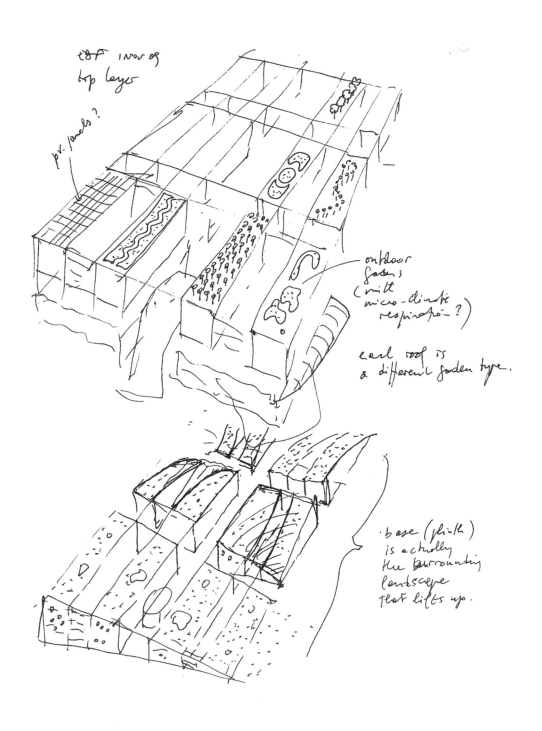

top 1 nov 09
top layer

p.v. panels?

outdoor
gardens
(with
micro-climate
respiration?)

each roof is
a different garden type.

. base (plinth)
is actually
the surrounding
landscape
that lifts up.

LDF 1 Nov 09

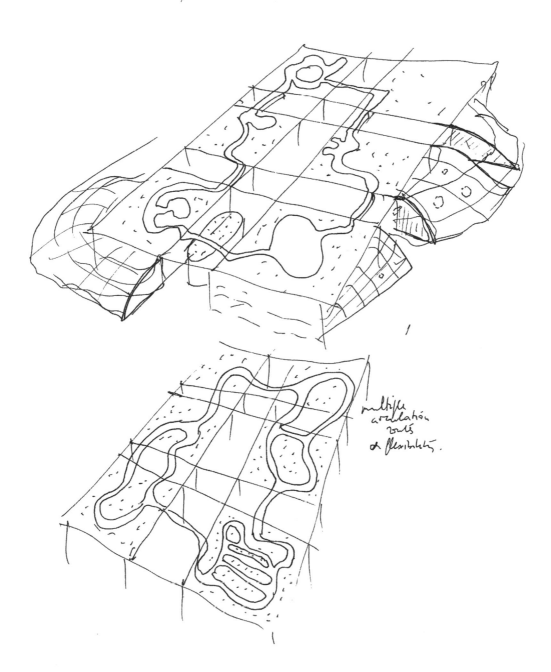

multiple
articulation
routes
& flexibility.

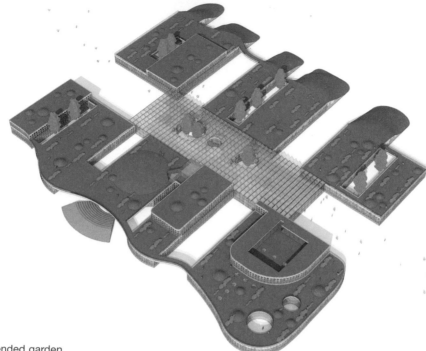

The suspended garden

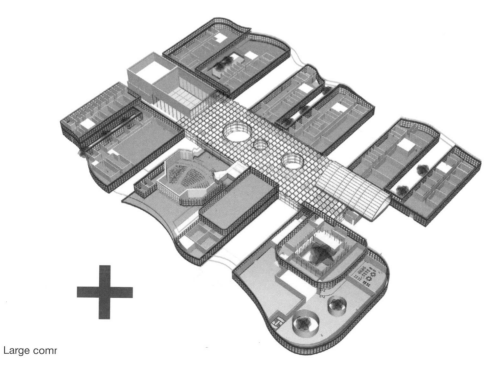

Large comr

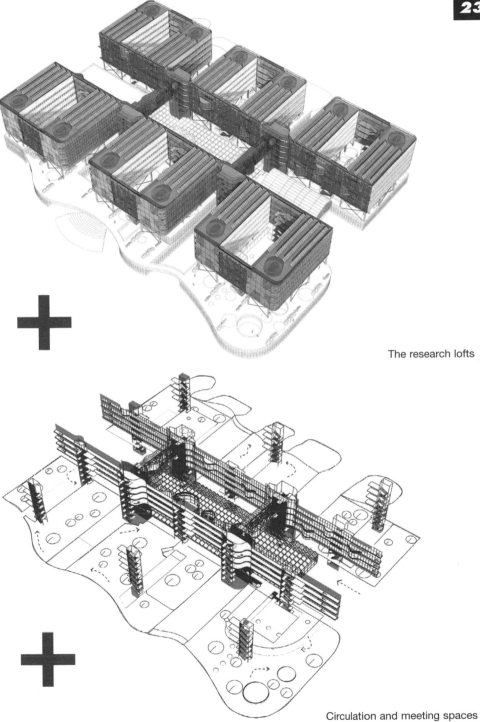

The research lofts

Circulation and meeting spaces

The Forum

The project's center is the planted public forum, which gives horizontal and vertical access onto all aspects of the program. Using passive heat and cooling, the forum is bordered by cafés and conference areas, and showcases the large halls used for mechanical demonstrations and showrooms. Four vertical cores located at each of the four corners of the forum control direct access to the research and administrative offices.

South

East elevation

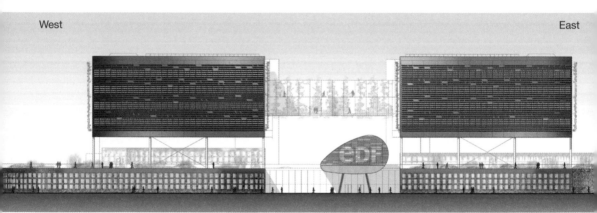

West

East

South elevation

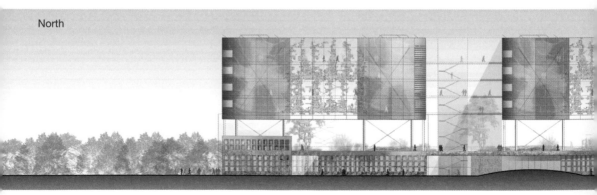

North

West elevation

North

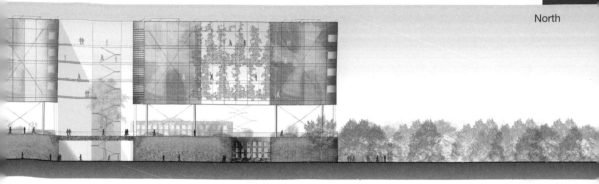

Color and Symbol

A colored facade costs the same price as a grey one. Nature is not monochromic. Electricity has no specific color; instead, it contains them all. The quality of life in the workplace can be heightened through differentiated spaces. We chose a wide-ranging color palette to give each block an individual identity. Six colors were studied to correspond to each block in the form of opaque tinted glass. Additionally, we designated silkscreened fritting for the glazing on the circulation corridors, ensuring effective solar protection. This patterned fritting could be based on 1931 film stills by the artist and photographer Man Ray that were originally commissioned by one of the electrical companies that later become EDF. The depicted "photogrammes" were inspired by new technologies, echoing the spirit of research and development that is central to the project.

South

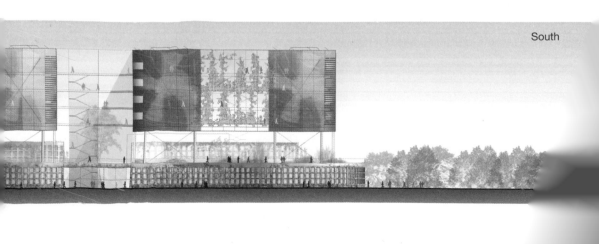

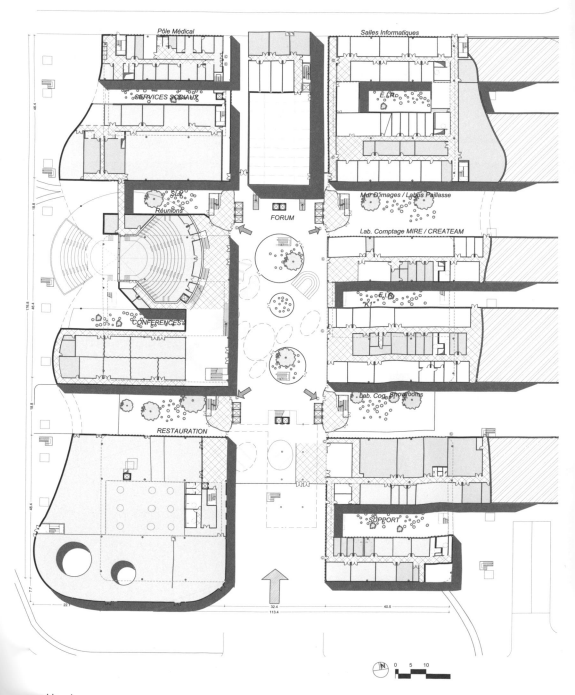

Pôle Médical   Salles Informatiques

SERVICES SOCIAUX

E.LRD

SLO
Réunions   FORUM   Mdr D'images / Labos Paillasse

Lab. Comptage MIRE / CREATEAM

E.LR
K1

CONFERENCES

Lab. Cog. Showrooms

RESTAURATION

SUPPORT

N   0   5   10

d level

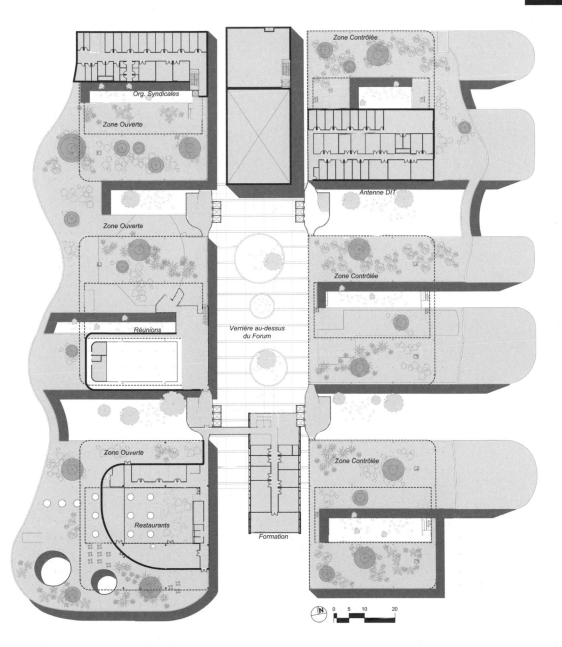

Org. Syndicales

Zone Ouverte

Zone Contrôlée

Zone Ouverte

Antenne DIT

Zone Contrôlée

Réunions

Verrière au-dessus
du Forum

Zone Ouverte

Zone Contrôlée

Restaurants

Formation

0   5   10   20

Suspended-garden level

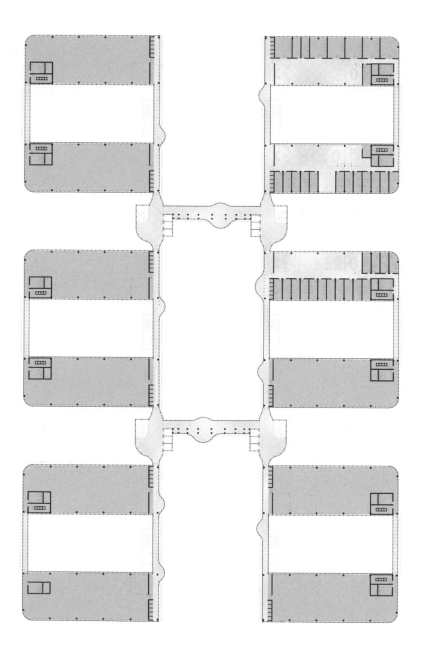

Typical office level (the lofts)

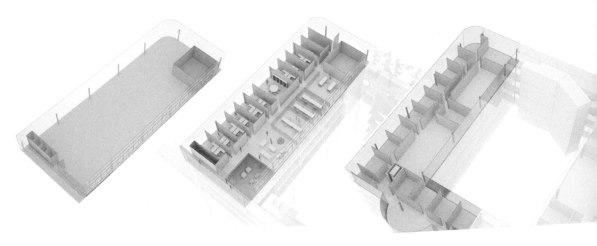

To encourage social exchange and collaborative work, the buildings are interlinked, creating relationships among different functional entities. These functional units can be organized horizontally (meaning, adjacent on the same level) or vertically (stacked and connected by elevators or stairs).

Model photographs

Ecological Suspension

The six office blocks located above the suspended garden are all organized around a planted terrace. The workspaces and relaxation areas are oriented along north-south corridors, while movement and meeting spaces have an east-west orientation and form a double skin. This strategy of combining orientation with the double envelope assists in providing energy sustainability as well as interaction among researchers.

Protected from direct sun by climbing plants and a silkscreened facade, the east and west corridors act as thermal filters. Maintaining a temperate buffer zone, they play an intermediary role between the outside climate and the internal office temperature, offering graded climatic environments. The corridors also open onto office spaces, conference rooms, and communal areas, encouraging researchers to stop and talk with colleagues.

Efficiency

A compact arrangement of programs concentrates thermal mass and increases efficiency.

Shading

Sun-shading made of green plantings mitigates the thermal side-effects of sunlight while providing a carbon sink.

Envelope

An energy-positive envelope means that it far exceeds the minimum thermal and shading requirements per code. Infiltration rates will be minimized due to reduction of thermal bridging. An optimized glazing ratio of 40% provides the balance between energy consumption in the building and high indoor environmental quality.

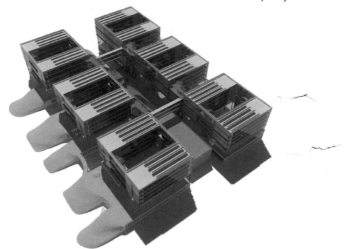

Orientation

The project is sited so that the offices all face north or south, which makes temperature management more pre-dictable and efficient. Circulation and communication spaces are located on the east and west facades, which are more difficult to control.

Daylighting

Borrowed light through offices to circulation spaces eliminates electrical lighting during the day. Corridors end in outdoor views. Courtyards and light wells to garage add to the natural-light strategy.

Thermal Mass

Exposed concrete, coupled with night purging, will take advantage of diurnal swings and thermal inertia of the structure, reducing cooling loads.

Energy Production

Photovoltaic panels on the roof contribute renewable energy to the electricity used by the building.

Natural Ventilation

Lifting the building facilitates breezes and fosters external and internal thermal comfort.

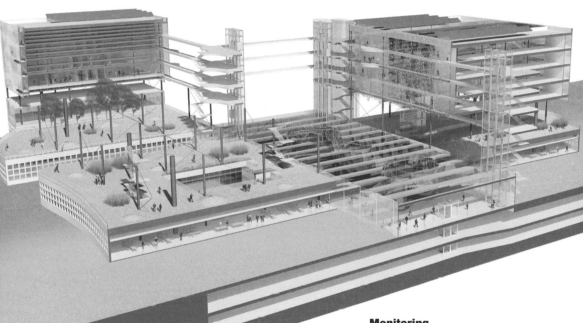

Garden Landscape

Level 1 "Secret Garden" provides natural carbon reduction and thermal insulation, while providing active social space for the entire complex.

Interactive

Display center in the forum provides public data on the building's performance through meter banks and interactive kiosks. Provides an overview of sustainable features for visitors.

Monitoring

Allows for links on strategy and performance, making the building a communicative education tool for the public.

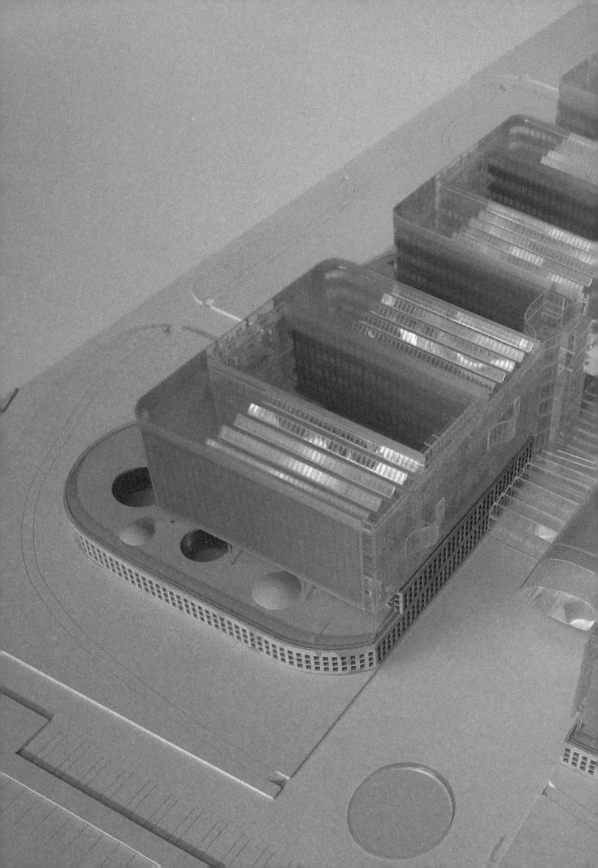

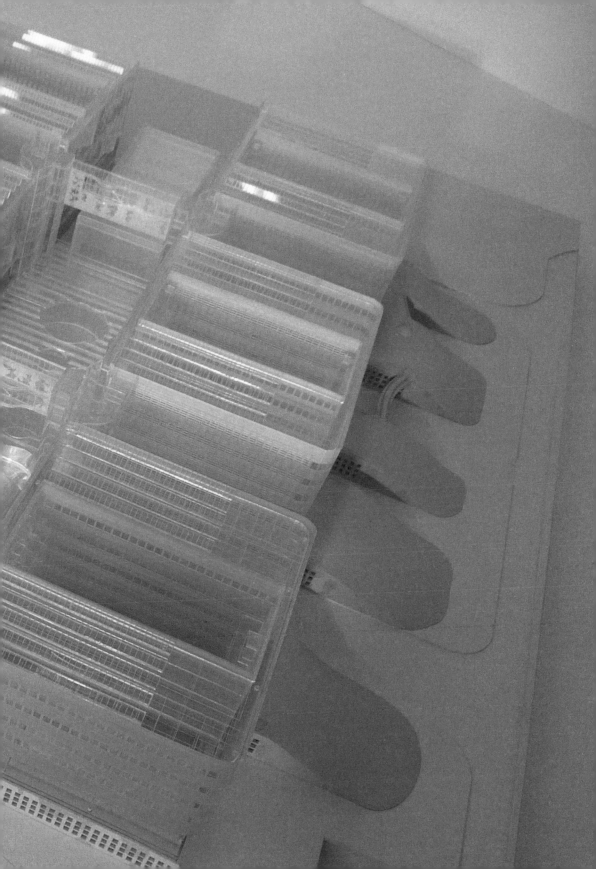

Abu Dhabi, Media Zone Master Plan, 2008-09

70 Days/35 Options

In 2008 Bernard Tschumi Architects was selected to design a master plan for a proposed media sector in the growing metropolis of Abu Dhabi. Intended to develop, produce, and provide content for the Middle Eastern and North African, or MENA, region, the media zone was to house facilities owned and leased by one company, twofour54, as well as the overall managing authority, the Abu Dhabi Media Zone Authority. Much like the master plan for Masdar City, the zero-carbon energy center planned by Foster and Partners in the same metropolis, the brief was intended to put in place a prototype for regional as well as global development. What ensued, for the architects, was a whirlwind of design options compressed into the relatively short period of two and a half months.

The Question
How to create a new urban quarter, a new piece of the city, that combines offices, housing, shops, production studios, hotels, and exhibition centers, so as to turn it into a buzzing metropolitan center—in other words, a city of energy and creativity? How can this new district be accommodated on a linear site that sits near a major hotel complex and a large arena, as well as the terminus of the Corniche?

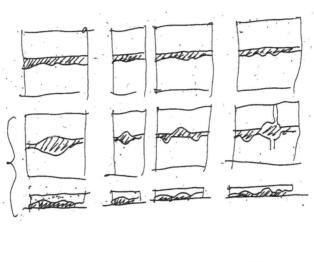

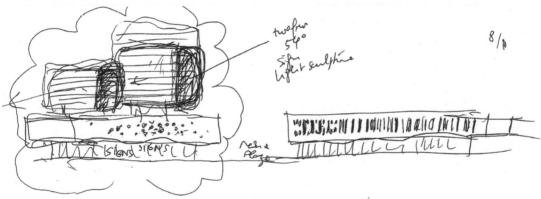

8/8

two fou
54°
Sikn
light sculpture

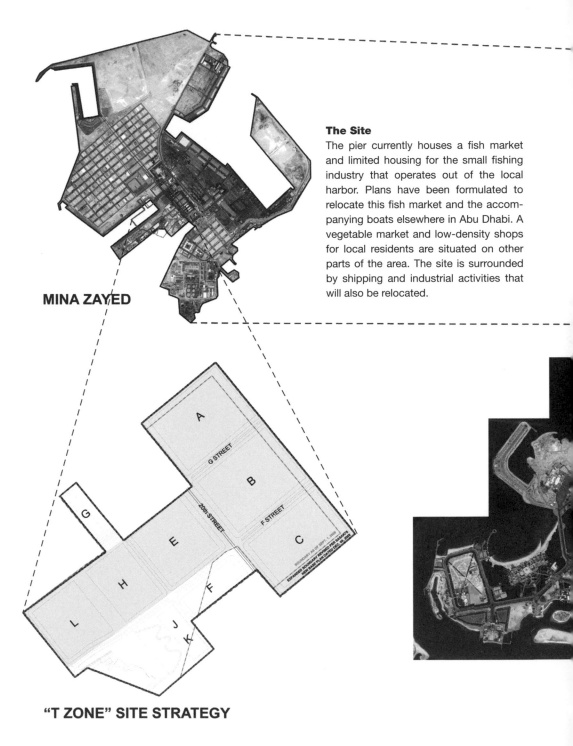

MINA ZAYED

The Site

The pier currently houses a fish market and limited housing for the small fishing industry that operates out of the local harbor. Plans have been formulated to relocate this fish market and the accompanying boats elsewhere in Abu Dhabi. A vegetable market and low-density shops for local residents are situated on other parts of the area. The site is surrounded by shipping and industrial activities that will also be relocated.

"T ZONE" SITE STRATEGY

MINA ZAYED
RESIDENTIAL
DISTRICT

SAADIYAT ISLAND +
CULTURAL DISTRICT

LULU RECREATION
ISLAND

ABU DHABI ISLAND

GREATER ABU DHABI REGION

We began by examining all of the program requirements and the available land, noting that many elements had to sit at ground level to accommodate deliveries and specific functional proximities.

We spent time testing as many strategies as possible, from superblocks and shaded mats to strips and banded schemes. We organized the program in as many ways as we could identify, some logical, some fanciful, but always with an eye to identifying all possibilities before settling on an image or concept.

We came up with a matrix of typologies with over 21 variants that described the project. We attempted to work with ideas that we knew would ultimately shape the project: pedestrian routes, studio space on the ground floors, offices above the program, retail located near pedestrian corridors, and the general constraints of the pier in terms of zoning and neighboring development.

The Site

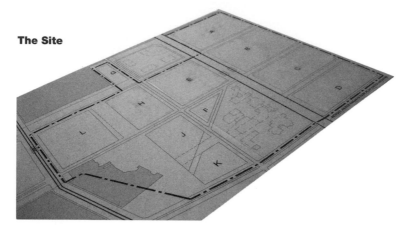

The Deck

The program mandated that 92% of the site would be covered with services that were required to be at street level. This suggested a dense, three-level block that we called the "Deck."

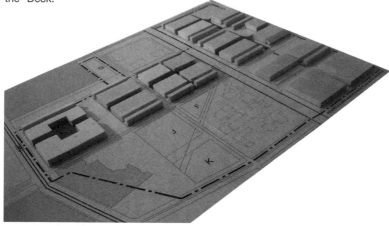

The Towers

The remainder of the program, which consisted mainly of offices and the two hotels, could be configured above the Deck in any arrangement, provided that the depth allowed for natural light.

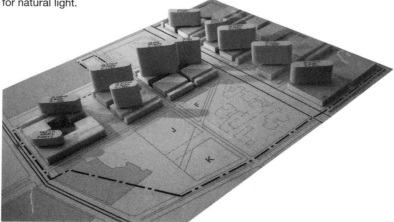

The Connector

In order to link all of the different activities located on the ground floors, we looked for a common denominator. The Connector is conceived of as an urban sequence, an architectural promenade, or a narrative that describes a journey through space.

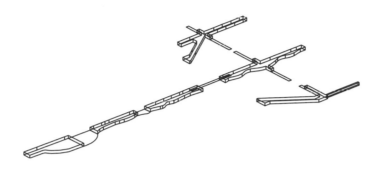

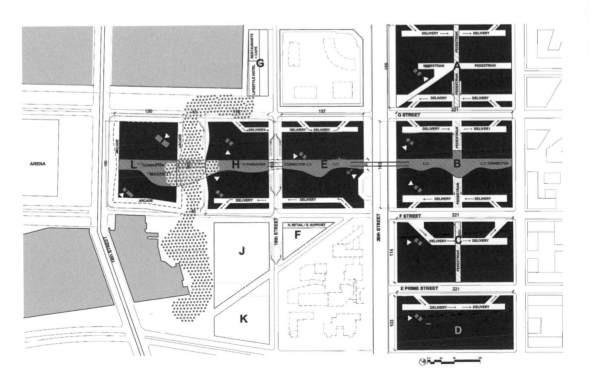

Plan showing the Connector

The Towers

A defining characteristic of the project is its focus on sustainability. Cognizant of the harshness of the Abu Dhabi sun, we decided to orient the Towers in the east-west direction so that the main dimensions of the facades would be open to the north and the south. The wide north and south facades are easy to protect in the latitude in which Abu Dhabi is located. The north facade has indirect exposure to the sun, while the high-noon sun that occurs during most seasons can be controlled easily by using small, horizontal *brise-soleils*. Thanks to the orientation of the Towers, the east and west facades are narrow and can be designed so as to filter out penetrating sun rays by using precast concrete screens and/or white spandrel glass, thereby maximizing energy savings and emphasizing sustainability.

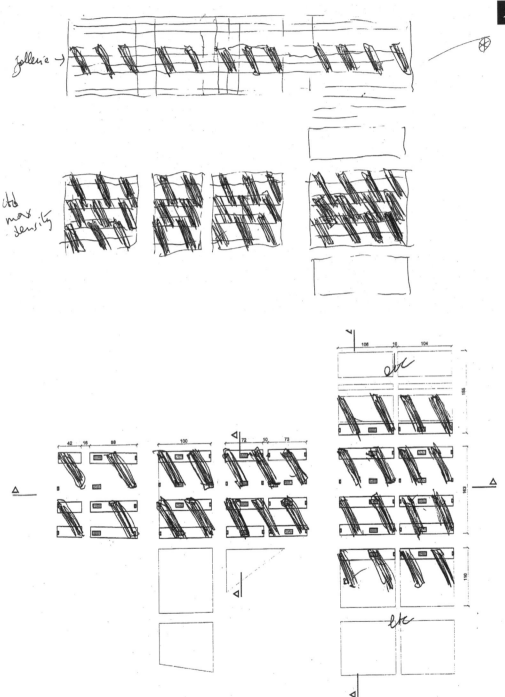

Concept sketches of the upper levels

A New Urban Typology

As opposed to traditional master plans that focus on scale and densities but remain relatively abstract in their implementation, the master plan for the Media Zone combines an intricate play among the terms of urban design, architecture, and programmatic requirements. From the onset, designing a new media quarter in Abu Dhabi meant inventing a precise programmatic mechanism that could simultaneously work as a dynamic urban concept and read as an inspiring architectural expression.

The project's programmatic specificity suggested a clear configuration. With triple-height production studios on nearly every block, the most coherent strategy involved the deck rising three stories above the street, surmounted by individual towers that could give character and interest to each block.

A common denominator that animates the space below the Deck at street level is the Connector, a horizontal, enclosed pedestrian avenue with retail, performance spaces, restaurants, cafés, and interactive stations. This linear street becomes the interface for media and its public, a rapidly growing audience in the Arab world. Interactive installations can broadcast content but also become generators of interest in media, its production, and its cultural impact on Abu Dhabi and the surrounding region.

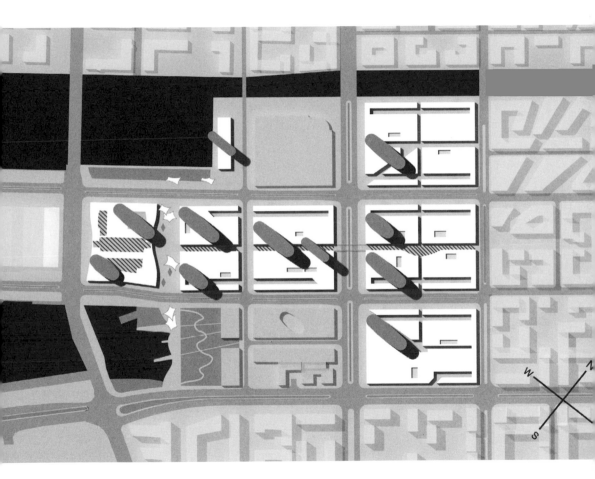

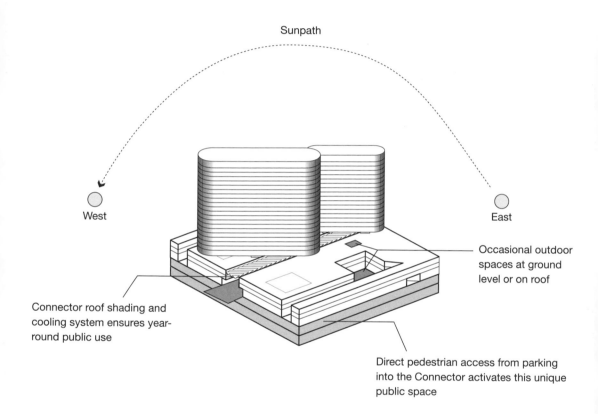

Sunpath

West

East

Connector roof shading and cooling system ensures year-round public use

Occasional outdoor spaces at ground level or on roof

Direct pedestrian access from parking into the Connector activates this unique public space

The building orientation maximizes views to the north and south and protects long facades against the harsh Abu Dhabi sun.

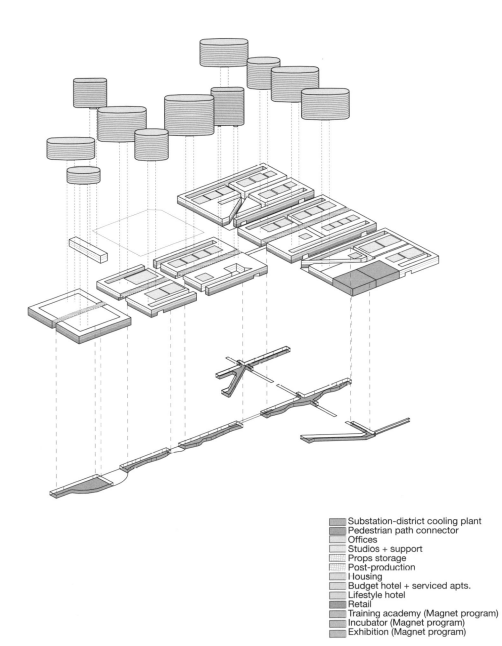

Substation-district cooling plant
Pedestrian path connector
Offices
Studios + support
Props storage
Post-production
Housing
Budget hotel + serviced apts.
Lifestyle hotel
Retail
Training academy (Magnet program)
Incubator (Magnet program)
Exhibition (Magnet program)

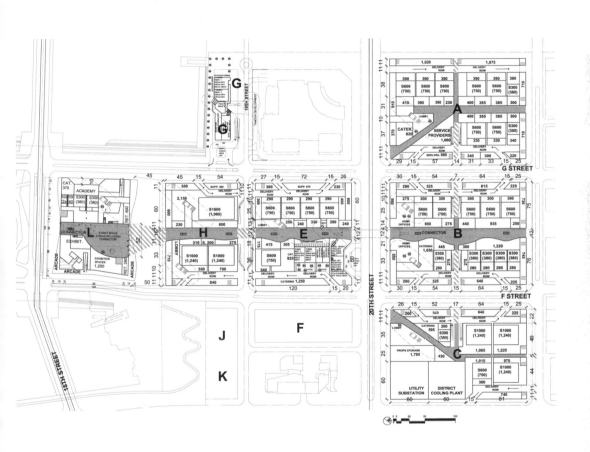

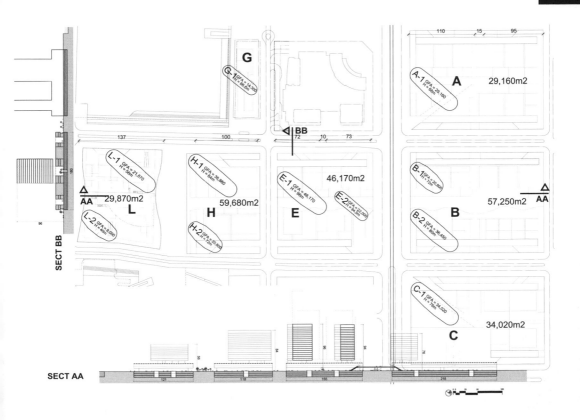

SECT BB

SECT AA

G

G-1 GFA = 14,300 H = 66.6m

A-1 GFA = 29,160 H = 66m

A 29,160m2

110 15 95

BB 72 10 73

L-1 GFA = 21,870 H = 56m

H-1 GFA = 38,880 H = 84m

E-1 GFA = 46,170 H = 96m

E-2 GFA = 32,000 H = 64.50m

B-1 GFA = 20,800 H = 72m

B-2 GFA = 36,450 H = 84m

B 57,250m2

AA

137 100

AA 29,870m2

L

L-2 GFA = 8,000 H = 40m

H 59,680m2

H-2 GFA = 20,800 H = 72m

E 46,170m2

C-1 GFA = 34,020 H = 76m

C 34,020m2

96

121 118 155 218

96 84 96 76

Upper floor (above the Deck)

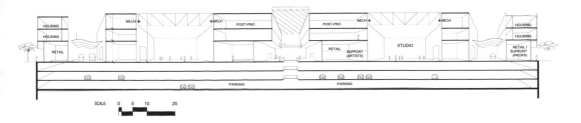

HOUSING
HOUSING
RETAIL

MECH

MECH POST-PRO

POST-PRO MECH

MECH

HOUSING
HOUSING
RETAIL / SUPPORT (PROPS)

RETAIL SUPPORT (ARTISTS)

STUDIO

PARKING PARKING

SCALE: 0 5 10 20

Transverse section

The "Pavilion" Cliché
Point of view. The viewer on the arrival
zoopolis arrival "capture d" within the city

Dining Zoo
Review
Columbine

Nov 24, 88

2

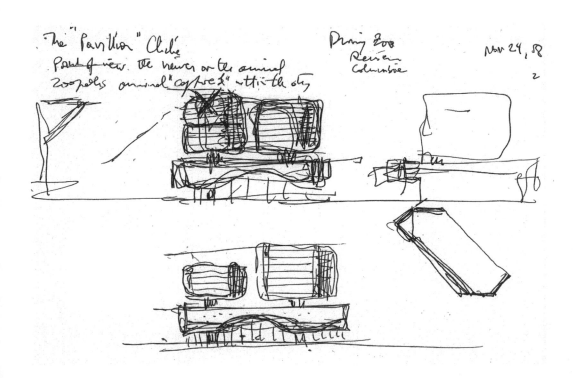

Cross programmed landscape (college city)
Can a tool do a cliché

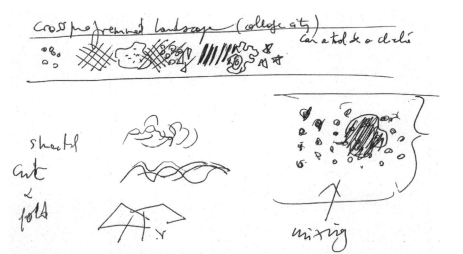

shuttl
cut
&
fold

mixing

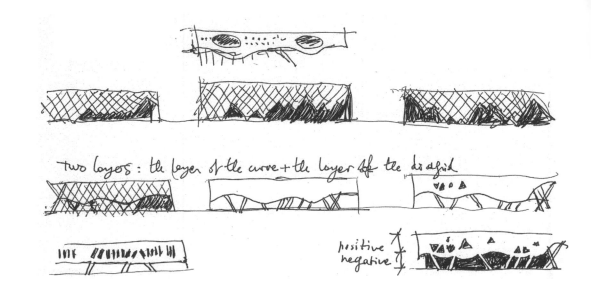

two layers: the layer of the curve + the layer of the diagrid

positive
negative

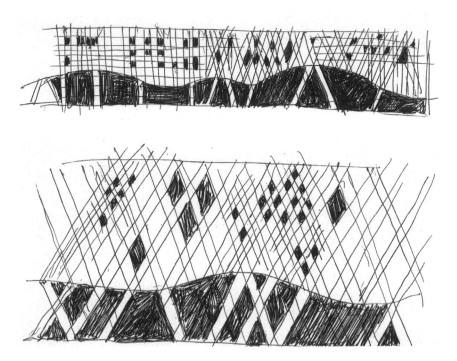

A concept-form is a-formal; it is not hierarchical and does not reflect a rigid set of rules. It is, instead, a specific moment in a thought process when an architectural strategy becomes the generator for making buildings.

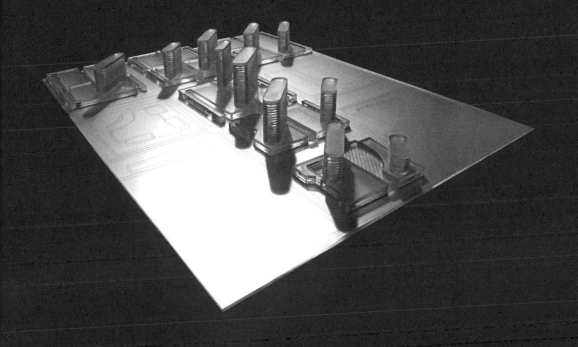

Plexiglass model

Signal Bdg

This height is so " low " that

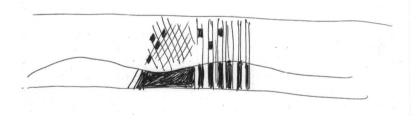

the overlap of
the horiz &
the diagonal
allows for
the construction of
the appearance of chaos.

A concept-form is, by definition, demate-rialized, minimal, and transient. Concept-forms can eventually become icons, symbols, or indexes, but they do not "represent" or stand for something else. Whether they are "real" or "simulacral" is of little importance; they are always abstractions.

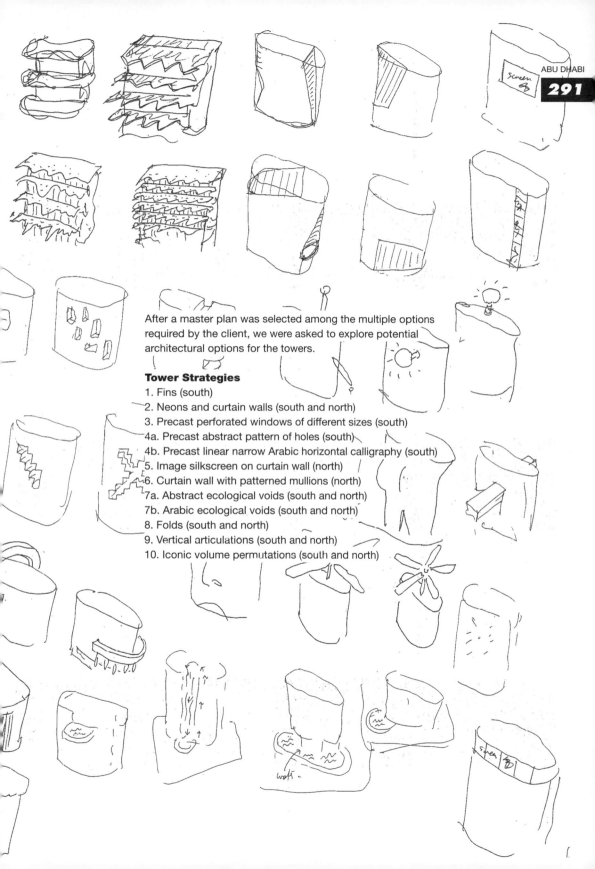

After a master plan was selected among the multiple options required by the client, we were asked to explore potential architectural options for the towers.

Tower Strategies

1. Fins (south)
2. Neons and curtain walls (south and north)
3. Precast perforated windows of different sizes (south)
4a. Precast abstract pattern of holes (south)
4b. Precast linear narrow Arabic horizontal calligraphy (south)
5. Image silkscreen on curtain wall (north)
6. Curtain wall with patterned mullions (north)
7a. Abstract ecological voids (south and north)
7b. Arabic ecological voids (south and north)
8. Folds (south and north)
9. Vertical articulations (south and north)
10. Iconic volume permutations (south and north)

Digital facade: horizontal band

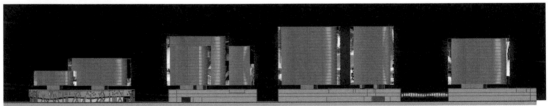

Digital facade: vertical band

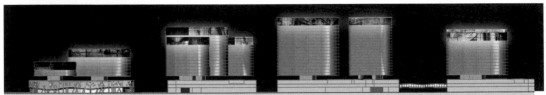

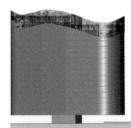

Digital facade: horizontal band

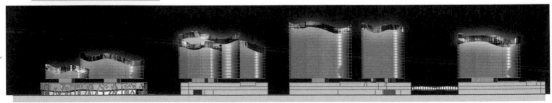

Strategies for the Towers: artists' murals and electronics (south and north)

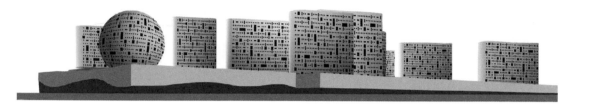

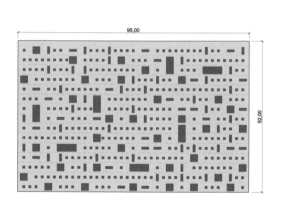

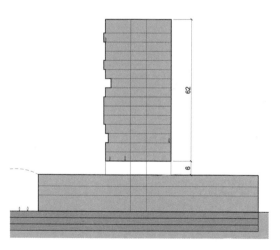

Strategies for the Towers: precast perforated windows of different sizes (south)

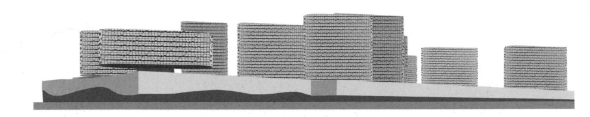

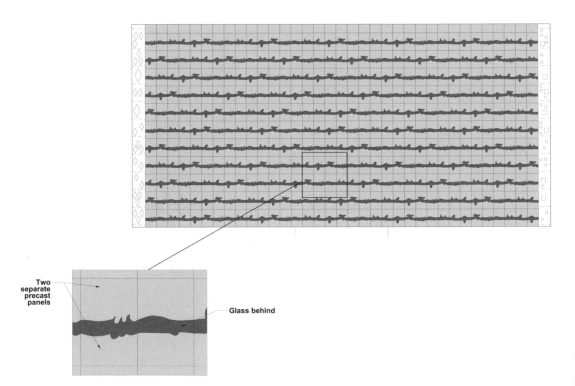

Two
separate
precast
panels

Glass behind

Strategies for the Towers: precast linear narrow horizontal calligraphy (south)

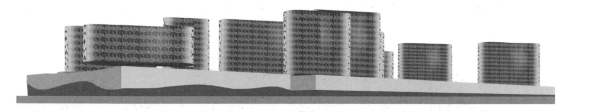

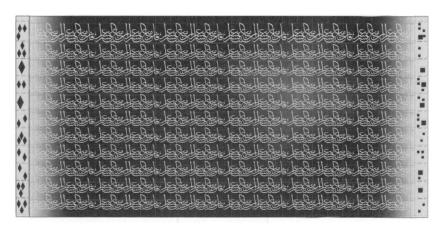

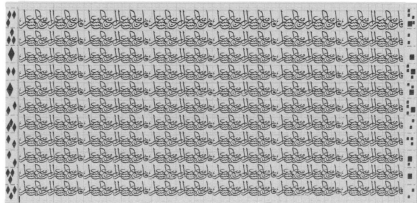

Strategies for the Towers: dark glass with fritted abstract calligraphy (north)

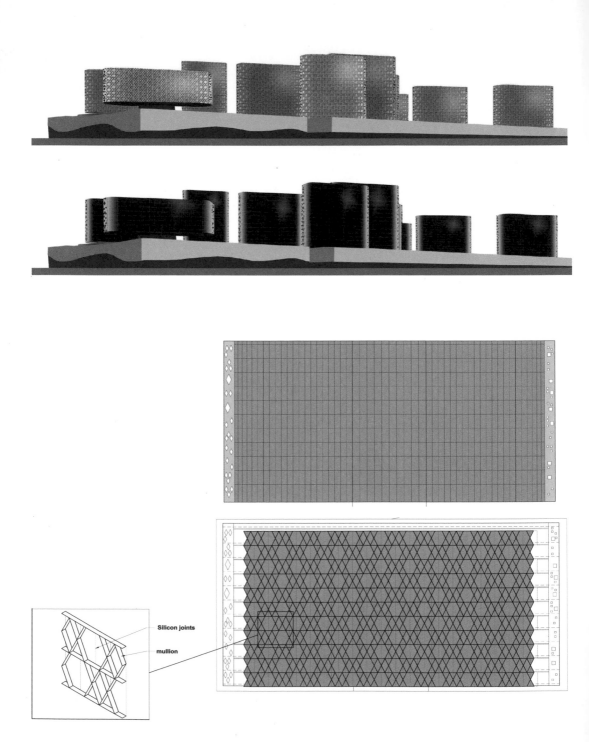

Strategies for the Towers: curtain wall and patterned mullions (north)

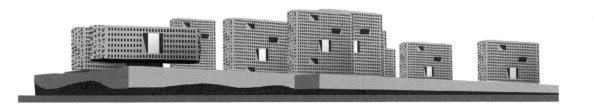

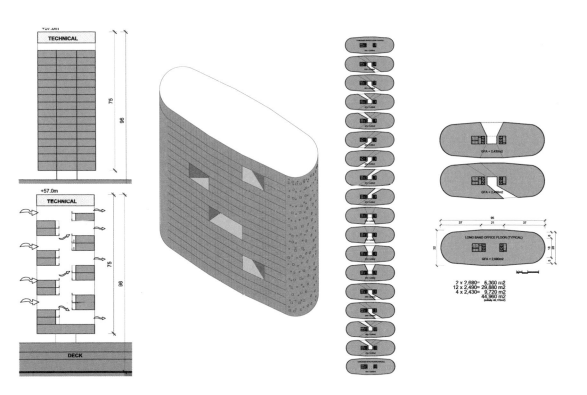

Strategies for the Towers: abstract ecological voids (south and north)

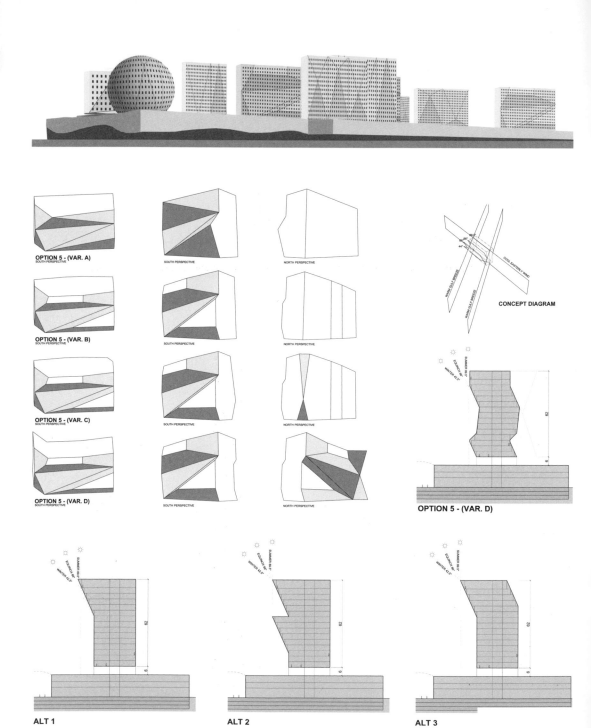

OPTION 5 - (VAR. A)
SOUTH PERSPECTIVE

OPTION 5 - (VAR. B)
SOUTH PERSPECTIVE

OPTION 5 - (VAR. C)
SOUTH PERSPECTIVE

OPTION 5 - (VAR. D)
SOUTH PERSPECTIVE

SOUTH PERSPECTIVE

SOUTH PERSPECTIVE

SOUTH PERSPECTIVE

SOUTH PERSPECTIVE

NORTH PERSPECTIVE

NORTH PERSPECTIVE

NORTH PERSPECTIVE

NORTH PERSPECTIVE

CONCEPT DIAGRAM

OPTION 5 - (VAR. D)

ALT 1

ALT 2

ALT 3

Strategies for the Towers: folds and curtain wall (south)

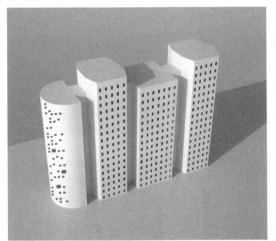

South

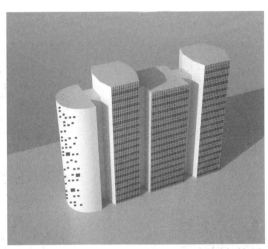

North

Strategies for the Towers: vertical articulation (south and north)

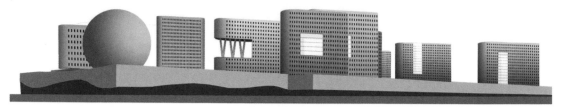

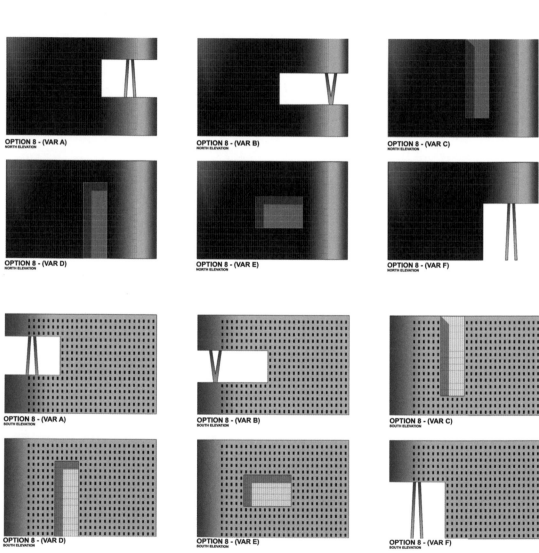

OPTION 8 - (VAR A)
NORTH ELEVATION

OPTION 8 - (VAR B)
NORTH ELEVATION

OPTION 8 - (VAR C)
NORTH ELEVATION

OPTION 8 - (VAR D)
NORTH ELEVATION

OPTION 8 - (VAR E)
NORTH ELEVATION

OPTION 8 - (VAR F)
NORTH ELEVATION

OPTION 8 - (VAR A)
SOUTH ELEVATION

OPTION 8 - (VAR B)
SOUTH ELEVATION

OPTION 8 - (VAR C)
SOUTH ELEVATION

OPTION 8 - (VAR D)
SOUTH ELEVATION

OPTION 8 - (VAR E)
SOUTH ELEVATION

OPTION 8 - (VAR F)
SOUTH ELEVATION

Strategies for the Towers: iconic volume permutations

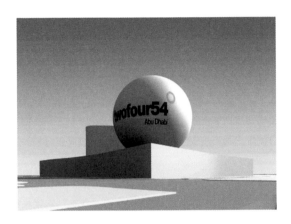

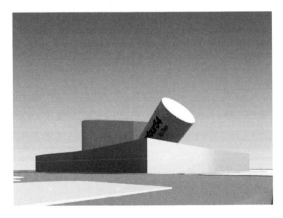

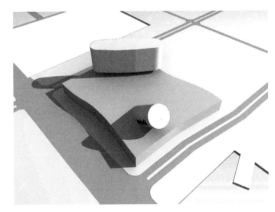

Strategies for the Towers: Magnet Tower, options 1 and 2

Abu Dhabi, Media Zone, 2009
Links-Shabaka

Process

Our master plan for the Abu Dhabi Media Zone was finalized in winter 2008-09. Intended as a new urban quarter combining production studios, offices, housing, shops, and education and exhibition facilities, its precise strategy was developed by distinguishing a base (the "Deck") and a top (the "Towers"). The three-story base contained all facilities that required immediate access from the ground level, such as production studios, shops, and exhibition facilities. The Towers were oriented exactly east-west so as to encourage passive solar protection and low energy consumption.

Reverse Option

Our clients selected a generic curtain-wall option from the nearly three dozen options that we developed during the master-planning phase, but they still felt that additional iterations were needed. In order to see more options, the client organized a competition among six architects, asking us and the other five teams to provide two more options each, while following our now-"official" master plan.

Perhaps because we were tired of exploring so many multiple options and felt that successive options would only become cosmetic derivations of earlier studies, we decided to use the competition as a chance to explore the exact opposite of our previous research, even if it meant excluding ourselves from the very rules that we had set in motion with the master plan. Instead of designing passive energy systems aimed at conserving energy, we would design an "active" energy system in which the Towers would be oriented in such a way as to produce, rather than save, energy.

Rotating the Towers in our master plan by 90 degrees not only provided the possibility of active solar energy production in the sun-drenched east and west facades, but also resulted in a radically different appearance for the master plan when the site was approached from the Abu Dhabi Corniche. Although identical, the towers now appeared thin and slender, rather than massive and short. Simultaneously, the competition's budgetary constraints of an off-the-shelf curtain wall were lifted by the client's political and cultural voices.

Parametric Concept-form

While freed of immediate budgetary constraints, we remained bound by a given set of programmatic requirements and environmental constraints that were outside of our control. Still, we felt that we could now re-organize views and transparencies, as well as create new horizontal links, in what had been a homogeneous system of vertical towers. From the simple vertical extrusions on the Abu Dhabi skyline that had been aimed at providing guidelines for future commercial development, we were now able to introduce flexibility into the system.

We looked for a concept-form that could be almost infinitely transformative. Still based on the master plan principle of towers on a plinth, we began to generate a set of variables to apply to the building envelope: an adaptive set of parameters. Using computational techniques, the original typological volumetrics became a new topological framework. Algorithmic design techniques allowed for the possibility of rapid transformative moves that eventually led to a new architectural expression of the master plan. So-called "media bridges" and a "mediascape" brought a new programmatic dimension to the scheme along with an entirely new identity for the Media Zone.

We took the existing master plan...

with its towers oriented away from the sun...

and turned them to face the sun, using solar collectors.

We gave the towers a more organic shape...

and linked them together high above the street.

The linked towers provide a sense of identity for each block, and by extruding them we discovered a dramatic new form.

Views inside the project reinforced this sense of identity...

and established a presence for the Media Zone brand.

We paid close attention to the feeling of being inside the project, looking out...

and of looking up...

while paying particular attention to the way the project would look from the city.

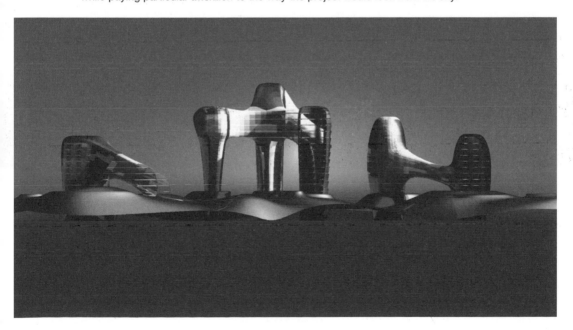

Links: Shabaka

The resultant Links-*Shabaka* project radically revised the master plan. Orienting the Towers north-south, rather than east-west, not only allowed for a streamlined silhouette from the water, but also gave maximum sun exposure to their east and west facades. These facades were then treated with a full mesh of photovoltaic panels, which filter light while producing energy. Linking several towers together added a dynamic dimension of world communication.

We then extended the idea of energy production to the world of media. We created a "Mediascape" by turning the roof of the Deck into a multipurpose horizontal surface, protected from the sun by a "Media Membrane." This in-between Mediascape extends down to the new iteration of the Connector derived from our original master plan and formulated here as the "Media Souk." Based on the idea of mesh, web, or links, our project became about the interconnectivity and reciprocal interaction of the Media Zone.

The Magnet Link

Closest to the water is the Magnet Link, which contains exhibition and conference spaces, offices, incubators, classrooms, and educational production studios. A dynamic, arched, magnet-shaped building acts as the centerpiece of the entire urban quarter. The Magnet itself serves as a link, beginning with the "Media Promenade" that starts on the ground level and ascends into the air, connecting both sides of the block. Under the suspended link, a large outdoor space located on the roof level is reserved for film screenings, parties, special newscasts, and the like. The Magnet Link brands itself as a future-oriented work and learning experience.

The Tower Link

The Tower Link takes the form of three interconnected towers on Block H and one tower on Block E. On Block H, the theme of linkages leads to a new building type, unique to the needs of media companies: from floors 5 through 17, each floor plate is approximately 1,600 square meters in size, but from floors 18 through 21, the floor plates can be as large as 5,400 square meters, easily accommodating the free-plan needs of such large media companies as Google or the BBC while benefiting from extraordinary views over the entire city. The bridges participate in the synergy among enterprises and help to foster cross-firm collaboration.

The Office-Hotel Link

On Block E, a smaller link connects the office tower to the hotel. This link contains a café and meeting rooms that can be rented out to office workers and hotel visitors. Together with the restaurants located on the ground level, the swimming pool and sport facilities on the intermediate level, and the media café on the 12th floor, Block E becomes a work-live complex for residents of Abu Dhabi as well occasional visitors on business. Far from simple "timeless" sculptural forms, the linked towers are conceived of as a direct expression of the need for interaction within a media ecosystem. They celebrate the media industry's appetite for innovation.

The Media Membrane, Mediascape, and the In-Between

Located atop the roofs of the Media Souk, the Media Membrane is a protective element that unifies the roof and the Media Souk below it, creating an in-between space for interaction with endless possibilities. Made out of a synthetic fabric that is alternatively opaque and translucent, it provides protection from the sun while offering a lively landscape when seen from above.

Underneath the membrane is an "in-between" media space—a space of broad capacity, equally welcoming to small or large events and media displays, all the while providing protection from the sun. Special cooling devices refresh parts of the covered membrane area without having to cool the entire space.

Blending digital media into its physical fabric, the Mediascape is in direct visual connection with the Media Souk below, confronting people with a 24-hour, three-dimensional creative world. To cite one example, it will be possible to look into production studios from the Mediascape on the way to the Media Souk.

We arrived at a scheme whose image reflects the connectivity that modern media de-mands and depends on—a visual and programmatic metaphor for the activities that take place inside.

The design emphasizes points of junction and interaction, employing multiple links, connecting passages, a solar membrane, incubator bridges, and a fluid roofscape. All of these features make up the connective tissue of the project. The forms are designed to emphasize the experience of connection rather than the shapes themselves.

Sun-Soaked Climate

Abu Dhabi receives more than two times the annual solar radiation of London. As a city defined by its exposure to the sun, Abu Dhabi receives almost 12 hours of continuous sun per day during the hottest months of the year. When considered including their high-sun angles, Abu Dhabi's buildings are literally bathed in light from morning to evening. Any architectural strategy that concerns Abu Dhabi must examine how to engage responsibly with the sun.

The Links-*Shabaka* design focuses on active sustainability through energy production. The Towers are rotated 90 degrees away from the master plan, orienting their long facades toward the sun. The solar membrane wraps the blocks and towers so as to convert the sun's rays into energy. The project follows the spirit of the original master plan while shifting from passive to active sustainability and from low energy use to energy production.

The Solar Membrane

The Solar Membrane builds on the physical network of bridges and links. As a semi-transparent solar panel surface that wraps around the outside of the project, it captures the sun's energy, generates power, and creates shaded spaces for social exchange.

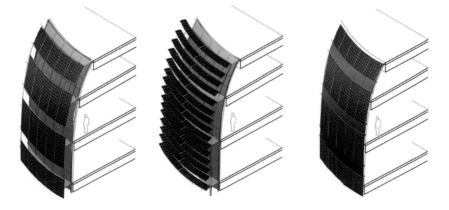

Solar energy production (PVs on
roofs, facades, and membrane)

Round envelope to
reduce turbulence

Close
access
to public
transit

Wind turbines:
vents capture winds
at technical floors

Accessible
green space

Close access to
bicycle racks

Native
vegetation

Shield toward
south: precast
concrete or metal

Permeable horizontal membrane:
natural ventilation and natural lighting

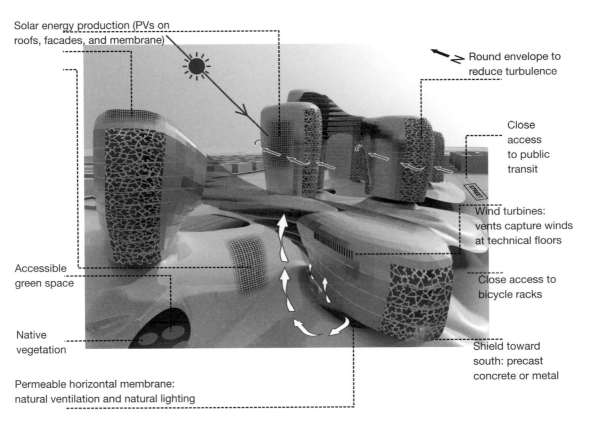

Linked Towers

The bridges give the identity of a destination to the project. They provide physical links between the Towers in order to promote cross-firm interaction, and act as incubator-galleries where experimental digital designs and media can be displayed. Public routes through the promenade extend from the Media Souk below to the shaded spaces of the Solar Membrane and the bridges up above.

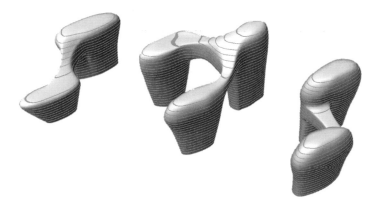

Incubator-Bridges

Media companies have always been quick to recognize the diverse needs of today's multitasking workforce, perhaps because they are not bound to traditional office settings. Break-out rooms, spaces for play and innovation, and ubiquitous wireless connectivity are as important as dedicated rooms for concentrated production. The bridges enable both large and small companies to work in and across several buildings.

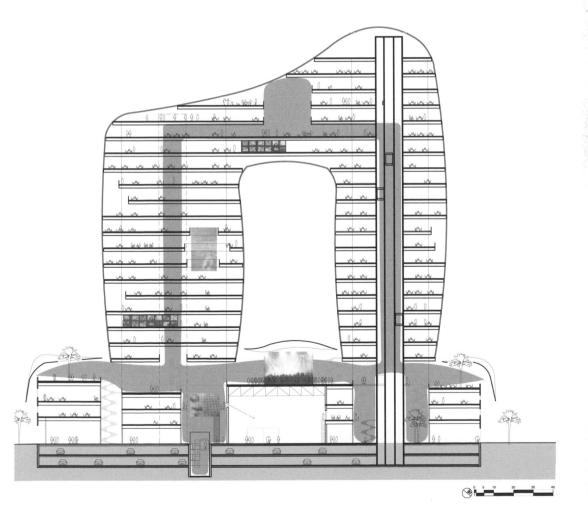

0 5 10 20 30 40

The Media Membrane

Above the podium, a membrane covers and shades the roofs of the recording studios and the programs located in the Deck. The membrane creates dynamic spaces both above and below that enliven and activate the semi-public spaces at the base of the linked offices. This area is reserved for the creative professionals in the Media Zone—for work and play. All share common semi-public spaces located above the podium.

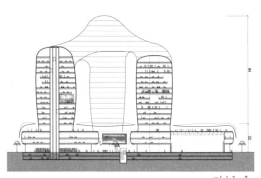

Block H: Offices

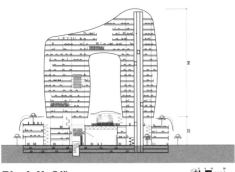

Block H: Offices

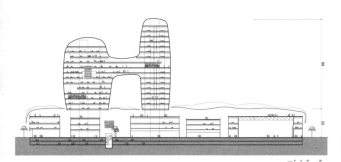

Block E: Offices/hotel

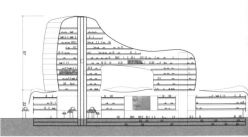

Block L: Magnet

Sections

The Media Promenade

The Media Promenade extends from the Media Souk to the undulating, complex spaces of the roof through the arterial web of the Towers. A public visitors' route moves from the media plaza through the networking spaces of the roof deck, dipping down to offer views into the studios and moving along an elevated skybridge that is equipped with experimental media stations featuring work by small firms or incubators.

The muted hierarchy of the new "Connector" allows for multiple paths, chance encounters, and diverse experiences such as might take place in a traditional souk or in a vibrant city neighborhood. The inner workings of the studios may be exposed, or visitors might catch glimpses of the unloading or installation of studio stage-sets. The resulting Media Souk affords diversity through the variety of its spatial experiences.

Retail outlets, a visitors' center, office lobbies, the academy, hotel amenities, and publicly accessible studio spaces with transparent walls are arranged so as to encourage exploration.

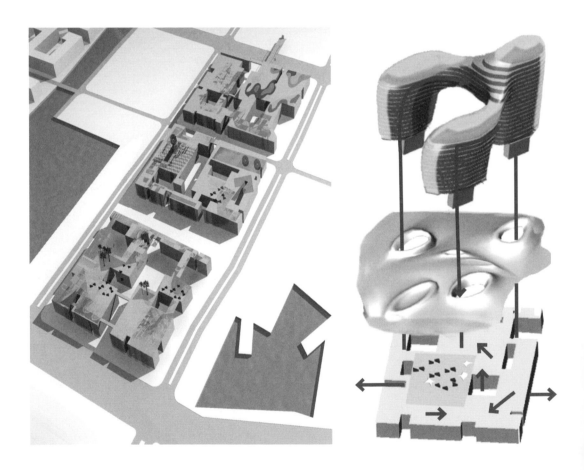

Circulation among the office links, the Media Membrane, the Mediascape, and the Media Souk

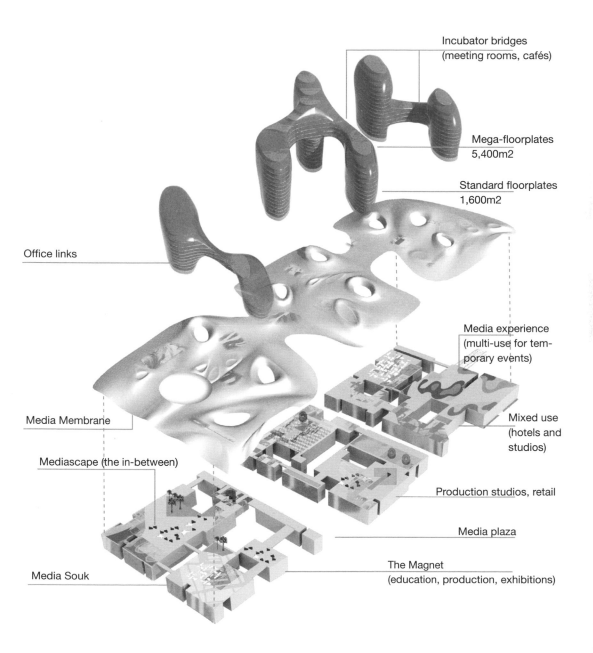

Incubator bridges
(meeting rooms, cafés)

Mega-floorplates
5,400m2

Standard floorplates
1,600m2

Office links

Media experience
(multi-use for tem-
porary events)

Mixed use
(hotels and
studios)

Media Membrane

Mediascape (the in-between)

Production studios, retail

Media plaza

Media Souk

The Magnet
(education, production, exhibitions)

The Media Souk

As we developed the idea of links or connections for the towers and the Media Membrane, we felt that the Deck should be re-imagined as a Souk so as to enrich the Media Zone experience for workers and visitors alike. We refined the idea of the Connector, transforming it from a linear experience to a more random and three-dimensional one with visible connections to the towers and the Media Membrane above it. At the ground level, various program spaces, including studios and retail, are broken down into discreet elements that can be approached and viewed from multiple directions.

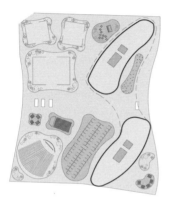  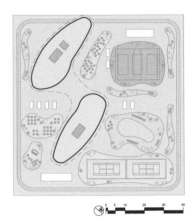

The Mediascape

Shared tenant amenities are located under the Media Membrane. The membrane weaves over and under the programs on the roof of the Media Souk, creating interesting spaces that define the characteristics of each block. Each block is meant to contain facilities that address a different creative lifestyle.

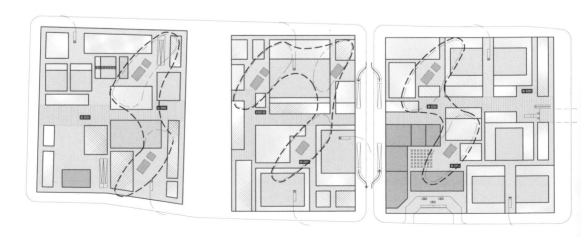

Block L: performance and exhibition   Block H: idea-generating facilities   Block E: creative lifestyle center

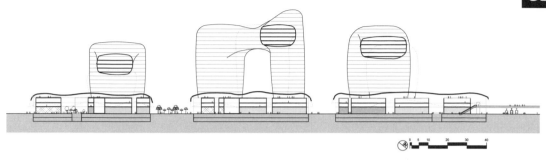

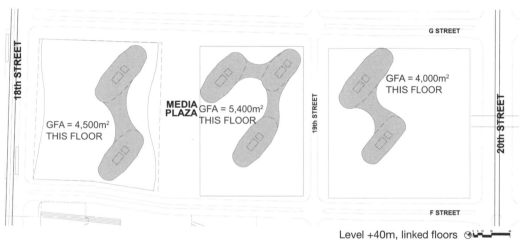

18th STREET

G STREET

GFA = 4,500m²
THIS FLOOR

MEDIA PLAZA GFA = 5,400m²
THIS FLOOR

GFA = 4,000m²
THIS FLOOR

19th STREET

20th STREET

F STREET

Level +40m, linked floors

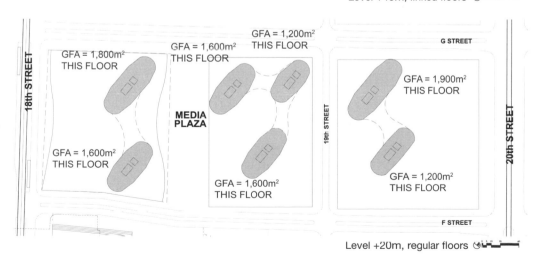

18th STREET

GFA = 1,200m²
THIS FLOOR

GFA = 1,600m²
THIS FLOOR

GFA = 1,800m²
THIS FLOOR

G STREET

GFA = 1,900m²
THIS FLOOR

MEDIA PLAZA

GFA = 1,600m²
THIS FLOOR

GFA = 1,600m²
THIS FLOOR

19th STREET

GFA = 1,200m²
THIS FLOOR

20th STREET

F STREET

Level +20m, regular floors

Block L: performance and exhibition   Block H: idea-generating facilities   Block E: creative lifestyle center

Epilogue

Master plan, 2008-09

Selected design for Zone 1 by UN Studio, press release 2010

A **concept-form** is a generator of new conditions. It freely uses or invents forms to locate activities or generate events.

C2. Raised

Abu Dhabi,
Sheikh Zayed National Museum, 2007

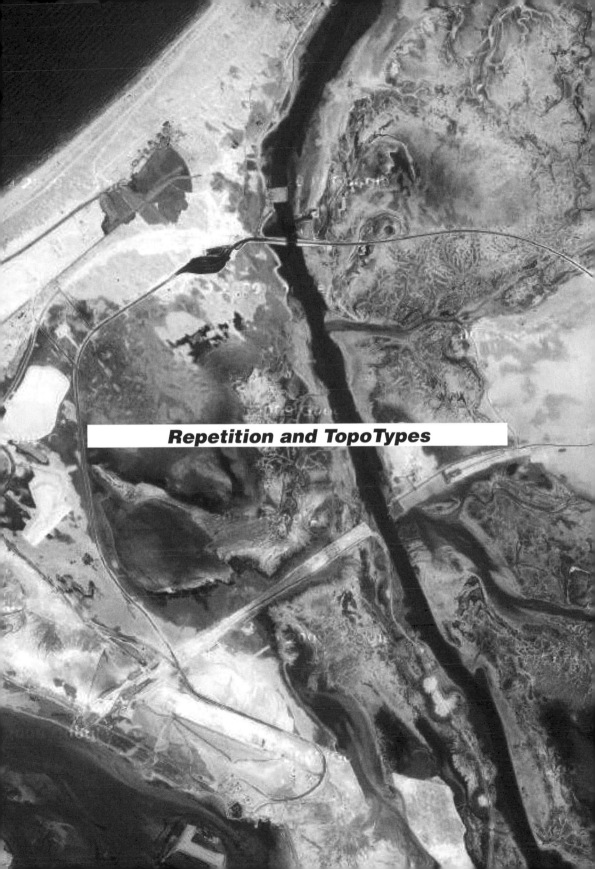

Repetition and TopoTypes

The New Abu Dhabi Cultural District

Like all new cities, the new Abu Dhabi cultural district needs a center of gravity, a meeting place where different aspects of culture converge. The site for the new Sheik Zayed National Museum and the two Biennale pavilions provides an opportunity for such a focal point. Our intention was to create one of the great cosmopolitan spaces, comparable to Venice's Piazza San Marco but conceived in the round, with the Sheikh Zayed Museum providing an equivalent to its Basilica.

We turned the traffic circle into an urban plaza, a circular "galleria" with art galleries and venues, designer shops, cafés, restaurants, and boutique hotels. Critical mass is this Ring's strength, serving as the dynamic heart for the lively cultural center of the new Abu Dhabi. A continuous stone-like screen along the inner facade of the Ring filters light inside and gives scale and urbanity to the circular plaza.

8 Aug 07

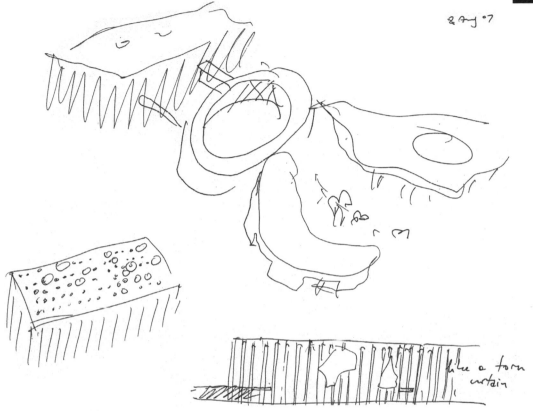

like a torn
curtain

Concept sketches

Rather than simply adding to the disparate collection of prestigious icons in the new Abu Dhabi, we felt the need to provide a suitable context for the museum and the pavilions so as to give them the urban focus they merit.

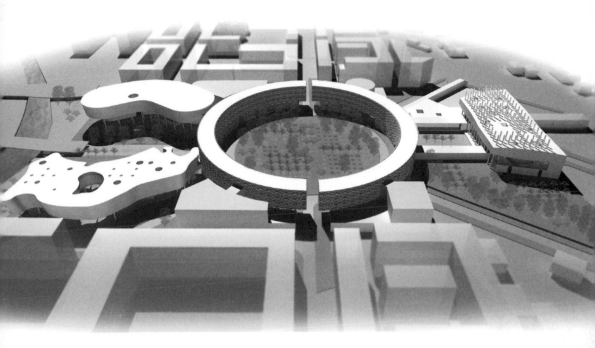

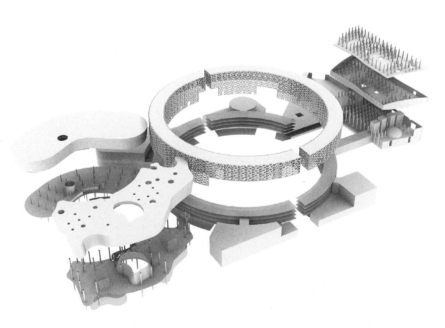

Three architectural themes inform our Abu Dhabi project. The first, "Concept-form," is best exemplified by the Ring as an organizing common denominator for the various activities located inside and around it. The Ring structure can either be integrated into the master plan requirements or added to the existing plan as an envelope-facade.

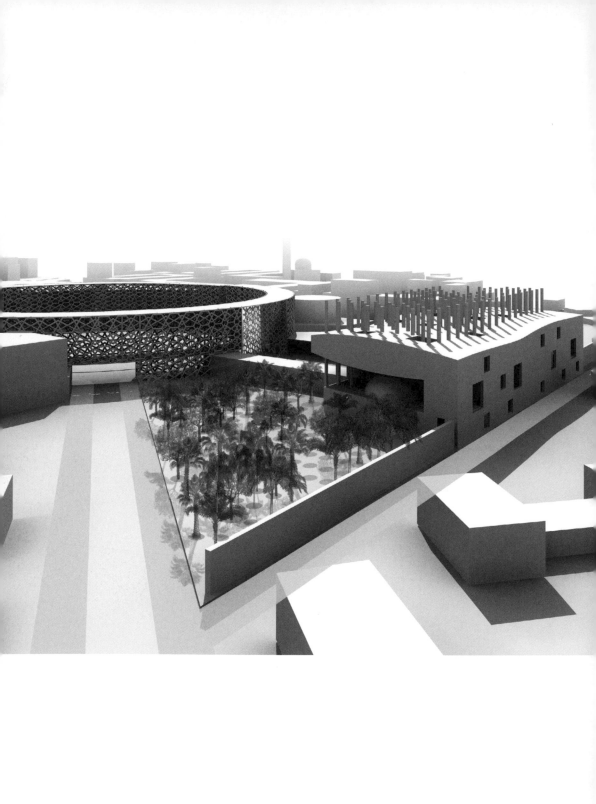

As one approaches the museum, the Ring stops and the galleries end. The stone screen now opens onto a large and quiet courtyard, providing the entrance to the museum with independence and dignity. Located next to the courtyard is a large orchard that is open to the public, but clearly part of the museum. The museum is designed as one of the world's great columnar spaces, interpreted in a secular and contemporary manner. The museum combines the interiority characteristic of Islamic architecture with the assertiveness of an architectural destination point.

Made out of concrete the color of the surrounding sand, the museum is conceived as a forest of columns supporting a slender horizontal volume, whose gentle curve meanders as if floating through the stark vertical elements. An exhilarating ten meter-high hypostyle lobby is a major moment in the visitor's experience. The columns and some of the palm trees growing in the patios extend upward through the roof, affording a singular external identity for the museum.

The second architectural theme is "singular iteration." In our scheme for the Sheikh Zayed National Museum, the repetition of columns provides a modern interpretation of an
Islamic space, expanding on the activation of architecture by the rhythm and repetition of
colonnades that is evident in major mosques. Continuing some of the columns into the
sky in a way never seen before gives the museum a unique and iconic identity.

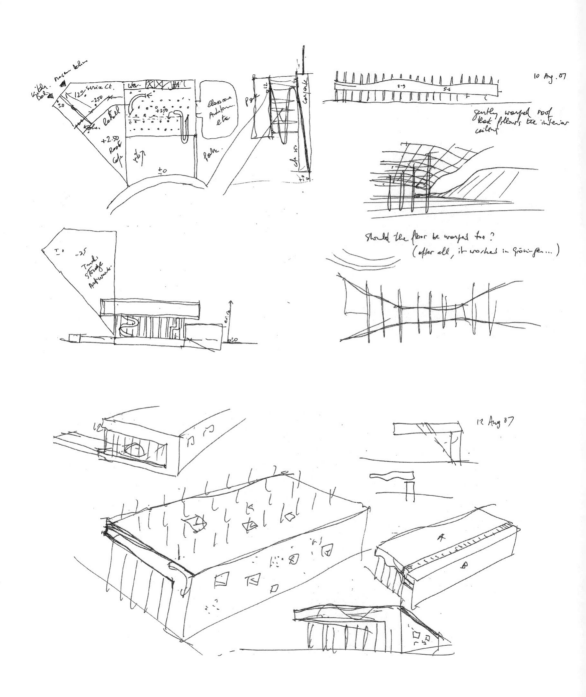

gently warped roof
Roof follows the interior
ceiling

10 Aug. 07

Should the floor be warped too?
(after all, it worked in Groningen...)

12 Aug 07

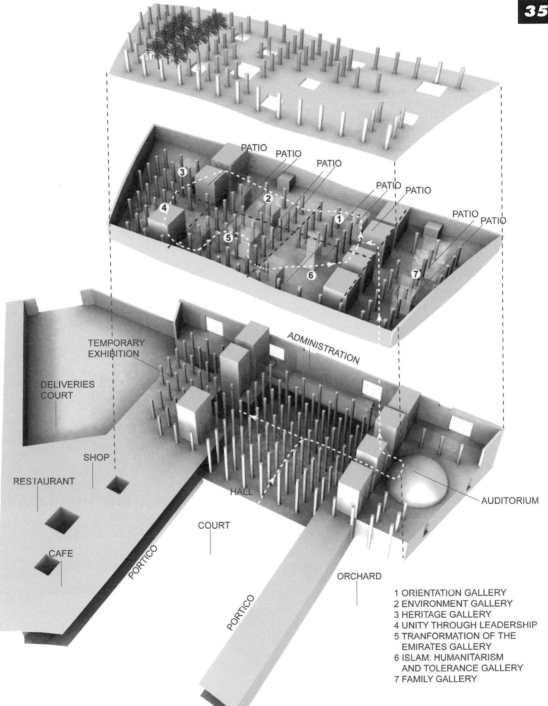

PATIO
PATIO
PATIO
PATIO
PATIO
PATIO
PATIO

ADMINISTRATION

TEMPORARY
EXHIBITION

DELIVERIES
COURT

SHOP

RESTAURANT

HALL

COURT

AUDITORIUM

CAFE

PORTICO

ORCHARD

PORTICO

1 ORIENTATION GALLERY
2 ENVIRONMENT GALLERY
3 HERITAGE GALLERY
4 UNITY THROUGH LEADERSHIP
5 TRANFORMATION OF THE
  EMIRATES GALLERY
6 ISLAM. HUMANITARISM
  AND TOLERANCE GALLERY
7 FAMILY GALLERY

B -> Nefeli 8 August 07

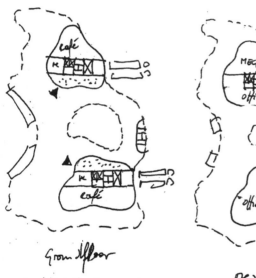

Ground floor

////// = Back of House
·.·.· = Public Amenities.

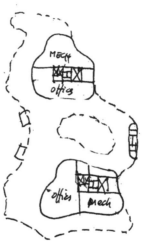

mezzanine

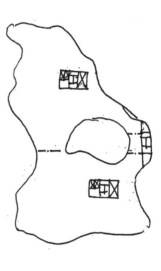

R1 1

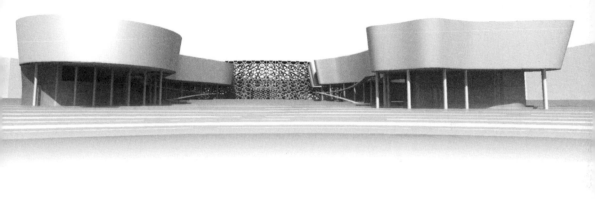

The two Biennale pavilions are accessible from both the Urban Ring and the Canal. If the Ring provides an urban entry to the exhibition space sequence, the Canal acts as a thread linking our pavilions to the others (19 are proposed in total). Hence this specific group of pavilions is simultaneously a support for the "urban" culture of the Ring and a "garden-like" feature of the general Canal promenade. This dual proximity allows for potential relationships between commerce and culture.

We have called our third architectural theme "Topotype," referring to an architecture that takes on different architectural configurations while remaining generally unchanged in program. In the pair of Biennale pavilions, the relatively simple typological geometry of one pavilion is transformed through "topological" distortion, generating a second and distinct pavilion.

The subtle architectural differences between Typo and Topo, including the several smaller, irregular-shaped spaces in the latter that are suitable for film, video, and media-based art, may find echoes in the works exhibited in them.

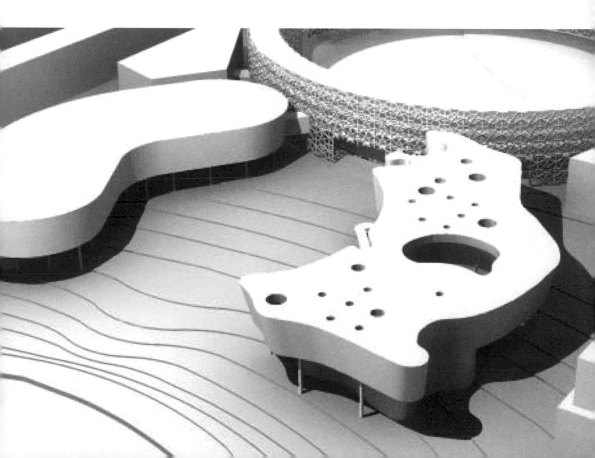

Busan, Cinema Complex, 2005

Real Simple

Looking for Sobriety: Program Becomes Form

The Busan International Film Festival is the most renowned film festival in Asia and among the eight largest film gatherings in the world. A major cinema complex was planned to accommodate the event and to foster Busan's identity as venue for the film industry and a hub of visual culture.

In keeping with these aims, we wanted to design a building that would respond to the established history of film-making as well as its on-going experimental nature. We wanted a building that would be both a magnet of culture and a generator of public life. Finally, we wanted to devise a building that would be as clear and evident as possible, avoiding the debauchery of excessive form-making. Instead of the motto, "Why be simple when architecture can be complicated?," we wanted sobriety.

For some of us, education in architecture began with the cinema. We learned more about architecture from studying the film directors Sergei Eisenstein and Dziga Vertov than from the treatises of architectural history. Jump cuts, fade-ins, fade-outs, and dissolves held no secrets for us. Traveling, panoramic, and close-up shots have informed our architecture since the day we started to design.

But instead of literally transposing aspects of film theory and filmmaking into the architecture of the Busan Cinema Complex, it seemed important for the genre of film to operate in a subliminal, emotional way. In no sense should the building compete with film. On the contrary, it should enhance film by contrast. For example, film is about movement, so a very "still" building was needed to frame film—still, but not static.

An Active Park

First, we landscaped the site on a slight incline toward the adjacent river so as to provide a comfortable seating area for an outdoor cinema surrounded by trees and recreational spaces. We then elevated the five required film theaters into the air and located them in the simplest way possible around a common "cinema hall." Thanks to this hovering platform, we defined a covered outdoor public space and a large public concourse on the ground. We slid the park under the building so as to offer a continuous public space to the city. The concourse entrance acts as an animated hub, giving access onto the lower level with its *cinemathèque*, visual arts center, and offices, as well as to the upper levels.

Cinema Hall with a View

In the air, the five theaters define a central meeting space—a cinema hall dedicated to film culture, with an impressive view toward the river. The configuration of the theaters also allows for a promenade around its periphery that gives panoramic views over Busan. We located the convention center between the public ground level and the cinema level, on a balconied mezzanine overlooking the concourse. Finally, we proposed a large roof garden with a bar, a restaurant, and a view onto the whole city.

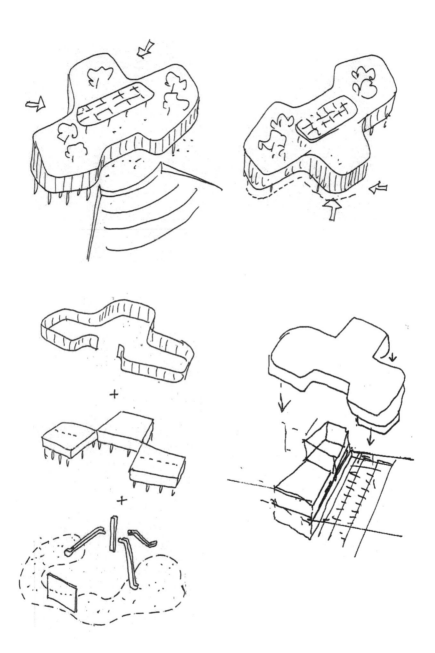

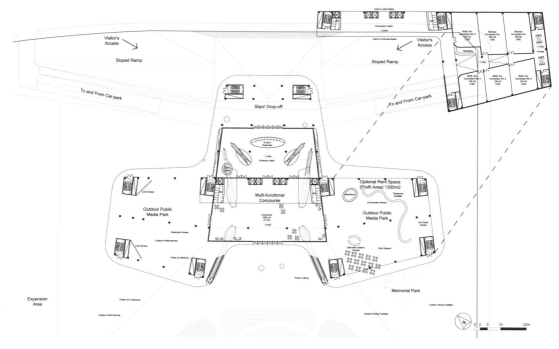

Level 1 (Concourse) with mezzanine level (Convention Center)

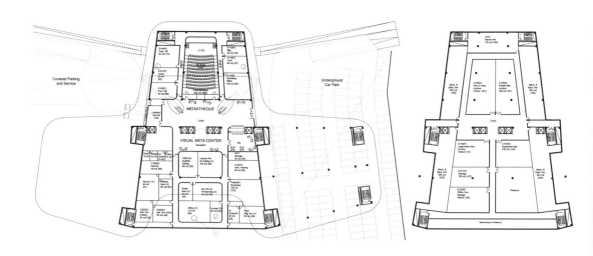

Level 0 (Theater, Visual Arts) and Level -1 (Support)

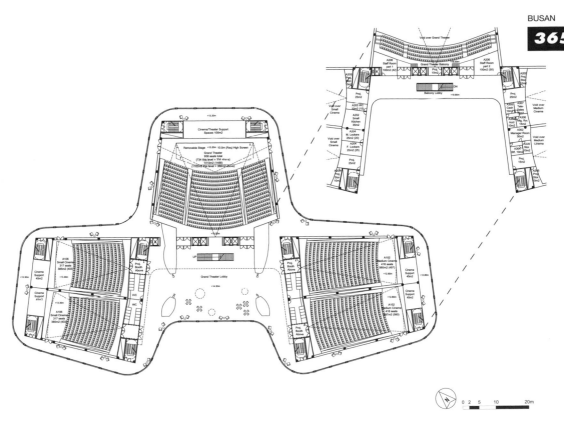

Level 2 (Cinemas) with mezzanine level (Balcony)

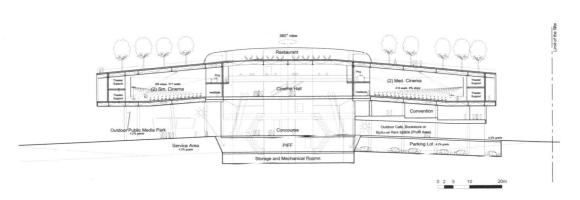

Section

A public space, filled with experimental images, for the city of Busan

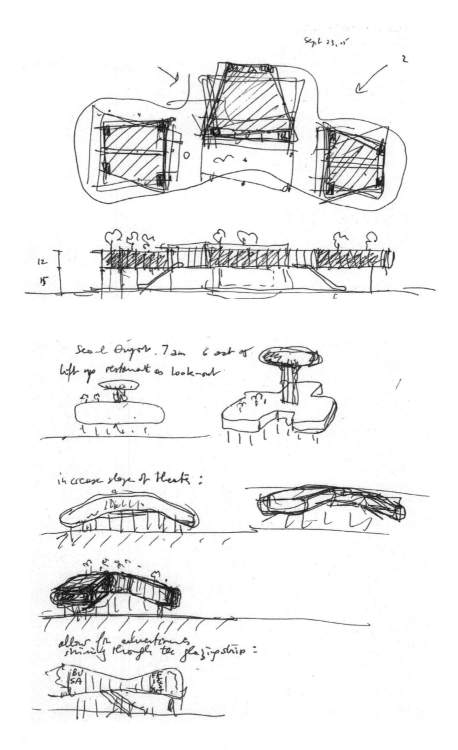

Sept 23, 05

2

12
15

Seoul August. 7 am   6 out of
lift up restaurant as look-out

increase slope of theatre :

allow for advertisements
shining through the glazing strip :

BU
SA

Arriving from the river, a park combined with an open-air cinema.
The hovering facade displays constantly changing light effects.

D. Gridded Loop

Our project for Mediapolis in Singapore is located within a general district plan by Zaha Hadid Architects. Our plan turns the original grid into an urban strategy of rigorous street fronts and flexible rear yards.

Singapore, Master Plan, 2008

Mediapolis

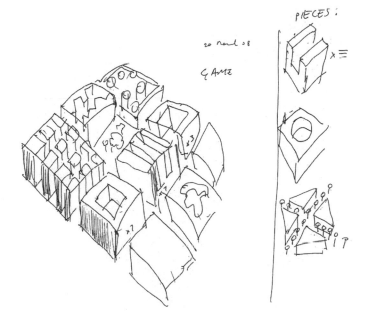

There is no great city quarter without contrast and calculated tension. Like all good stories, we wanted the media park to resonate with surprises and to register as a unique Singapore experience, both in terms of climate and energy. We wanted to be both global and local. So, we devised a double strategy, like two sides of a coin.

On the "heads" side, we implemented a "narrow street" loop as a common denominator, distributing all active local vehicular and pedestrian traffic, shops, and restaurants. We aimed at a climate of excitement, with multi-colored electronic banners visible at all times of the day, comparable to the most active and dense street life of the most metropolitan cities of the world. It is simultaneously shaded, protected from rain, and well-lit day and night.

On the "tails" side, namely on the area not directly in contact with the street loop, we encouraged ultimate creativity of forms, volumes and architectural expression. In contrast with the street side alignments, here invention is encouraged: a feeling of playful freedom.

We want the tension between these two sides to be a challenging and constantly provoking environment for film-makers and multimedia designers, underlining today's paradoxical aims of urban density and architectural free play. Hence, the media park is developed with the awareness that media production in the 21st century depends not only on dedicated facilities but also on constant innovation and creative collaboration. The media park aims at nurturing a production ecology of both local and international activity.

The system of urban paradox—both free-form and densely continuous—produces pragmatic benefits, as well. The plan facilitates the development of the studio complex and dedicated facilities as lower-scale developments in the first phase. Landscaping integrates itself into the strategy as a diffused network. The free-form breaks in the street wall provide opportunities for iconic architecture and signature elements, whether for corporate branding or residential luxury. At the same time, the regularity of the street wall facilities a thorough organization of access routes and support services. Perhaps most significantly, the density of urban space defines an active and porous ground plane for inhabitants to work, learn, and engage in creative and collaborative play.

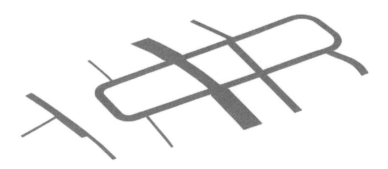

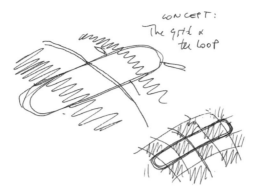

CONCEPT:
The grid &
the loop

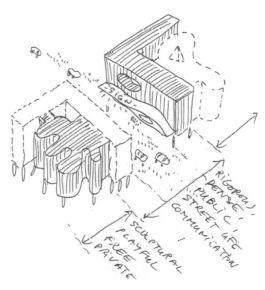

RIGOROUS
DENSE
PUBLIC
STREET LIFE
COMMUNICATION

SCULPTURAL
PLAYFUL
FREE
PRIVATE

-SIGN-

Concept sketches: the grid and the loop

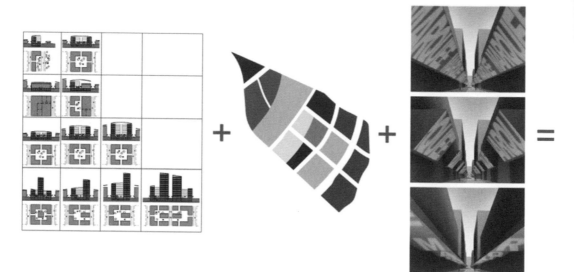

The Game
The pieces + the board + the net

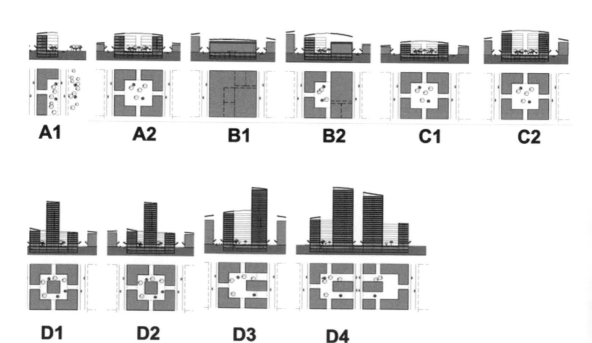

A1 A2 B1 B2 C1 C2

D1 D2 D3 D4

The Pieces
Typical block variations in section

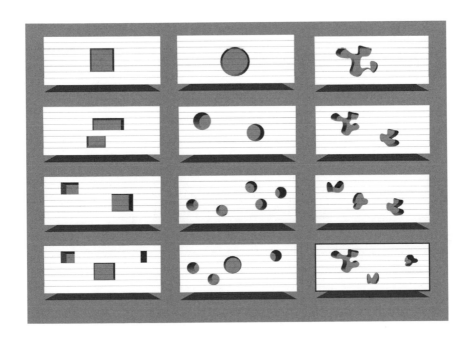

Possibilities for a 10% elevation void, with 406 square meters voided
10% void as minimum requirement in elevation; frame may not be voided; 100% border as indicated

Concept-forms are situated between diagrams and types, since a diagram can be purely conceptual and have nothing to do with form, while a type is always represented by a form.

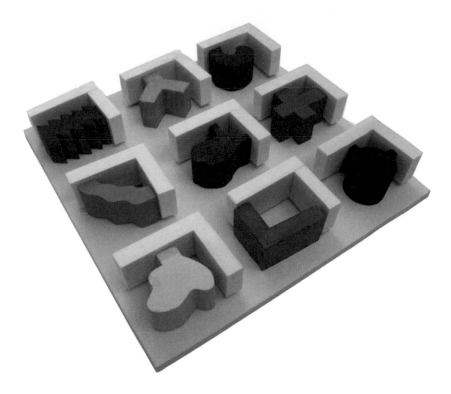

Material Concept

Glass makes up the exterior surfaces, while freedom is exercised in the inner courts and toward the periphery. Within the frame of the glass street-wall, the architect may play games—of holes, voids, balconies, loggias—to animate the inner facade.

Green glass/steel facade   Blue glass/steel facade   Purple glass/concrete facade

E. Discontinuity/Repetition

Part E explores how a discontinuous concept-form can give the appearance of continuity. In the case of the Paris Ile Seguin project, the strategy makes use of a cinematic device in order to convey the illusion of a continuous urban envelope.

The design for an exhibition about new architectural projects in Paris takes small advertising billboards—an urban artifact familiar to all Parisians, called the "*sucette*," or lollipop— and locates them at random throughout a large exhibition hall to create dynamic readings between the moving visitors and the exhibition panels.

Pavillon de l'Arsenal, Paris, 2005

Concept-Form as Objet-Trouvé: Paris Lollipops

The Pavillon de l'Arsenal in Paris is run by city authorities and focuses on urban and architectural exhibitions related to the metropolitan area. In 2005 we were asked to design an exhibition dedicated to recent urban proposals for the Paris region by a range of local architects. How could we celebrate the dynamism of a city in constant transformation when most of the materials submitted were static documents like master plans and written descriptions of roadside improvements?

Our concept was simple: we decided to bring city life into the exhibition space. Paris is known for its "*sucettes*," lollipop-shaped advertising billboards that punctuate the city streets and sidewalks. These billboards are operated mechanically so that two or three images rotate at 20-second intervals, providing a constantly changing advertising message. We convinced the Pavillon de l'Arsenal to borrow about three dozen *sucettes* and to replace their usual commercial content (advertisements for cough syrup, women's underwear, and so on) with architectural drawings.

The constant rotation of the *sucettes* provided image and sound animation to the space. Positioned at seemingly random locations throughout the exhibition, the billboards were not "composed," but instead simply arranged to offer a dynamic reading between the movement of visitors and the content of the exhibition panels.

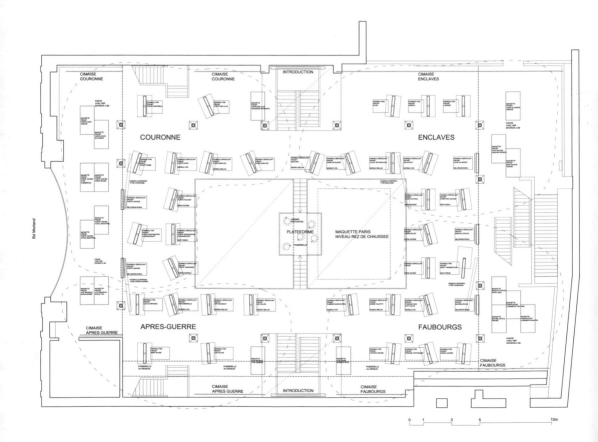

Paris, Ile Seguin II, 2004

Cinematic Envelope

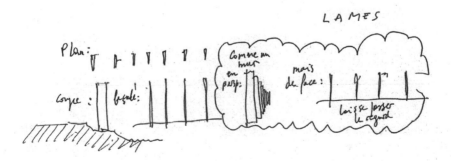

The 2004 competition for the Ile Seguin, the fourth international architectural competition for the area in a decade, asked for an adaptive re-use strategy for a dramatic abandoned industrial site located on an island in the Seine River. We responded with an attempt, at once historical and sentimental, to preserve both the memory of the place (which was formerly home to the first Renault automobile factories) and the visual coherence of its old buildings, which were nostalgically reminiscent of a steamship frozen in the water.

For technical and logistical reasons, it was impossible to conserve the "hull" of the ship in the way that one preserves the facades of Haussmann buildings in Paris by emptying them out and installing new commercial standards. It also was impractical to impose rigid facade rules on future private investors without a strong sense of the future uses of the site. Therefore, our challenge became to imagine a facade-envelope—a coherent, organizing assemblage/packaging/wrapper—that would restore the visual unity of the Ile Seguin without requiring costly restoration, even absent any clear vision of the programmatic needs of its future users.

A New Question
How to give to both urbanity and identity to the Ile Seguin? How can a facade-envelope lead to a public space?

To avoid making a frozen block-plan, we imagined a strategy rather than a project. The strategy consisted of offering both continuity and discontinuity to the exterior vision. We situated a series of wedge-shaped blades a dozen meters in height at ten-meter intervals along the island periphery, enacting a well-known optical effect: the blades appear as a continuous surface when viewed from an angular perspective, but allow the gaze to pass between interior and exterior, assuring permeability and openness, when sighted from a position perpendicular to them. The blades provided markers, permitting way-finding all along the periphery of the island.

In addition, we drew the dotted rhythm of the blades in toward the interior of the island, providing locations for the public spaces proposed in the existing master plan. This embodied an urban strategy as much as a visual one: the blades became points for collecting and exchanging information. Thus, our facade-envelope articulated a space that was neither open nor closed, representing a permeable periphery—at once continuous and discontinuous.

Technical Strategy

The visual strategy lent itself to innovative materials capable of expressing the double nature of the facade-envelope as a presence that is alternately opaque and transparent, depending on one's perspective. Additionally, the structure and envelope of the blades could be constructed using very light and resistant materials, akin to the alloy composites employed in naval architecture and aerospace, or light mesh membranes inset with planes of stainless steel, glass, aluminum panels, and so on.

The Riverside

Our strategy was dependent on continuity, rhythm, and flatness as well as light and its reflection in water, which dominates the site due to its proximity to the Seine River. The elements make up a panoramic and rhythmic view that is at once transparent to the buildings on the island and (from certain angles) completely opaque. Indeed, the scroll of the blades across dozens of meters almost offers a smooth, closed wall, much like an actual facade.

The general scale of the project is such that the perception of the blade-system induces movement by the user. The manner in which the openings are perceived creates different dimensions and results in wide-ranging scales in perpetual flux that can only be appreciated by direct engagement with the architecture.

Ile Seguin II represents a spatial strategy that is neither open nor closed; the periphery is permeable.

From Hanging Points to Public Space

The blades mark the presence of a public space on the (privately developed) Ile Seguin. They suggest possible uses of the space for private or public initiatives, including festivals, concerts, and exhibitions. They jostle the frozen limits between built and non-built spaces, making a lively public space emerge.

The strategy of hanging points can extend to many different types of contemporary events in the city. For example:

> A ring of dynamic lights
> A ring of sound, turning the island into a simulacrum of an automobile race-track
> A pyrotechnic ring of flares
> Banners by artists, creating a "gallery in the wind"
> Multi-screen projections of films or fixed images
> A technical grille supporting light and sound projections
> A curtain of light, water, or sound

The system of blades or posts represents, first and foremost, a "contemporary architecture installation" that situates public space as a place of collective action, cultural innovation, confrontation, and urban cooperation.

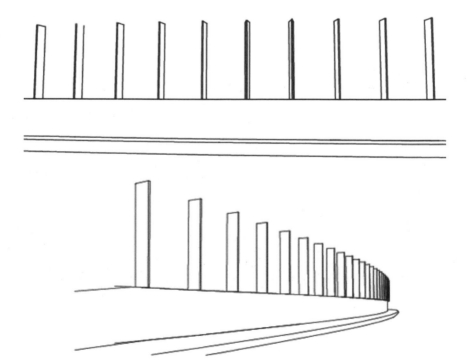

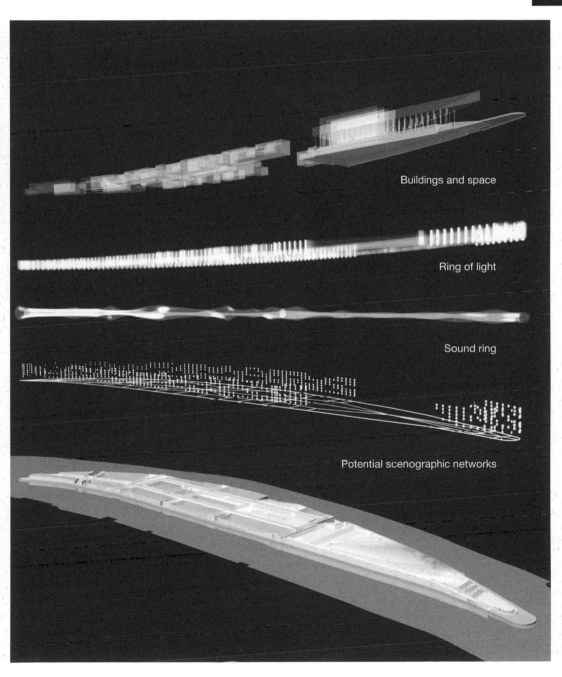

Buildings and space

Ring of light

Sound ring

Potential scenographic networks

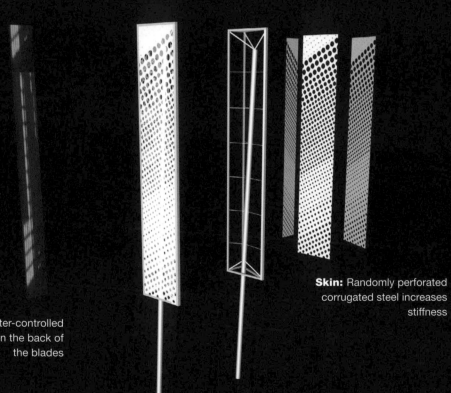

L.E.D.: Computer-controlled lighting panels on the back of the blades

Skin: Randomly perforated corrugated steel increases stiffness

Structure: Tension frame transfers loads to the mast

Fin

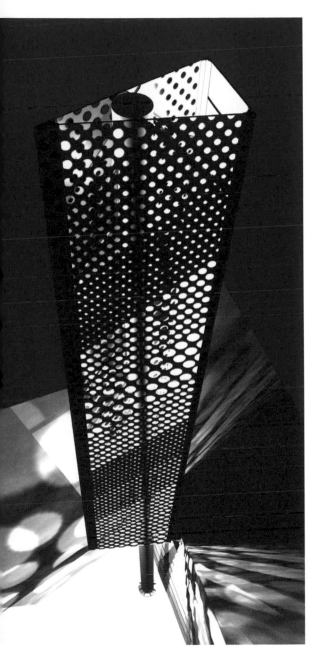

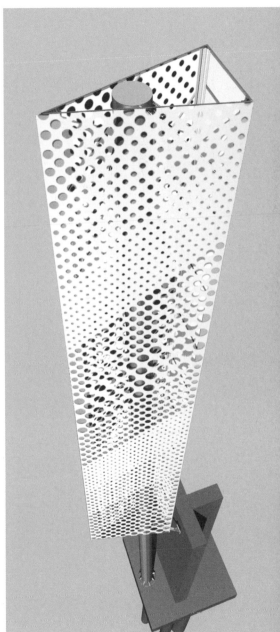

The blades

The envelope accommodates spectacular and temporary transformations.

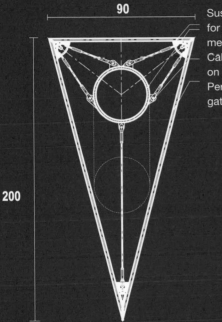

90

200

Suspension cable
for perforated
metal
Cables' anchors
on the mast
Perforated corru-
gated metal plate

Suspension cable for
perforated metal plate
Cast-steel anchor for
suspension cables

Full-height extrusion
Fastening for perforated
metal sheet
Stainless-steel extrusion
Rail for lighting
Fluorescent lighting

Details (Hugh Dutton Associates)

There is no architecture without something that happens in it. Once an abstract concept-form is built, it is confronted with its contents and therefore it is no longer abstract. It now assumes an unstable and changing role, far from the permanence of its original diagram.

F. Linear/Sequential/Continuous

Here, linearity is the theme. Determined by the program or by site conditions, the line is never arbitrary but instead engages specific conditions in a sequential form. Passageway, linear atrium, "great hall"—each archetype acts as a common denominator for all of the other programmatic elements.

**The Hague,
Passage and Department Store, 2005-**

Dutch Tiles

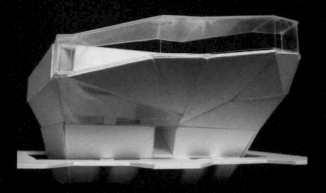

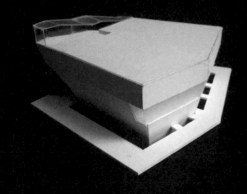

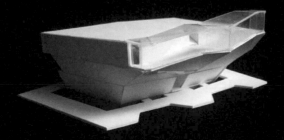

Perspective of entrance, perspective from southwest, perspective from northeast

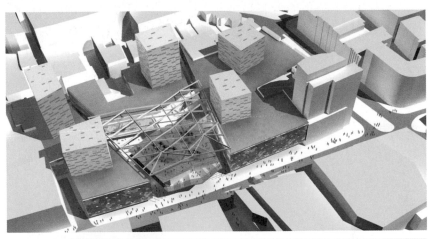

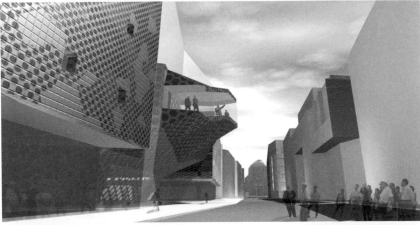

First scheme, on a full urban block, with housing and a cultural center

The site is located in the heart of The Hague, at the intersection of heterogeneous city fragments: vertical and horizontal, subways and streets, administrative and commercial sectors. At this intersection, we wanted to create a three-dimensional place capable of linking together these disparate surroundings. The program consisted of a commercial complex containing both large and small shops as well as a main department store. It offered two passageways between the large Grotemarktstraat and the smaller but very busy Spuistraat, which has its own existing covered passage. It also offered a link between an underground tramway stop and carpark designed by OMA and restaurants and a garden located on the roof of the complex.

First Scheme

The angular configuration of the passageway defines a polygonal block that has been lowered by one level to allow for a suspended garden. The passageway is itself covered by a skylight, and its interior takes the form of a "rock" set in a large atrium that has been distorted according to programmatic needs. It provides a balcony onto the Grotemarkt, covers the entrance, contracts in order to bring light underground, and carves in and out, creating space for vertical circulation like escalators, elevators, and ramps.

The rock can house special uses like galleries, cafeterias, jazz clubs, or community gathering spaces. The garden atop the rock is protected from rain, offering a suspended, quiet piece of nature in the city. It is surrounded by restaurants and terraced bars. An inner court located at the center of the complex offers a plaza for public events.

At street level, the building is open and transparent so as to showcase changing store-front displays. The blue and white facade on the upper floor is reminiscent of Delft tiles. The housing towers on the roof are turned and angled, providing excellent views and permitting sunlight to penetrate inside. The roof is landscaped and linked to the restaurants and bars underneath, creating an urban plaza above the city.

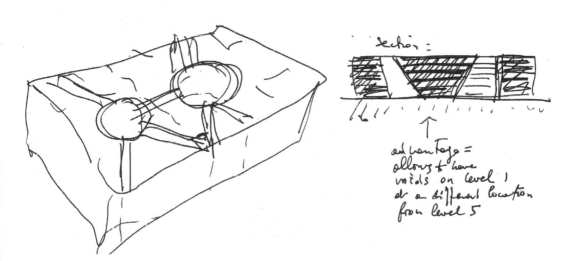

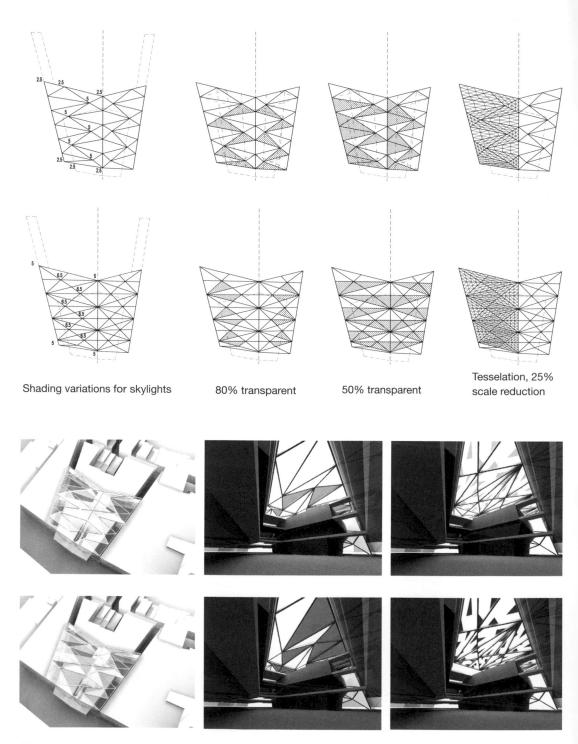

Shading variations for skylights   80% transparent   50% transparent   Tesselation, 25% scale reduction

Alternative skylight schemes at 80% transparency

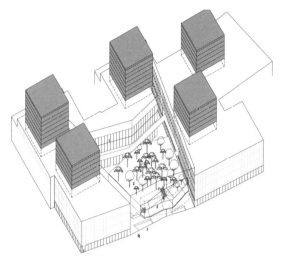

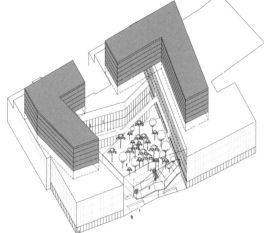

Orthogonal Towers
(10,600 sq. meters, 40 and 50 meters high)

"C" Shape Closed
(13,000 sq. meters, all at 40 meters high)

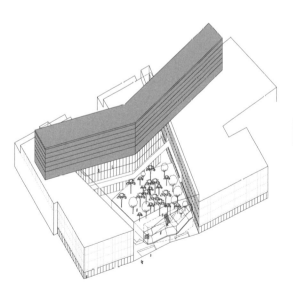

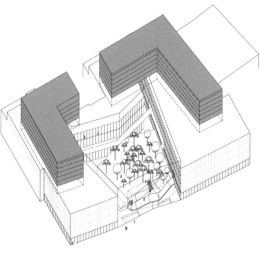

"V" Shape
(10,000 sq. meters, all at 40 meters high)

"C" Shape Open
(13,000 sq. meters, all at 40 meters high)

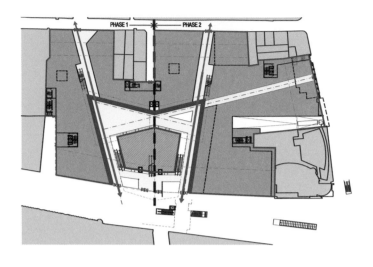

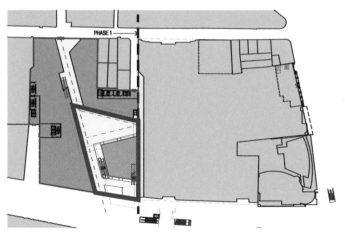

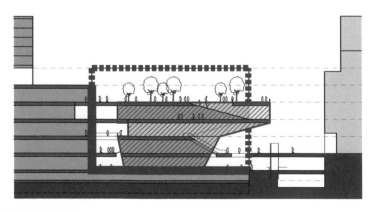

Spatial strategy for the main space

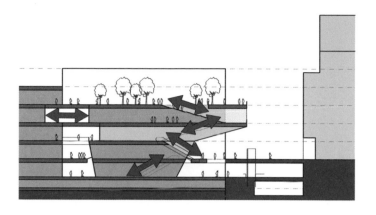

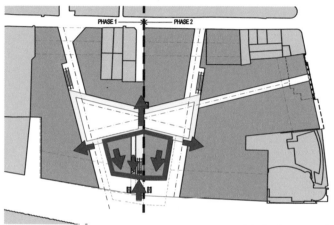

A hub of communications at the entrance

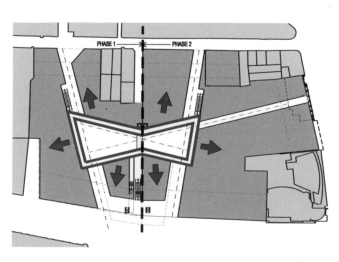

An upper-level distribution ring

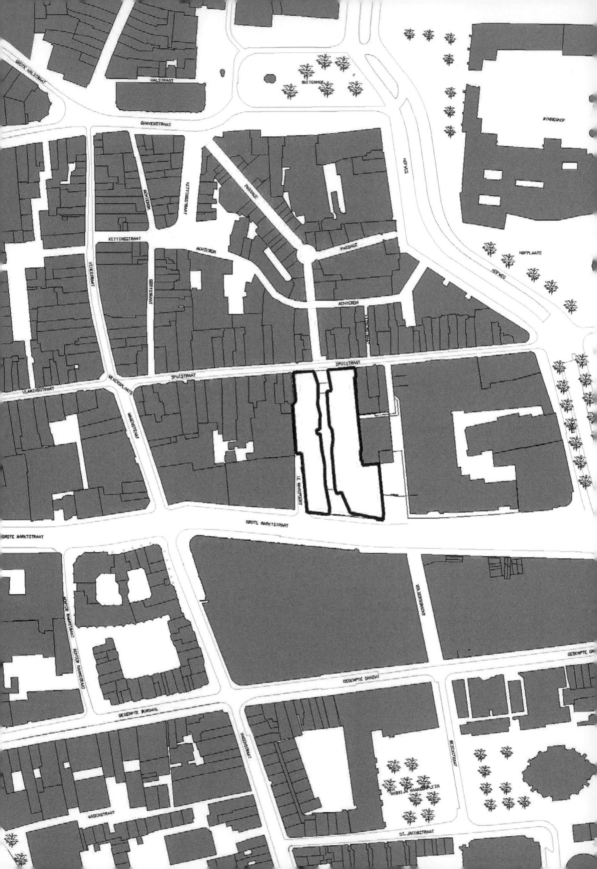

Second Scheme

As the project developed, the site became smaller, and the program became less socially ambitious but more specialized. Its aim was now to create a new urban passageway comparable to the historic Hague Passage to the north as well as to the great passageways throughout Europe.

With this new program came new questions: How could we update this urban typology for contemporary uses? How could we do it in such a way that the resulting passageway could be located only in The Hague? We wanted to approach the project as a building that was incontrovertibly Dutch, but also had an international flavor—a combination in keeping with the role of The Hague among other European cities.

The "*passage*" has a great tradition with a variety of spatial configurations. Passageways are not identical: their ceiling heights, colors, openness, and pedestrian traffic all vary. They can be wide or tight. There is no homogenous configuration (in marked contrast with the 20th-century enclosed shopping mall, whose typology is similar, no matter where on the globe you are located). Controlling signage in passageways is obviously of great importance.

The blue of the tiles was originally suggested as a way to bring a sense of light and openness into the passage interior. The tiles are light blue—close in color to a blue sky on a sunny day—which, in combination with the white tiles, will give a clean, airy feel to the space, drawing customers in from the bustle of the streets.

The use of ceramic tiles is also a nod to Dutch history, suggesting the tin-glazed Delftware tiles that were ubiquitous in 17th- and 18th-century architecture in The Netherlands. Our strategy appropriates them in a contemporary way that references the traditional significance of The Hague as the internationally recognized home of Dutch culture. The particular shade of blue used could also be viewed as an oblique reference to the original light-blue flag of Prince William of Orange.

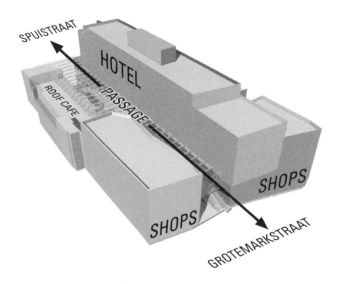

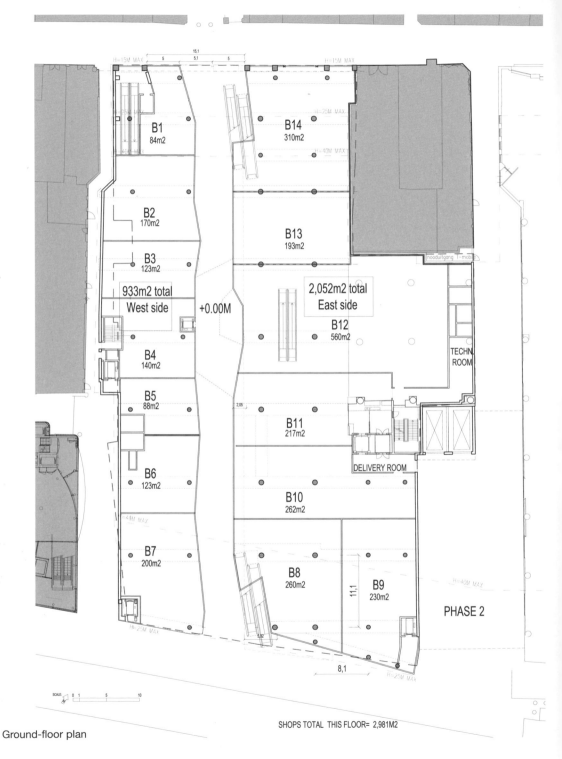

B1
84m2

B14
310m2

B2
170m2

B3
123m2

B13
193m2

933m2 total
West side

+0.00M

2,052m2 total
East side

B12
560m2

TECHN
ROOM

B4
140m2

B5
88m2

2,05

B11
217m2

DELIVERY ROOM

B6
123m2

B10
262m2

B7
200m2

B8
260m2

11,1

B9
230m2

PHASE 2

8,1

SCALE 0 1   5   10

Ground-floor plan

SHOPS TOTAL THIS FLOOR= 2,981M2

View from Grote Marktstraat

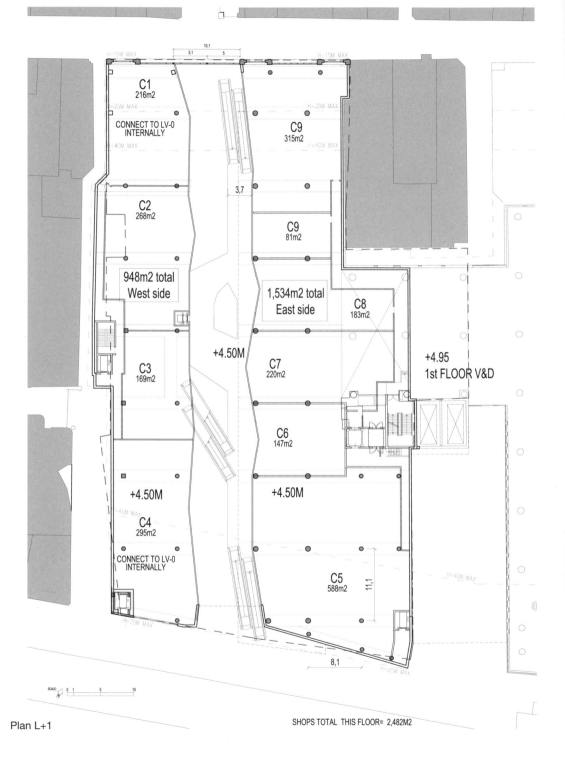

C1
216m2

CONNECT TO LV-0
INTERNALLY

C9
315m2

C2
268m2

C9
81m2

948m2 total
West side

1,534m2 total
East side

C8
183m2

+4.50M

C7
220m2

+4.95
1st FLOOR V&D

C3
169m2

C6
147m2

+4.50M

+4.50M

C4
295m2

CONNECT TO LV-0
INTERNALLY

C5
588m2

11,1

8,1

Plan L+1

SHOPS TOTAL THIS FLOOR= 2,482M2

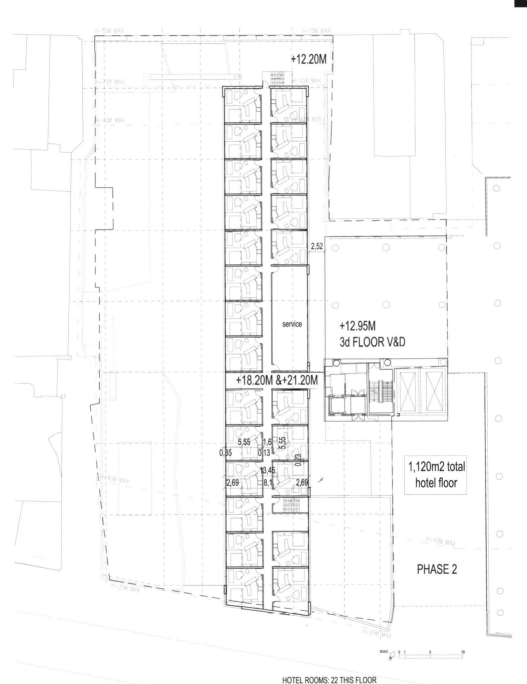

+12.20M

2,52

service

+12.95M
3d FLOOR V&D

+18.20M &+21.20M

5,55   1,6   5,55
0,85   0,13   0,23

13,45
2,69   8,1   2,69

1,120m2 total
hotel floor

PHASE 2

SCALE 0 1 5 10

HOTEL ROOMS: 22 THIS FLOOR

Plan L+5, +6

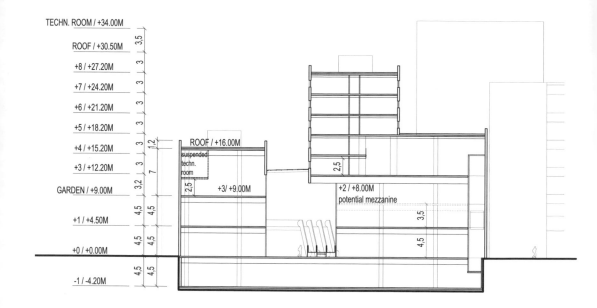

TECHN. ROOM / +34.00M

ROOF / +30.50M — 3,5

+8 / +27.20M — 3

+7 / +24.20M — 3

+6 / +21.20M — 3

+5 / +18.20M — 3

+4 / +15.20M — 3 / 1,2 — ROOF / +16.00M

+3 / +12.20M — 3 / 7 — suspended techn. room

GARDEN / +9.00M — 3,2 / 2,5 — +3/ +9.00M — +2 / +8.00M potential mezzanine — 2,5

+1 / +4.50M — 4,5 / 4,5 — 3,5

+0 / +0.00M — 4,5 / 4,5 — 4,5

-1 / -4.20M — 4,5 / 4,5

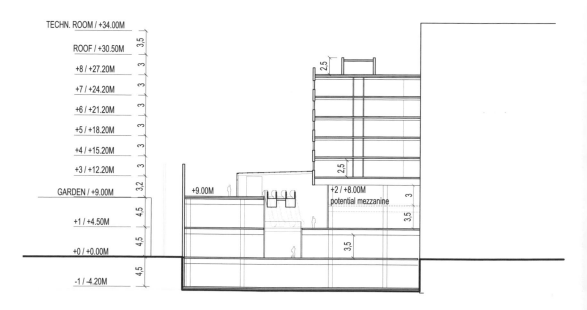

TECHN. ROOM / +34.00M

ROOF / +30.50M — 3,5

+8 / +27.20M — 3

+7 / +24.20M — 3

+6 / +21.20M — 3 — 2,5

+5 / +18.20M — 3

+4 / +15.20M — 3

+3 / +12.20M — 3 — 2,5

GARDEN / +9.00M — 3,2 — +9.00M — +2 / +8.00M potential mezzanine — 3

+1 / +4.50M — 4,5 — 3,5

+0 / +0.00M — 4,5 — 3,5

-1 / -4.20M — 4,5

Sections

Step 1: Generate template

Step 2: Insert tiles

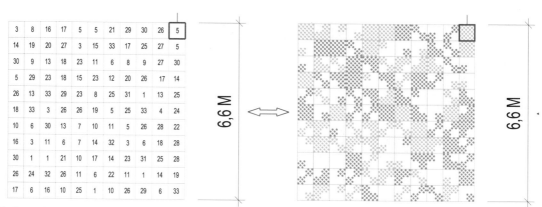

3	8	16	17	5	5	21	29	30	26	5
14	19	20	27	3	15	33	17	25	27	5
30	9	13	18	23	11	6	8	9	27	30
5	29	23	18	15	23	12	20	26	17	14
26	13	33	29	23	8	25	31	1	13	25
18	33	3	26	26	19	5	25	33	4	24
10	6	30	13	7	10	11	5	26	28	22
16	3	11	6	7	14	32	3	6	18	28
30	1	1	21	10	17	14	23	31	25	28
26	24	32	26	11	6	22	11	1	14	19
17	6	16	10	25	1	10	26	29	6	33

6,6 M

⟺

6,6 M

Each number above represents a specific
tile and its rotation.

60 x 60cm

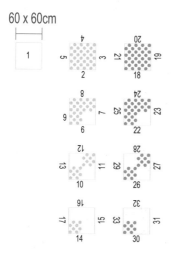

1

Total: 9 different tiles,
all to be oriented in 4
possible positions

60cm tiles: 1 white, 4 light blue, 4 dark blue

Step 3: Arrange

13,2 M

60 x 60cm

COPY 1 | COPY 2

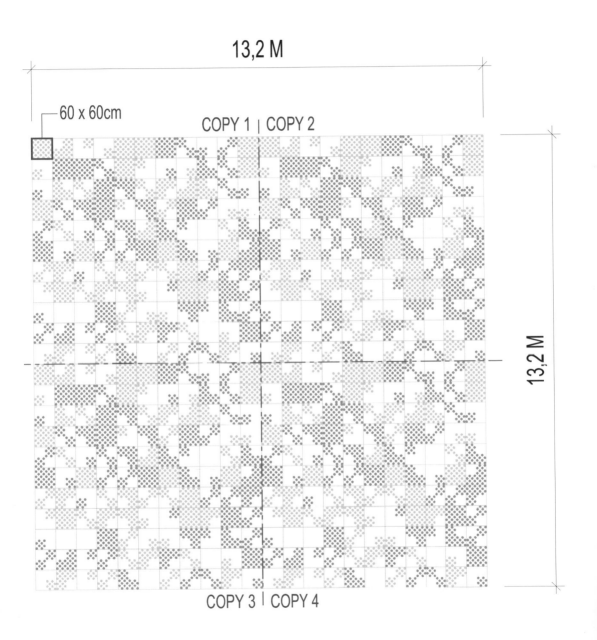

COPY 3 | COPY 4

13,2 M

The above scaled study of "pixels" is related to the approximate width of the hotel.

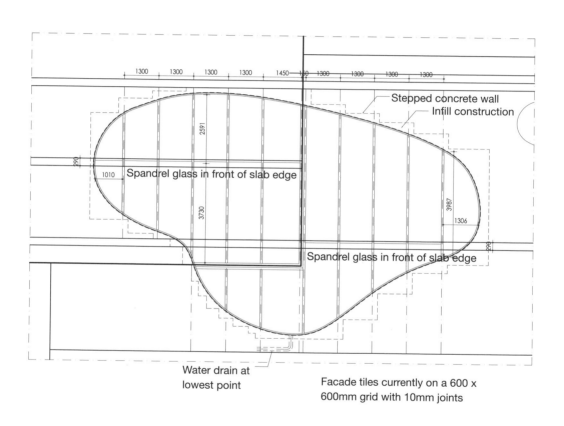

1300 1300 1300 1300 1450 150 1300 1300 1300 1300

Stepped concrete wall
Infill construction

2591

290

1010 Spandrel glass in front of slab edge

3730

3987

1306

Spandrel glass in front of slab edge

290

Water drain at
lowest point

Facade tiles currently on a 600 x
600mm grid with 10mm joints

Construction detail (curved window)

Toulouse, Airbus Delivery Center, 2004

Production Sequence

Forces Made Evident: Tracing the Flow of the Aircraft

Our Airbus Delivery Center was intended as an emblematic group of buildings for an exceptional plane, the A-380. The Center forms a whole that showcases the new plane in its best light through the main buildings and satellites. A prism-shaped central building acts as the main reception space in which clients are presented with the new planes that they have ordered.

Located at the middle of a functional axis created by the orientation of the principal building, the central prism distributes different users toward their respective destinations while simultaneously creating spaces to allow visitors to discover the advanced technologies developed by Airbus. The architectural concept offers the clarity of a linear master plan and optimizes circulation, security requirements, and future options for extension.

Lit at night by the colors of individual clients, the prism was intended to become a presentational theater for airline representatives upon the arrival of each new aircraft. The prism has a crystal-like focus point where clients, media representatives, and engineers gather to celebrate the delivery of the highest-performing civilian aircraft in the world. The presentation theater opens up to reveal each new plane, stationed behind a large, uninterrupted glass expanse. The theater allows some 500 visitors and professionals to hear and see all of the necessary information about the plane while enjoying an impeccable view of it. The prism is built on three levels, with departure lounges, VIP rooms, and dining halls.

The two office wings are designed on five levels with additional satellite buildings for manufacturing, each located on two levels that are 19 meters wide with a 7.20-meter structural frame. All of the buildings in the complex are centered on a long logistical axis that follows the functional assembly of each plane and the necessary circulation flows of the airplane delivery process. The prism acts as a pivot. A common reception area distributes traffic to the various production spaces by assigning different flows to workers, visitors, and VIPs, much as a prism distributes light. The new delivery center presents a singular architectural image in the aviation industry, an image that can be customized for the many international clients that lend diversity to the sector.

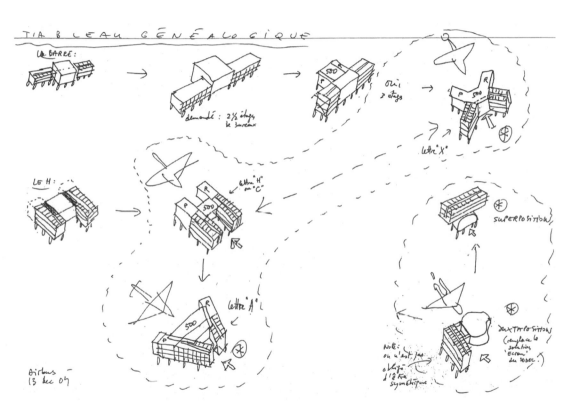

TABLEAU GÉNÉALOGIQUE

LA BARRE:

demandé : 2½ étages de bureaux

oui 3 étages

lettre "X"

LE H:

lettre "H" ou "C"

SUPERPOSITION

lettre "A"

Note:
on n'est pas obligé d'être symétrique

JUXTAPOSITION
(remplace la solution "écran" du 10 déc.)

Airbus —
13 déc 04

A common reception area organizes various spaces and ensures the distribution of circulation by simply distributing the flow of the various types of reception users.

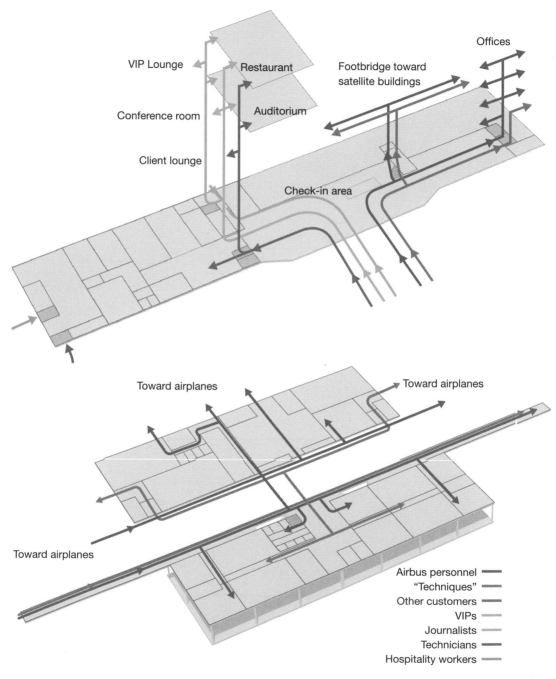

VIP Lounge

Restaurant

Footbridge toward
satellite buildings

Offices

Conference room

Auditorium

Client lounge

Check-in area

Toward airplanes

Toward airplanes

Toward airplanes

Airbus personnel
"Techniques"
Other customers
VIPs
Journalists
Technicians
Hospitality workers

Circulation diagram: main building and satellite buildings

L+4

L+3

L+2

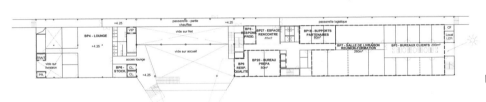

L+1

L0

Section and plans

Aix, Courthouse, 2007

Architecture Parlante

Architecture Parlante

Judicial architecture is often described in terms of frozen and authoritative monumentality, as if seeking to intimidate rather than invite. This observation led us to question how to use architecture to express the permanence of an institution that is central to democracy, while at the same time recalling that justice protects the rights of each and every citizen. In other words, we wished to remain attentive to the role of justice as an enduring ally and a foundation of our society.

The Site

At first glance, the site seemed ill-suited to housing a major civic building. Located off the Boulevard Carnot in Aix-en-Provence, France, its periphery is on a noisy boulevard that marks the rift between the historic and contemporary cities. However, the site also revealed several distinct opportunities, including three exceptional, nearly 20-meter-tall trees, an exploitable topographic gradient, and a potential dialogue with an important site in the civic history of Aix-en-Provence.

One corner of the site is located exactly along the axis of the Cour d'Appel, which was conceived of, but not realized by, Claude-Nicolas Ledoux several years before the French Revolution. Aix-en-Provence is also home to the Cours Mirabeau and one of the Marquis de Sade's residences. Ochre colors seem to permeate every building in the city, from stone to stucco. In short, from the scale of the majestic boulevards to its picturesque pathways, the city is indivisible from its architectural identity. Aix is a permanent architectural promenade.

The Challenge

The challenge was to reconcile urbanism, architecture, and justice into one single entity. Our concept is an architectural promenade through the trees, or a walk in the light (which references both the sunlight of Provence and the clarity of justice). The concept could also be described as a mathematical theorem. The three terms of the equation are equivalent to three independent circuits made up of judges and detainees (whose trajectories never intersect, except at determined points and particular times), and the general public. We proposed a particular architectural typology based on three axes: x, y, and z. Our courthouse is an architectural machine operating with rigorous precision, in which the building's form is the materialization of the equation, with each axis corresponding to one of the three variables.

Functional Circuits

The three completely independent circuits in the project occupy separate realms, a move that affords an architecturally determined level of security without closing off the building or creating onerous checkpoints. A large waiting room (referred to as "the Hall of Lost Steps" in French) incorporates an ambulatory circuit that is also an architectural promenade that facilitates private meetings and reflection. Adjoining the waiting room at the mezzanine level is a suspended garden that is sheltered from sunlight: a place of reflection and relaxation separated from the city and protected by the mass of the building's eastern side. A colonnaded entry gallery gently slopes to connect the tall trees in the public plaza at street level to the mezzanine and the waiting room. At the street corner, facing Ledoux's Cour d'Appel but at a distance, the large perforated cube of the main courtroom attempts to establish a permanent dialogue with Ledoux's utopian vision of an *"architecture parlante."*

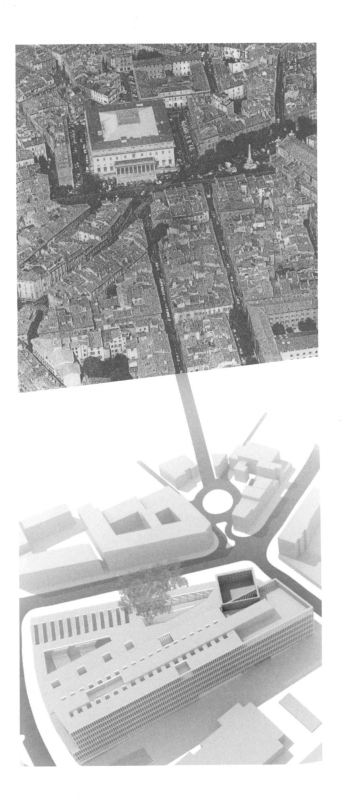

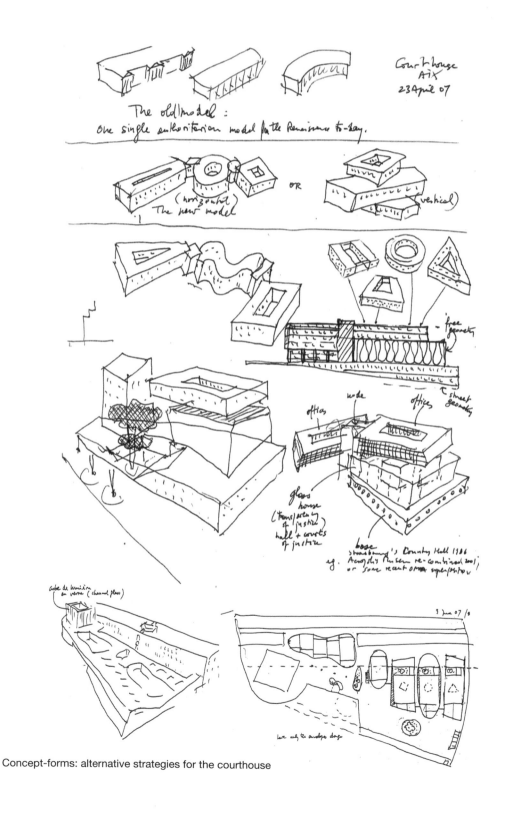

Concept-forms: alternative strategies for the courthouse

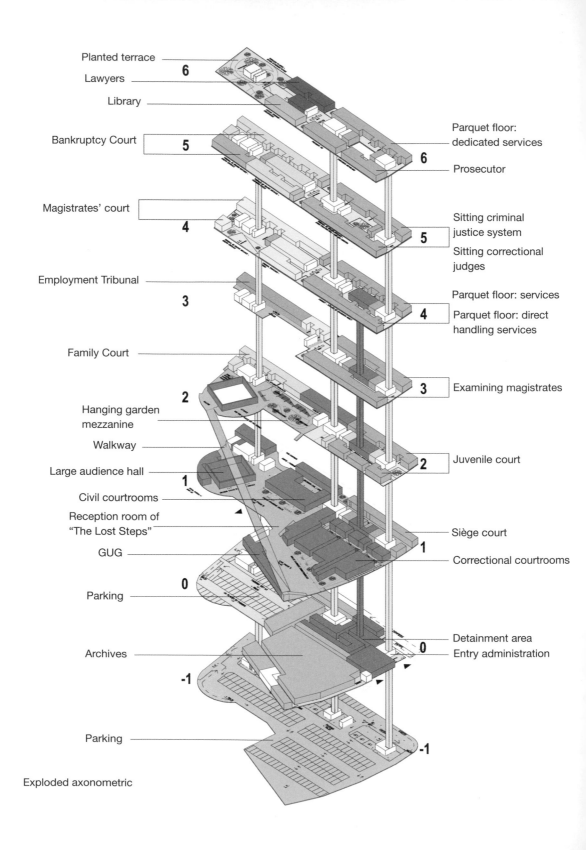

Planted terrace
Lawyers
Library
Bankruptcy Court
Magistrates' court
Employment Tribunal
Family Court
Hanging garden mezzanine
Walkway
Large audience hall
Civil courtrooms
Reception room of "The Lost Steps"
GUG
Parking
Archives
Parking

6
5
4
3
2
1
0
-1

Parquet floor: dedicated services
Prosecutor
Sitting criminal justice system
Sitting correctional judges
Parquet floor: services
Parquet floor: direct handling services
Examining magistrates
Juvenile court
Siège court
Correctional courtrooms
Detainment area
Entry administration

6
5
4
3
2
1
0
-1

Exploded axonometric

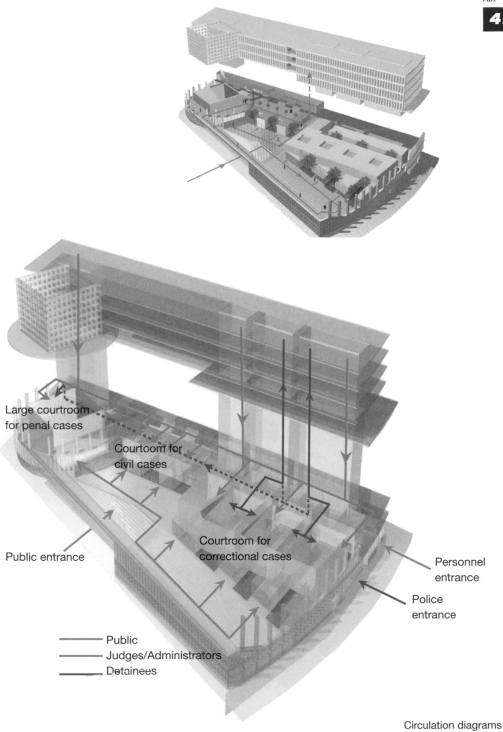

Large courtroom
for penal cases

Courtoom for
civil cases

Courtroom for
correctional cases

Public entrance

Personnel
entrance

Police
entrance

Public
Judges/Administrators
Detainees

Circulation diagrams

*University of Texas Student Services
Center, Dallas, 2008*

Inner Court

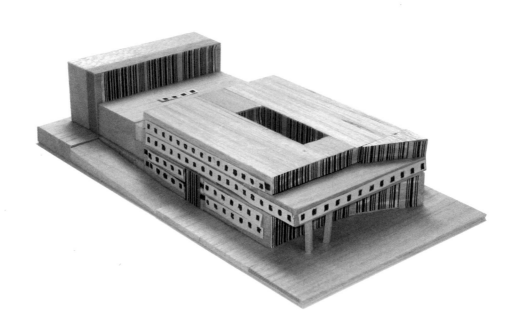

The proposed Student Services Center sits adjacent to two major green arteries and a pedestrian route, all recent campus construction efforts designed to encourage interaction among the university's users. The new building must acknowledge and engage with these pedestrian arteries while remaining mindful of how the evolution of landscaping will affect the way the building reads in its context over the next 10, 15, or 20 years.

The budget and complex program called for a solid block that could define the axis, with pieces carved away for student traffic (for example, to create a connection with the adjacent Student Union building) and to allow light to penetrate the center's inner court. The massing of the building derives from a desire to establish a clear central axis, as defined by the university master plan.

The new center is also engaged in a dialogue with the nearby site of the future Arts and Technology Building. Students, faculty, and other visitors can access the building from the two green axes that meet on the southwest corner of the site. At this critical junction, the frontage of the building recedes slightly to reveal a shaded area, energized by strips of glass. This shaded patio acts as a transitional space, mediating between the sunny public spaces and the vibrant interiors of the new building.

The "marquee" massing integrates certain gestures that are already a part of campus vernacular while responding to the very basic requirement of generating shade in front of the building, where students are most likely to congregate. Given the building's placement on the avenue, the "marquee" addresses the axis while suggesting more intimate spaces inside. New buildings along the avenue may play with or against this strategy. In this way, the new building both continues and enlivens a dialogue with existing campus buildings and promotes future interactions.

Two materials are juxtaposed: first, the beige concrete and bands of windows address the existing campus with a familiar language and massing. Second, the curtain wall's glass panes in alternating University of Texas colors create a playfully contrasting rhythm and energy that suggest the interior activities of the center.

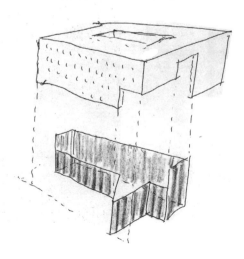

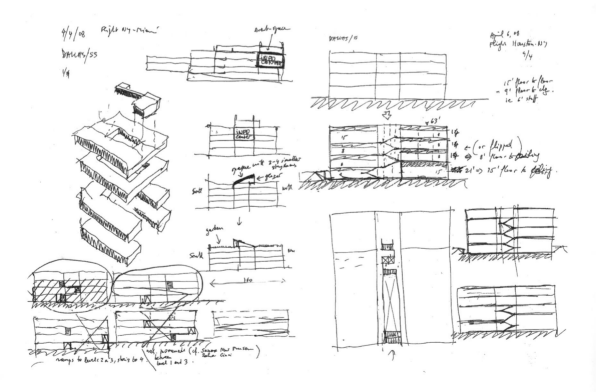

4/4/08   Right NY - Miami

DALLAS/55

1/4

April 6, 08
Flight Houston - NY
4/4

DALLAS/55

15' floor to floor
= 9' floor to clg.
ie 6' stuff

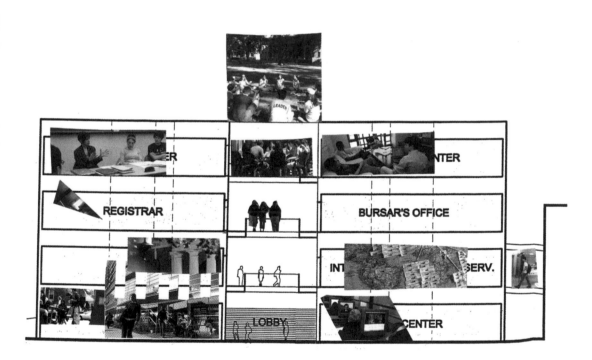

Section with collage

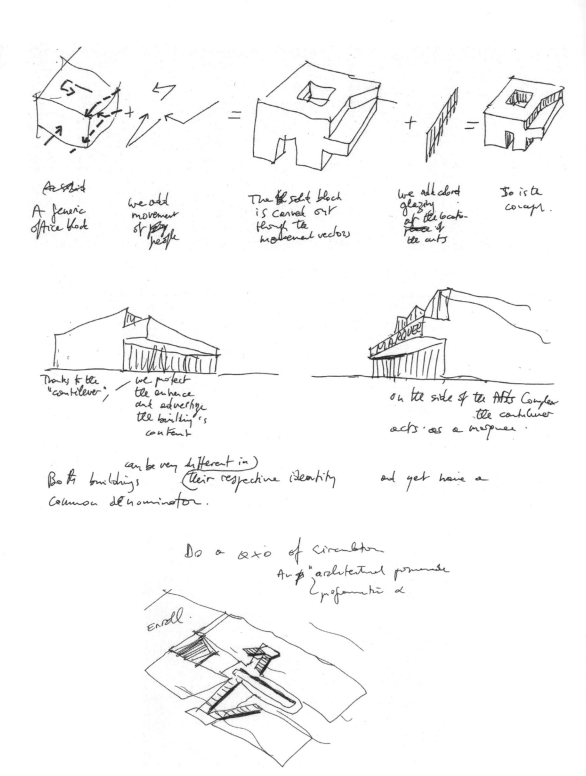

A generic
office block

We add
movement
of people

The solid block
is carved out
through the
movement vectors

we add colored
glazing
at the loca-
tion of
the cuts

So is the
concept.

Thanks to the
"cantilever",

we project
the enhance
and advertise
the building's
content

on the side of the Arts Complex
the cantilever
acts as a marquee.

Both buildings (can be very different in their respective identity) and yet have a
common denominator.

Do a axo of circulation
An "architectural promenade"
(programmatic a

Enroll.

parts that stick in

pieces that stick out

parts that stick in
parts that stick out

Boston NY
16 May 08
3

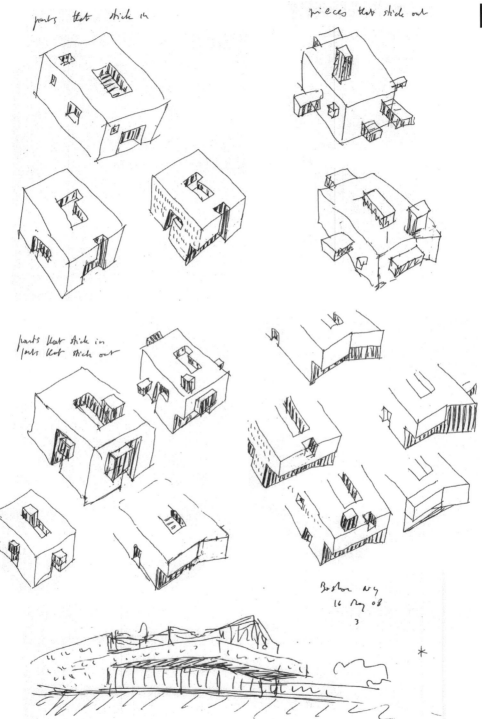

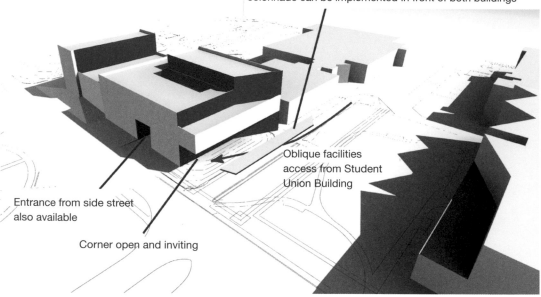

Depending on future plans for the Student Union, the light colonnade can be implemented in front of both buildings

Oblique facilities access from Student Union Building

Entrance from side street also available

Corner open and inviting

The massing of the Student Services Building encourages entry and interaction with the *allée*.

The massing and the *allée* facade of the Arts and Sciences Center can potentially establish a dialogue with the Student Services Building.

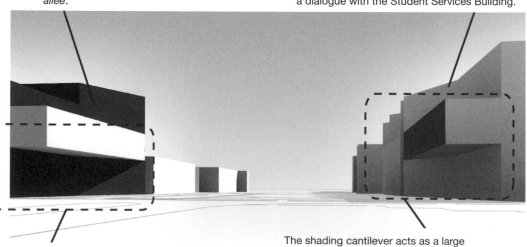

The shading cantilever can be used for gathered students or for expanding activities from the Student Services Building.

The shading cantilever acts as a large marquee, with potential information or visibility toward its activities.

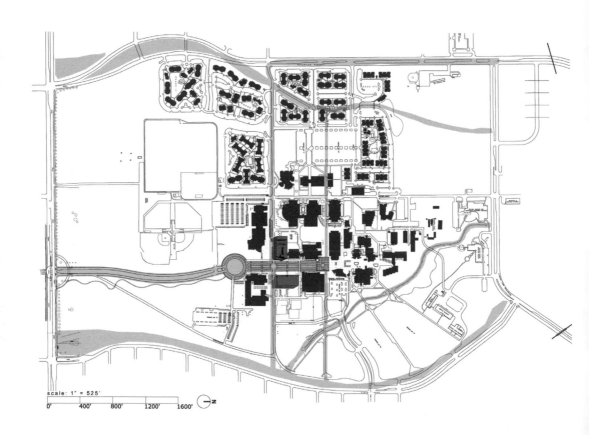

scale: 1" = 525'

0'   400'   800'   1200'   1600'   N

Campus plan

Existing context: 1960s modernism

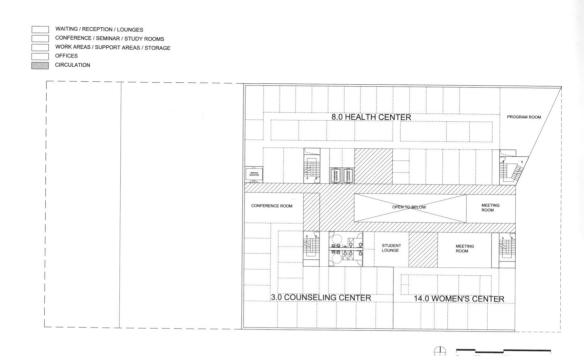

Legend:
- WAITING / RECEPTION / LOUNGES
- CONFERENCE / SEMINAR / STUDY ROOMS
- WORK AREAS / SUPPORT AREAS / STORAGE
- OFFICES
- CIRCULATION

8.0 HEALTH CENTER

PROGRAM ROOM

SERVICE ELEVATOR

CONFERENCE ROOM

OPEN TO BELOW

MEETING ROOM

STUDENT LOUNGE

MEETING ROOM

3.0 COUNSELING CENTER

14.0 WOMEN'S CENTER

0   10ft   25ft   50ft

Typical office layout plan, level 4

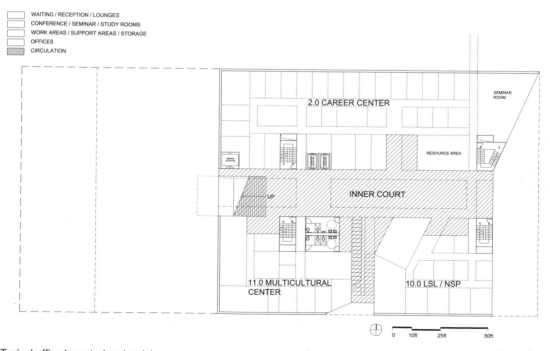

Legend:
- WAITING / RECEPTION / LOUNGES
- CONFERENCE / SEMINAR / STUDY ROOMS
- WORK AREAS / SUPPORT AREAS / STORAGE
- OFFICES
- CIRCULATION

2.0 CAREER CENTER

SEMINAR ROOM

SERVICE ELEVATOR

RESOURCE AREA

UP

INNER COURT

11.0 MULTICULTURAL CENTER

10.0 LSL / NSP

0   10ft   25ft   50ft

Typical office layout plan, level 1

WAITING / RECEPTION / LOUNGES
CONFERENCE / SEMINAR / STUDY ROOMS
WORK AREAS / SUPPORT AREAS / STORAGE
OFFICES
CIRCULATION

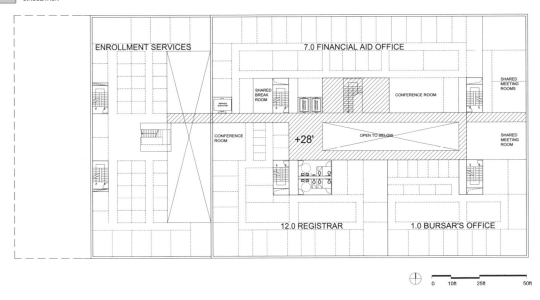

Typical office layout plan, level 3

WAITING / RECEPTION / LOUNGES
CONFERENCE / SEMINAR / STUDY ROOMS
WORK AREAS / SUPPORT AREAS / STORAGE
OFFICES
CIRCULATION

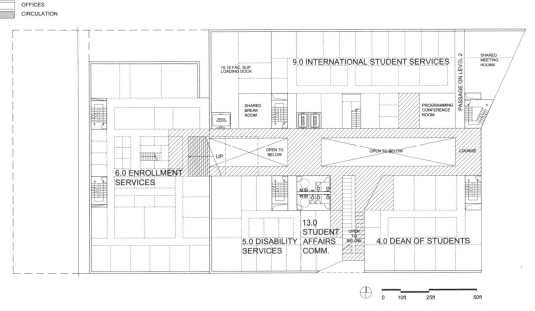

Typical office layout plan, level 2

Carving/Wrapping

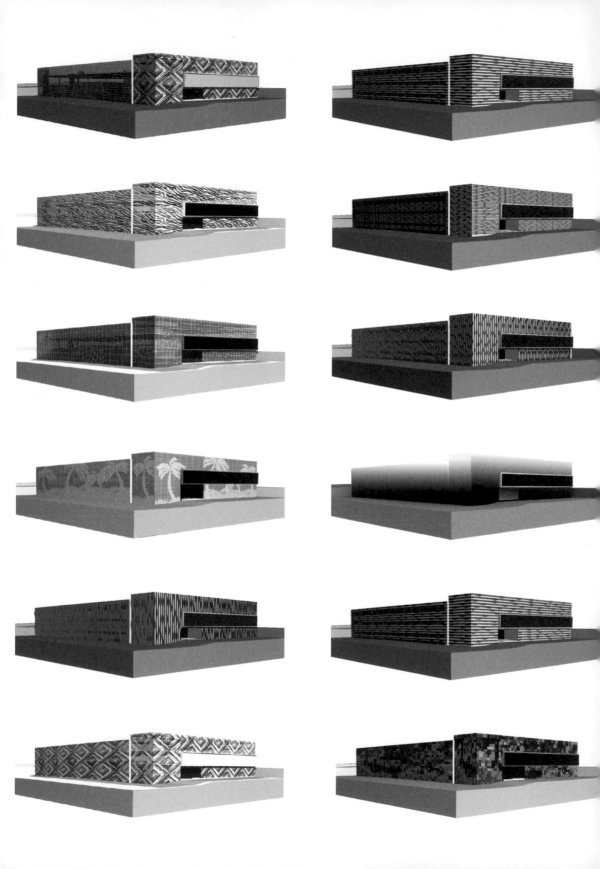

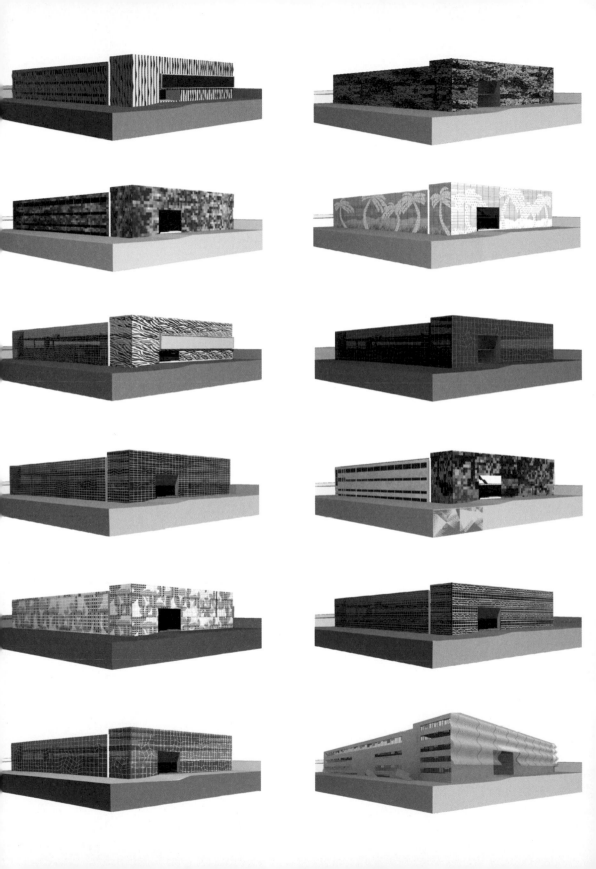

Old and New

The renovation and rehabilitation of the Ecole Cantonale d'Art de Lausanne (ECAL) in Renens, an industrial neighborhood at the edge of Lausanne, Switzerland, began with an existing building and reinterpreted its industrial context with a contemporary material approach that enlivens the old structure for new uses, fusing old and new through a limited architectural intervention.

Built in and around a former factory that housed IRIL (a knitwear company that produced women's stockings and other clothing), the new design transforms the existing 1950s-era structure, an enormous four-story building with floor plates as large as a football field. In order to bring sunlight into the new school, four slender atria or light wells were carved into the existing structure so as to distribute natural light throughout the building. A 200-foot-long exhibition hall on the ground floor, which is punctuated by light wells and

exposed stairs, provides circulation and divides the space into both large and intimate areas for study, work, and creative expression. A pattern of primary colors helps identify the interior spaces, demarcates circulation within the space, and unifies the interior spaces with the exterior. A variety of metal meshes and corrugated steel cover the existing factory structure, including a signature wavy screen over the length of the entrance facade. The color strategy, revealed in thin bands on the exterior, reflects the building's significance in the community as a civic hub, echoing the site's former role as the economic heart of the neighborhood.

ECAL occupies two-thirds of the space, while the remaining areas are shared by the architecture school of the Lausanne Polytechnic Institute, the ECAL Art Gallery, workshops for local artists-in-residence, and studios dedicated to emerging technologies.

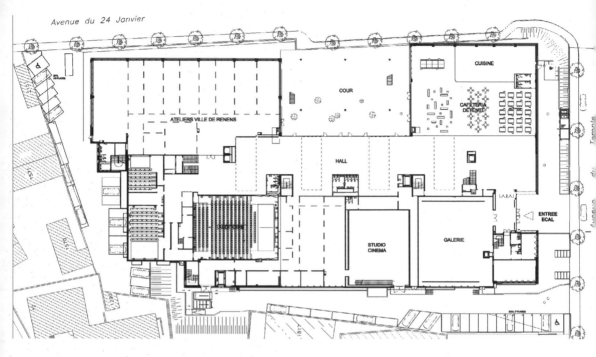

Avenue du 24 Janvier

CUISINE

COUR

CAFETERIA
DETENTE

ATELIERS VILLE DE RENENS

HALL

ENTREE
ECAL

AUDITOIRE

STUDIO
CINEMA

GALERIE

Plan L0

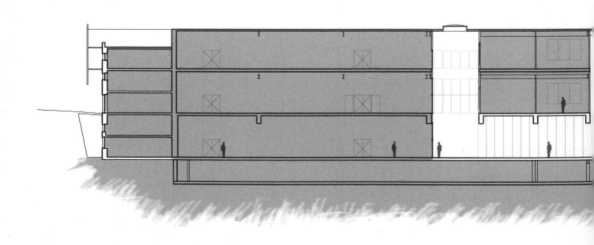

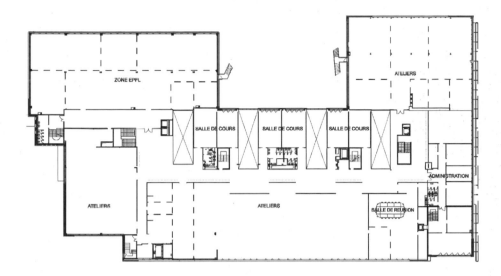

ZONE EPFL

ATELIERS

SALLE DE COURS SALLE DE COURS SALLE DE COURS

ATELIERS

ATELIERS

SALLE DE REUNION

ADMINISTRATION

Plan L2

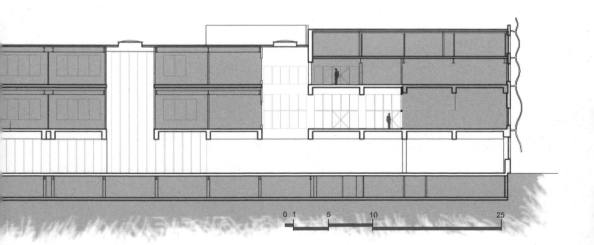

0 1   5   10   25

Longitudinal section: view toward the court

The form is as much about the concept as the concept is about the form. A concept-form takes its strength and justification from constraints and strives toward an economy of means. It works with and against the program, and never ignores it. It is characterized by the strength of the obvious ("la force de l'évidence"). WHAT REALLY COUNTS IS NOT ONLY WHAT IT LOOKS LIKE, BUT ALSO WHAT IT DOES.

G. Faceted/Folded/Angular

Each of the projects in Part G has in common a low-budget enclosure, together with specific volumetric particularities that result from program or zoning requirements. Simple faceted or folded envelopes respond to these constraints and are used to produce a distinct identity for each building. Our first folded envelope was designed and constructed at Le Fresnoy in 1991. (See *Event-Cities*.)

**Lausanne,
Interface Flon M2 Metro Station, 2003-09**

Green Politics

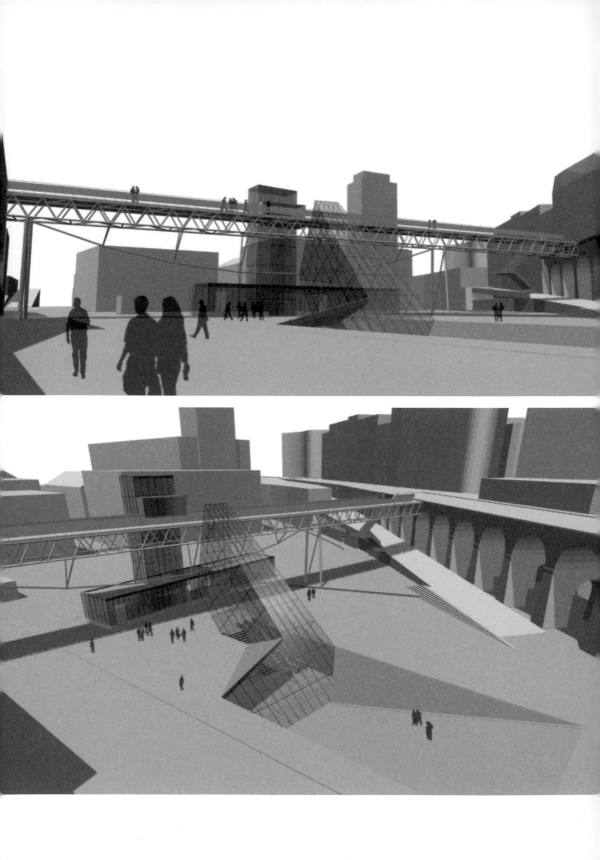

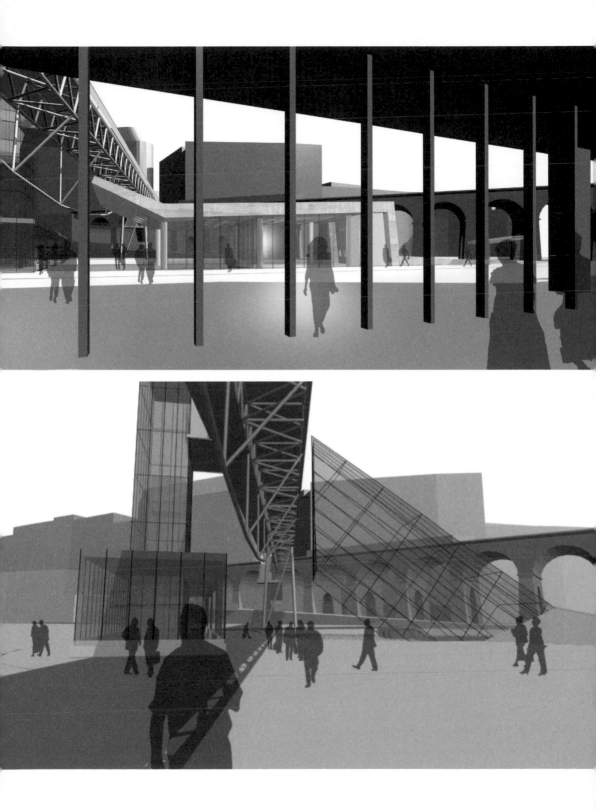

Above Ground

The M2 Transit Hub had a long incubation period, marked by two distinct phases. In the early 1990s Bernard Tschumi Architects, with Luca Merlini, submitted a competition for the redevelopment of the Flon Valley. The "Bridge-City" scheme included a series of inhabited bridges over the valley. When redevelopment lapsed due to lack of funding, local transit authorities approached us to design a new transit station. The first phase—a light-rail station characterized by red printed glass, a new pedestrian bridge, and connections to the valley at the Place de l'Europe—was completed in 2001.

The project's second phase was originally planned to add a major entrance to the new Lausanne Metro. We proposed an angular glass core that penetrated deep into the ground toward the track. "Too beautiful for Lausanne," said the chief city official. So as to force us to change our scheme, the official modified the program, turning it into an information center. Two days before we were due to present the new precast concrete scheme to the mayor, he was attacked in the press for allegedly covering the city with concrete buildings. So when the precast concrete project was presented to him, the mayor, of course, said "No." We showed him alternatives, and the mayor chose green.

The second phase incorporated a ticket counter, escalators, and a subway station into the transit hub complex. Designed with Merlini + Ventura, the building, which features a concrete fold covered with a green roof and a long pedestrian ramp, addresses these programs while expanding the first phase into the west in order to create new transit connections in the heart of the city.

As the main ticket office for Transit Lausanne, the building had to convey a public image for the transit authority and the city at large. Its main gesture is the folded concrete, which acts as if a strip of the plaza has been folded and bent back on itself to accommodate a ticket office to the east and a pedestrian ramp to the subterranean level on the west. The roof and west wall are covered with a green carpet of plantings, which addresses the client's environmental concerns (including the local Minergie Standard, similar to a LEED rating). This carpet also links the second phase with the first phase, which incorporated a landscaped berm into a sunken oval, opening up the subterranean light rail to natural daylight. The building houses some offices for the transportation authority, providing both privacy and natural light.

The program was resolved by using the strategy of the fold: the main structural gesture is made out of concrete, as though a piece of the plaza had been cut away and raised back on itself, with the sides of the "slice" materialized in glass. The building is treated with sturdy industrial materials and details that are well suited to the heavy traffic of a major transit center.

Below Ground

Underneath the Place de l'Europe, the M2 subway intersects with the earlier LEB (Lausanne-Echallens-Bercher) commuter rail line and the adjoining M1 subway. Regional rail lines and buses are located in adjoining facilities. With planned trolleys under study, the site is poised to become even more significant to Lausanne's transit infrastructure. Planning had to be as deliberate below ground as above it.

We became interested in the idea of an underground station as it relates to the "thickness" of the city. Lausanne has always been shaped by its topography and scale as a city situated on a sloping hillside along the Lake Léman. The new transit hub appropriates the resulting multiple levels of traffic as if a Cubist diagram of the city, in which bridges, houses, streets, and Alpine horizons fit together naturally. A program that is almost exclusively related to movement allowed us to view the visitors' constant shifts in perspective as they traverse the bridges, stairs, ramps, and glass elevators and ride the trains as a design opportunity.

The project required that new rail lines be created above the subterranean river that gives the valley its name. In essence, the Interface Flon project is about recreating and re-routing urban flows above the ancient river so as to better accommodate traffic at every level of the city and, in particular, to link the Bel-Air neighborhood with the industrial Flon district below it at ground level. Given that the first and second phase were to be completed almost ten years apart, the orchestration of these movements required an architectural perspective of the city that would account for its evolution over time, according to different transit conditions and needs.

The project was completed in 2009. We won the competition in 1988. If you want to be an architect, you better be patient.

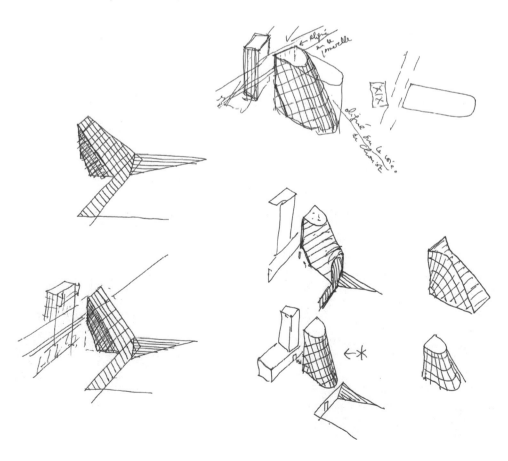

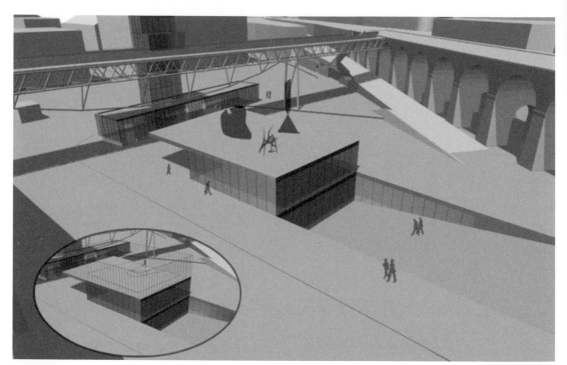

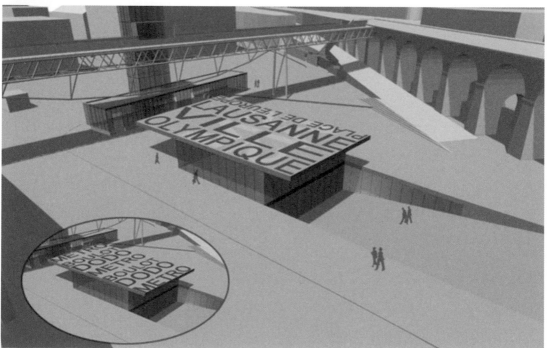

As the city had rejected our glass proposal, we tested other alternatives: a sculpture roof, a signage roof...

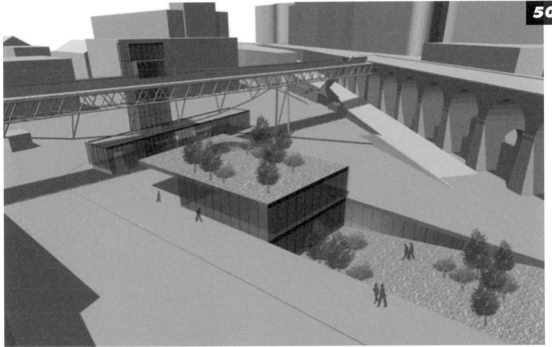

a garden roof, a folded plane. The mayor didn't want concrete, so we combined the garden and the fold.

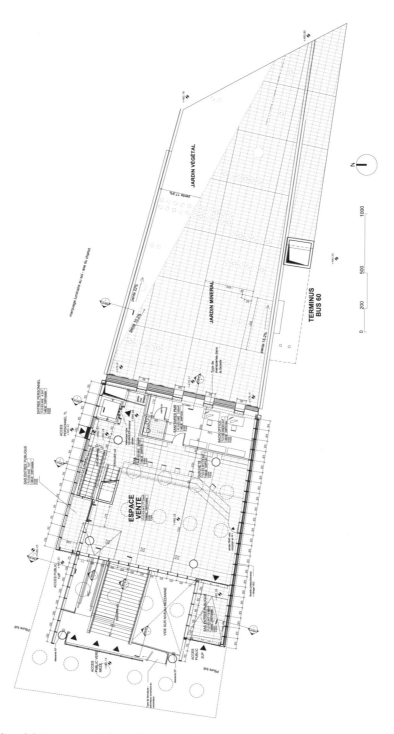

Ground-level plan: ticket counters, information center, lounge

Detail of first basement-level plan

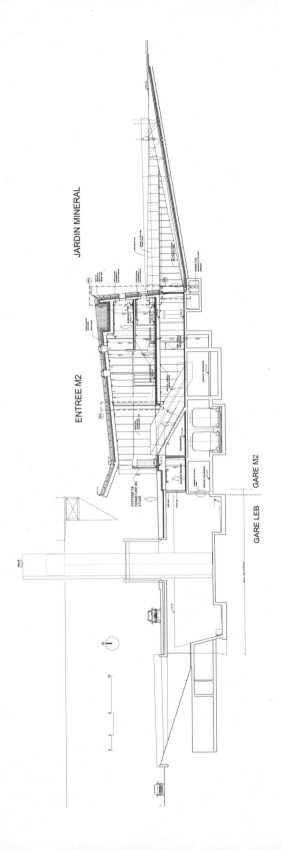

JARDIN MINERAL

ENTREE M2

GARE LEB

GARE M2

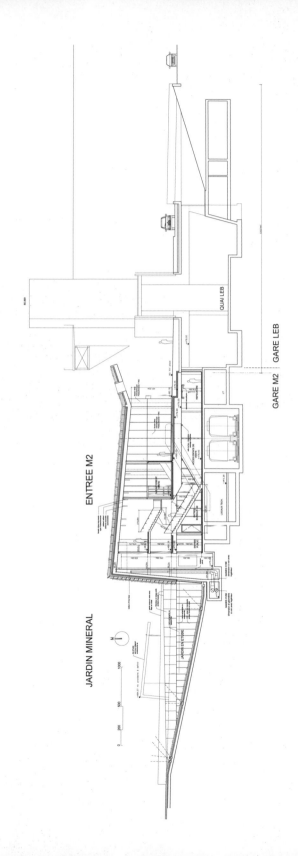

JARDIN MINERAL

ENTREE M2

QUAI LEB

GARE M2 | GARE LEB

Unless a concept-form is site-specific, it remains untested as long as it is without a site. The introduction of a site requires that the concept-form be sufficiently flexible in its configuration to allow for adjustment. The constraints inherent to a site become part of the definition of a concept-form. Any given concept-form can have several volumetric iterations, depending on its site constraints.

New York City,
BLUE Residential Tower, 2004-07

Code as Generator

Zoning Constraints as Generator

This residential mid-rise on New York City's Lower East Side presented a major design challenge: how to create an original architectural statement while simultaneously responding to the constraints of New York zoning codes, the developer's commercial requirements, and a low budget? In our solution, the base of the building occupies a lot zoned for residential use and cantilevers over an existing building designated for commercial use. The slightly angled walls facing the street and rear yard artfully negotiate the varying setback rules, crossing the line between the commercial and residential zoning districts. The sloped top of the building integrates the zoning district's two sky exposure plane requirements. The cantilever over the commercial space on the southern part of the building is also angled from base to top, thus enlarging the size of the units located on the upper floors, which have stunning river-to-river views of Lower Manhattan. This strategy additionally maximizes the amount of allowable residential square footage. The pixelated facades reflect the internal arrangement of spaces and the multi-faceted character of the neighborhood below.

BLUE does not start with a theory or formal gesture but instead takes the character of the site as its source, parlaying abstract zoning into angulated form, and form into a pixelated envelope that both projects an architectural statement and blends into the sky, simultaneously respecting and embracing the dynamism of the neighborhood.

The building consists of 32 residences ranging from one- and two-bedroom units near the base to full-floor units with large terraces higher up, crowned by a duplex penthouse. Many units feature a sloped window-wall. All units have full-height windows in the living and dining rooms. The apartments are fitted out using sustainable materials that include bamboo floors and wall panels, palm flooring, and river-pebble bathroom tiles. BLUE also recycles unused space on top of a neighboring commercial structure as an urban garden that provides communal space for residents and guests, with broad views of the Williamsburg Bridge.

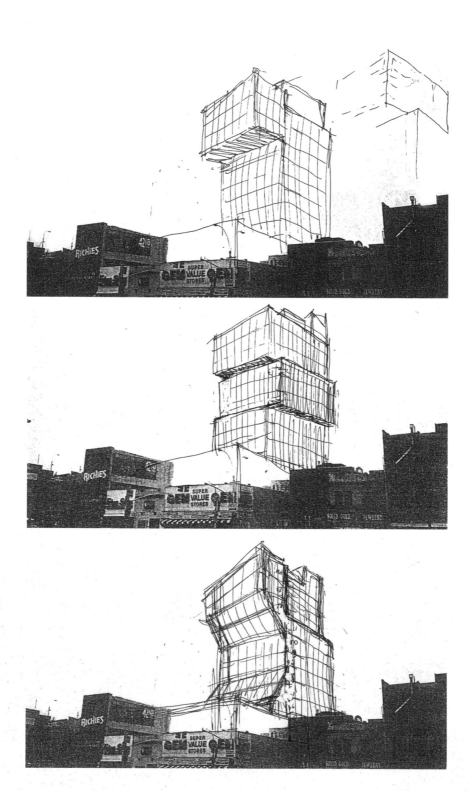

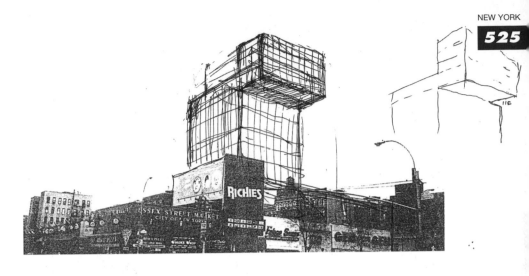

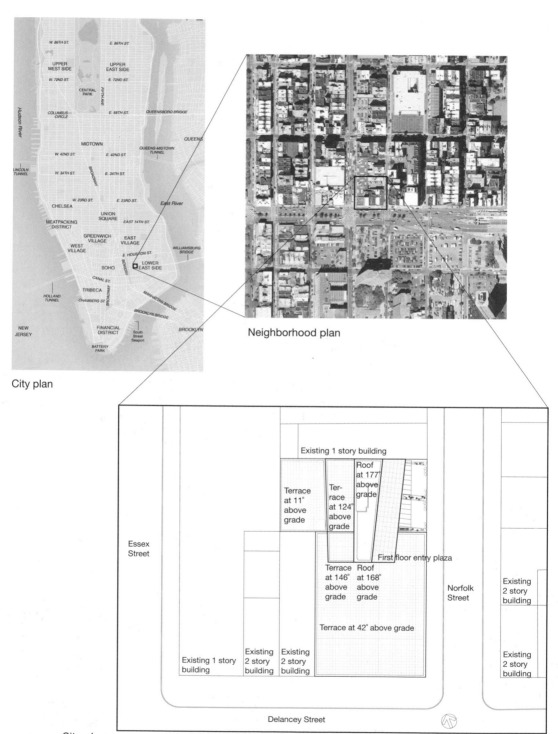

City plan

Neighborhood plan

Site plan

Existing 1 story building

Terrace at 11° above grade

Ter-race at 124° above grade

Roof at 177° above grade

First floor entry plaza

Terrace at 146° above grade

Roof at 168° above grade

Terrace at 42° above grade

Essex Street

Norfolk Street

Existing 2 story building

Existing 1 story building

Existing 2 story building

Existing 2 story building

Existing 2 story building

Existing 2 story building

Delancey Street

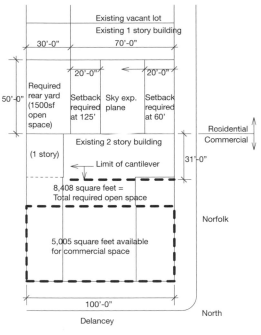

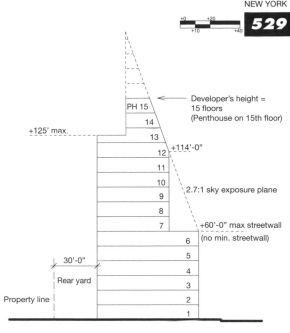

103-05 Norfolk St. zoning analysis

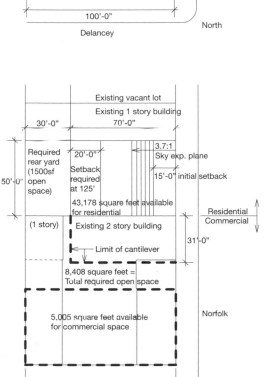

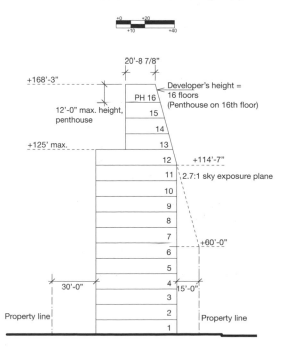

103-05 Norfolk St. zoning analysis (alternate setback)

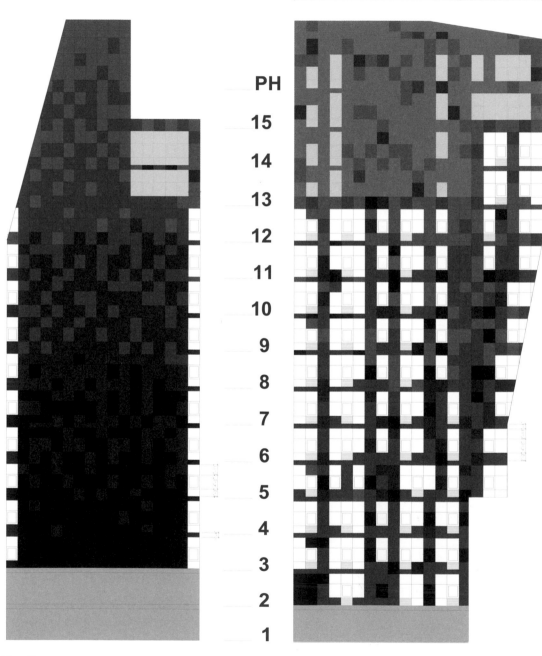

$71'-0\frac{1}{2}"$

PH

15

14

13

12

11

10

9

8

7

6

5

4

3

2

1

Elevations

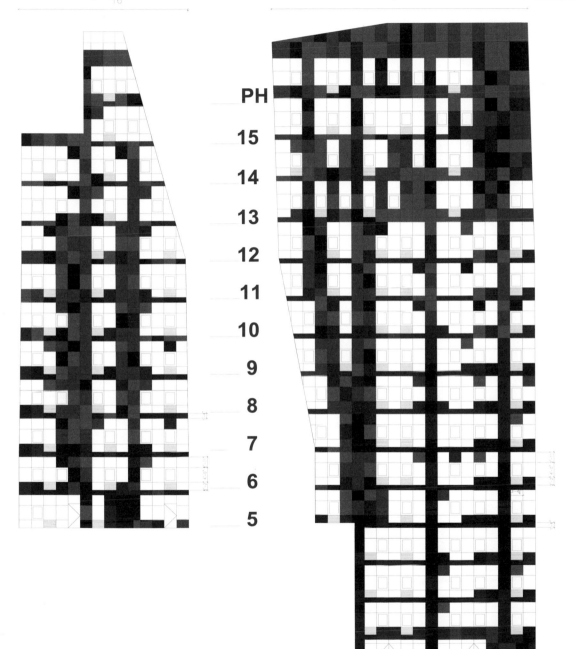

46'-9 13/16"

71'4-1/4"

PH

15

14

13

12

11

10

9

8

7

6

5

??? - OPERABLE——>

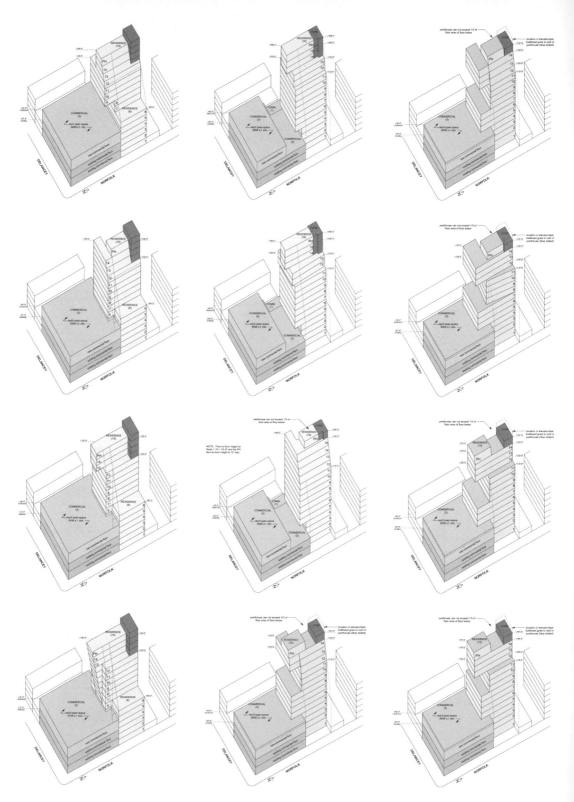

We tested multiple permutations within the local planning-code requirements.

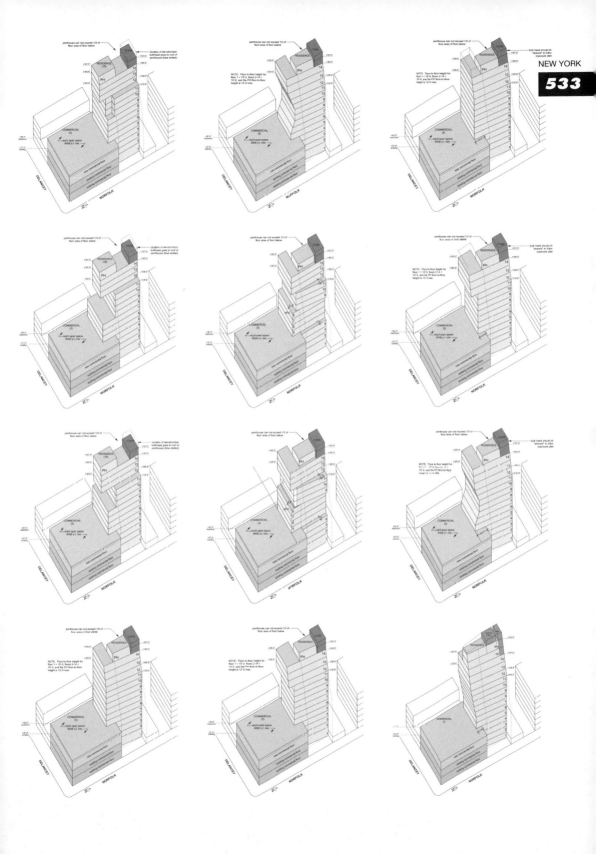

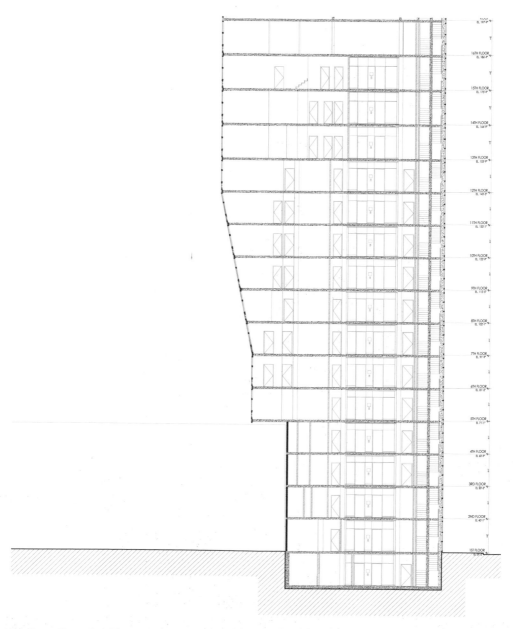

North-south section: The tower cantilevers over the existing building.

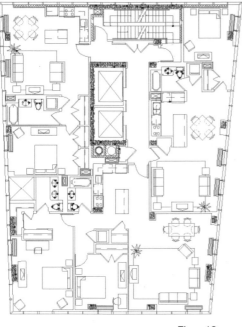

Floor 12

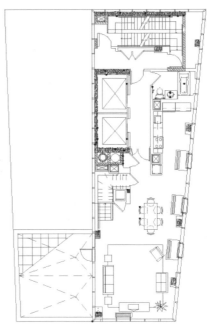

Floor 15

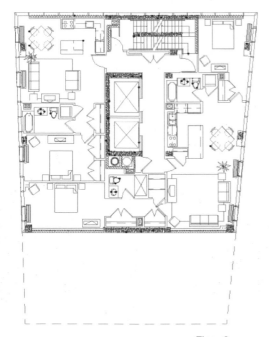

Floor 3

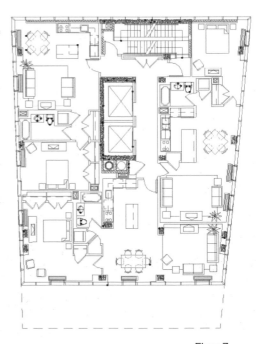

Floor 7

Plans are determined by the client's commercial advisors.

Beijing, West Diaoyutai Tower, 2004

Mixed-Use

View from the river

There are architects who think before they draw, and others who draw before they think. Both methods work. When you think before you draw, you first determine what your concept will be, then you draw it. When you draw before you think, you hope that the project will appear as you sketch along, whether or not you have a concept. (Digitally, as you let your computer-set parameters fold and unfold until you tell the design to stop.) One approach is more objective, the other more subjective.

549

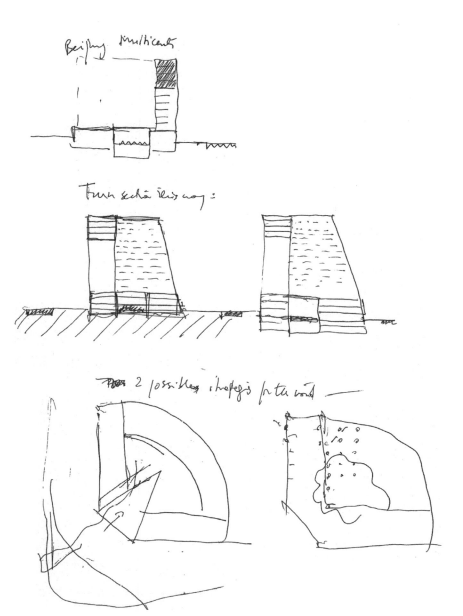

Three Programs, Three Architectural Components

Situated at a prominent bend in the Kunyu River in Beijing, China, our West Diaoyutai hotel and residential scheme features a distinct prow-like form and "liquid-bubble" facade.

We tested various options for the building's massing before settling on the prow shape, with its distinctive cut-out void. This configuration had the advantage of opening up sight lines across the site, enabling a dialogue between the city and the river. The building envelope and the organization of its interior functions were developed next. The organization of the building around a curvilinear atrium made sense because it both produced a dramatic space and allowed flexible partitioning. Considerable thought was given to the placement of the building's cores, including passenger and freight elevators, so as to allow the project's three user groups—hotel guests, apartment residents, and club users—to share some spaces easily while keeping other functions separate.

On entering the base of the building, residents and visitors encounter a triple-height atrium. The ceiling of the atrium is perforated with circular openings that reveal the bottom of the fish pond above. Sunlight filters through the water and into the atrium below. Multi-story waterfall elements also might be incorporated into the atrium. Curved handrails might feature "bubble-like" openings or be filled with water. The interaction of these light and water elements in the atrium creates an ever-changing environment for the club, hotel, and apartment users to share.

Several other amenities were designed to take advantage of the riverfront site. A swimming pool on Level 2 is enclosed in glass, affording its users a magnificent view of the river as they swim. A restaurant on Level 27 provides a dining space with views of the water below and the sky above.

Materials

The exterior skin of the tower is intended to be made out of perforated metal panels; precast or poured-in-place concrete could also be used. Where a portion of the tower has been carved away at its southeast corner, the incised, or "cut," surface is clad in a glass curtain wall so as to emphasize the unique building geometry. The base of the building can be thought of as a lush garden. It is carpeted in grass and mixed landscaping, and supported by a concealed frame.

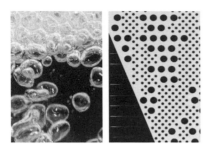

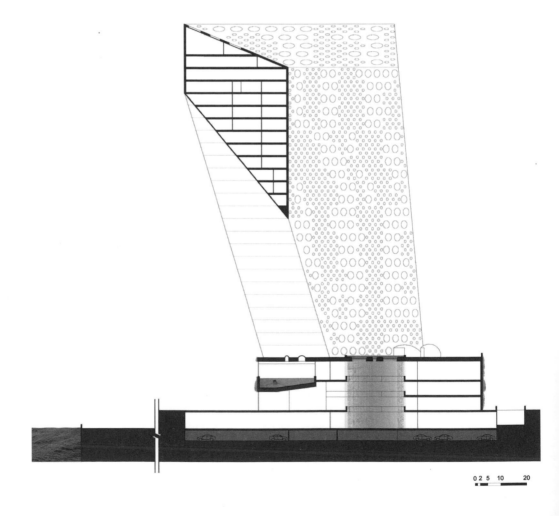

0 2 5 10   20

Programmatic section: water elements

Interior view

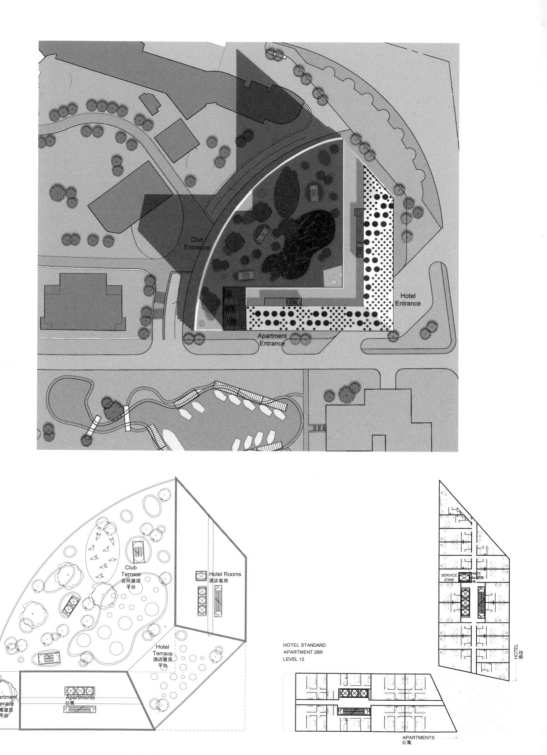

Site plan and hotel and apartment plans

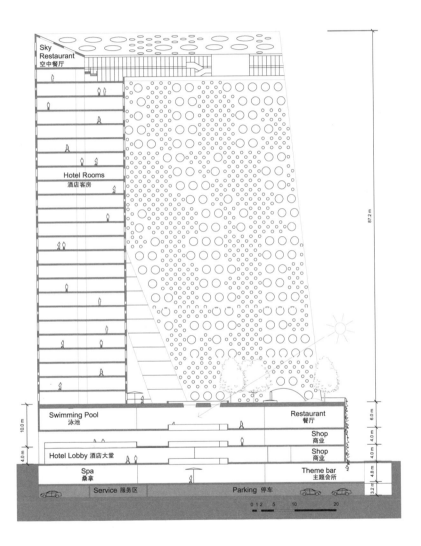

Sky
Restaurant
空中餐厅

Hotel Rooms
酒店客房

87.2 m

Swimming Pool
泳池

Restaurant
餐厅

6.0 m

10.0 m

Shop
商业

4.0 m

Hotel Lobby 酒店大堂

Shop
商业

4.0 m

4.0 m

Spa
桑拿

Theme bar
主题会所

4.8 m

Service 服务区

Parking 停车

3.2 m

0 1 2 5   10   20

Section

View from the river at night

Abu Dhabi, Housing Study, 2005

Duos

"Duos" starts from the typology of rectangular city blocks in Abu Dhabi. We first introduced the regular pattern of a screen made out of solids and voids, protecting the interiors by filtering the harsh desert sunlight in the mathematical form of a contemporary *mashrabiyya*. We then inserted chance into the precise volume of the block by carving an iconic vertical void through the building, thereby turning its rigorous geometry into a poetic challenge. The two interdependent halves created through this strategy are given different material identities: one in precast concrete, the other in shaded glass and opaque curtain wall. Shadows alternating with rays of light make each building a unique experience. The apartments are varied and flexible, and can be adapted to different client requirements.

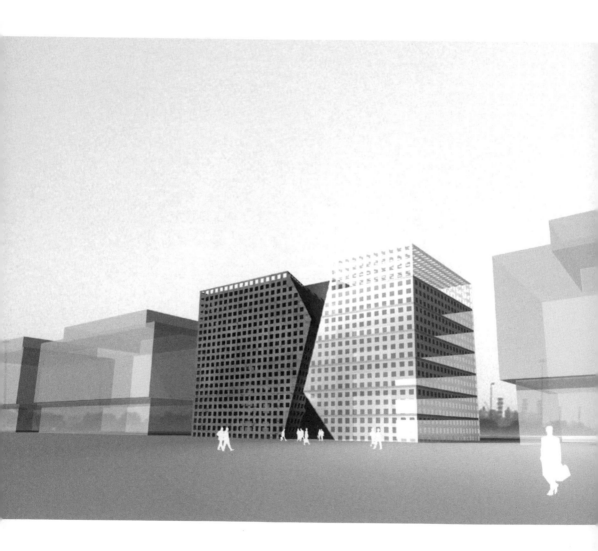

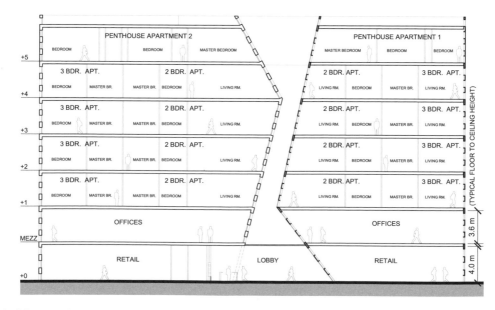

Low building: section

Low building

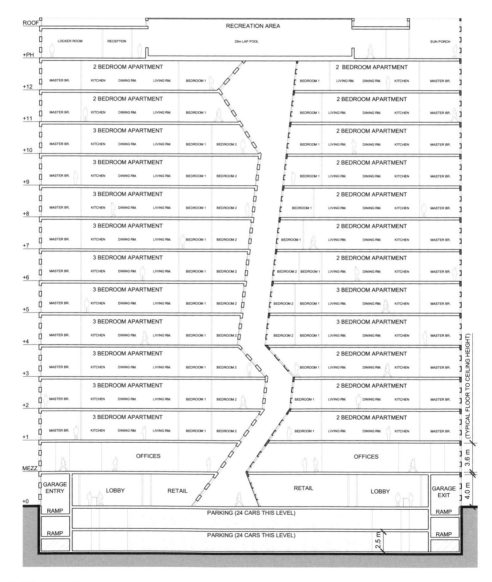

Tower building: section

Tower building

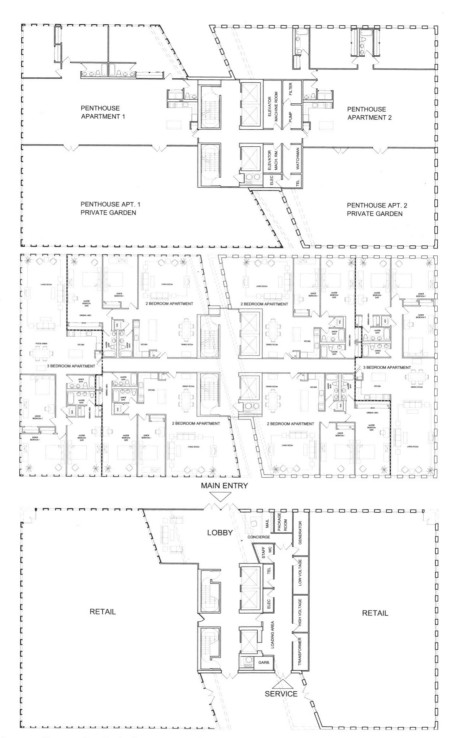

PENTHOUSE
APARTMENT 1

PENTHOUSE
APARTMENT 2

ELEVATOR
MACHINE ROOM

FILTER

PUMP

ELEVATOR
MACH. RM.

WATCHMAN

ELEC

TEL

PENTHOUSE APT. 1
PRIVATE GARDEN

PENTHOUSE APT. 2
PRIVATE GARDEN

LIVING ROOM

JUNIOR
BEDROOM 1

MASTER
BEDROOM
SUITE

2 BEDROOM APARTMENT

2 BEDROOM APARTMENT

LIVING ROOM

JUNIOR
BEDROOM 1

MASTER
BEDROOM
SUITE

MASTER
BEDROOM
SUITE

JUNIOR
BEDROOM 1

MASTER
BATH

DRESSING AREA

KITCHEN

DINING ROOM

KITCHEN

MASTER
BATH

DRESSING AREA

JUNIOR
BATH

POWDER DINING

3 BEDROOM APARTMENT

DRESSING AREA

KITCHEN

3 BEDROOM APARTMENT

MASTER
BATH

JUNIOR
BATH

KITCHEN

DINING ROOM

DINING ROOM

KITCHEN

JUNIOR
BATH

MASTER
BATH

DRESSING AREA

JUNIOR
BEDROOM 2

JUNIOR
BEDROOM 1

MASTER
BEDROOM
SUITE

2 BEDROOM APARTMENT

2 BEDROOM APARTMENT

JUNIOR
BEDROOM 1

MASTER
BEDROOM
SUITE

LIVING ROOM

LIVING ROOM

LIVING ROOM

MAIN ENTRY

LOBBY

MAIL

PACKAGE
ROOM

CONCIERGE

GENERATOR

STAFF
W/C

TEL

LOW VOLTAGE

RETAIL

ELEC

HIGH VOLTAGE

RETAIL

LOADING AREA

TRANSFORMER

GARB.

SERVICE

Low building: penthouse plan, typical apartment plan, ground-floor plan

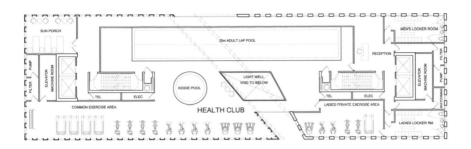

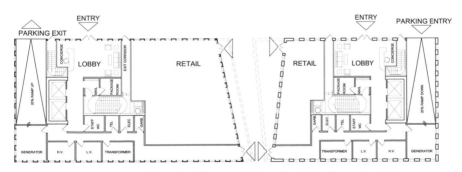

Tower building: penthouse plan, typical apartment plan, ground-floor plan

Typical apartment

Top-floor common spaces

Bordeaux-Cenon, Cultural Center, 2005-10

Black Glass Vector/Red Metal Envelope

Envelope and Vector

As a proposed generator of cultural and artistic activity located on a site overlooking the Garonne River, the Cultural Center in Palmer Park starts with a unique landscape. The facility is designed to accommodate up to 2,000 spectators and national and international touring productions.

The project's mandate was to create an extroverted architecture that opens onto the park while still deferring to the natural qualities of the site. The project needed to respect the landscaped park while simultaneously bringing a visible identity to the cultural ambitions of the city of Cenon. The pleated hulls of the cultural center's three performance volumes are sheltered by an outer shell of perforated steel. Their dimensions and geometries, while designed for the comfort of spectators and artists, also take advantage of the park topography.

Circulation vectors intersect the three large metal volumes and are identified by glass panels. These glass galleries lead the public in from the park toward the introverted performance spaces.

The interiors are designed to respond to the needs of live performance while echoing the vocabulary of the steel exterior. At night, light glows from the interior galleries and foyers. Garden patios may also be used for open-air performances. The center offers an architectural form that responds to and reflects both landscape and theater.

29-8-05

Cenon —

C'est vraiment un casse-tête, vu leurs contraints.
Effectivement l'option 5 n'est pas possible, les studios étant en
2e phase en plus. Ci-joint (page suivante), j'ai mis une option 6
qui correspond à leur organigramme de la p. 23 et suivantes.
Comme ceux-ci ont un croissant de flux malheureux, je
proposerai l'option 7 ci-dessous. Imaginez des
boîtes "à la Gehry", en différents matériaux.
                                    Bon travail.   R

(Note: la vue
aérienne est
bien utile)

OPTION
7

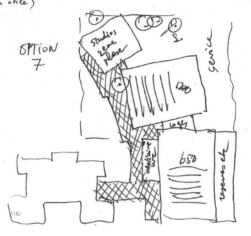

B → Véro, Antoine, Vincent, stagiaire 31 oct 05 Dans l'avion Paris N.7 —
Ci-joint qq notes pour essayer de clarifier le concept et par là-même
simplifier les décisions en cours.

C
E
N
O
N

+ diagramme
des listes
(à combiner avec
diagramme des
circulations
pages suivante)

(Je n'ai pas les plans avec moi. Tous
les diagrammes ci-joint sont
donc de principe)

carapace =
bardage tout
simple
moins angulé

seule
exception
au bardage
angulé les
boîtes : ici
la carapace "sort"
pour englober la galerie
de verre.

Trying to reconcile program requirements and site constraints

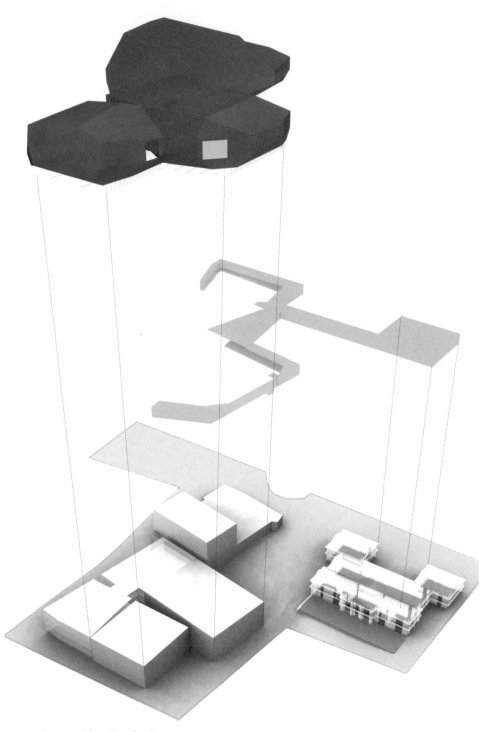

Envelopes, vectors, and functional volumes

Left: the new cultural center
Right: existing stables converted into a restaurant and conference center

A CONCEPT IN FIVE POINTS   Cenon

1. THE LARGE   2. GLASS GALLERY
PROGRAMMATIC   (PUBLIC CIRCULATION)
VOLUMES

                                            The gallery connects to the new
                                            pavilions. It seems to levitate above
                                            the park.

3. THE ENVELOPE   4. SUPPORT SPACES
(THE SHELL)

Note: The envelope follows the
outline of the new volumes exactly,
except in Point A.

5. THE ACTIVE PARK

                                            = THE PROJECT

a) cineslope
b) performance patio
c) video-terrace

BORDEAUX
581

UN CONCEPT EN CINQ POINTS. Cenon

1 LES GRANDS VOLUMES PROGRAMMATIQUES

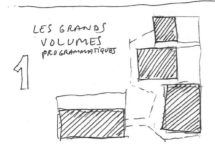

2 LA GALERIE DE VERRE (= CIRCULATIONS DU PUBLIC)

vista vers le château et le parc

La galerie de verre commence par l'auvent, traverse le vieux pavillon et enserre les nouveaux volumes. Elle semble flotter en lévitation au-dessus du parc.

on un autre nom plus écolo-culturel, comme "le camouflage" "le caméléon"

3 LA CARAPACE

A

Note: la carapace suit "exactement" les contours des nouveaux volumes sauf au point A. ("exactement" = avec 99 facettes)

4 LES ESPACES-SUPPORT

les espaces-support sont sur la voie de service

LE PARC ACTIF

5

a. - la ciné-pelouse
Sur cette pente engazonnée, on peut s'allonger les beaux soirs d'été et regarder un film projeté sur le "nez" de la carapace

b. le patio-performance.
Pour de petits spectacles en plein air mais dans un espace intime, abrité du vent.

c. la terrasse-vidéo [ou autre: à inventer]

(éventuellement, élargir l'idée en faisant une proposition quant au paysage du parc)

LE PROJET

=

BON COURAGE !

October 2005 fax

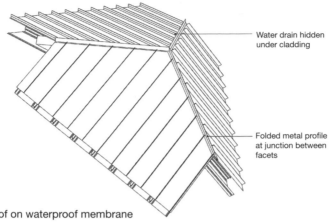

Water drain hidden
under cladding

Folded metal profile
at junction between
facets

Axonometric: metal roof on waterproof membrane

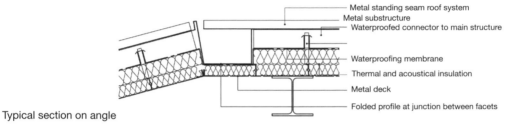

Metal standing seam roof system
Metal substructure
Waterproofed connector to main structure

Waterproofing membrane

Thermal and acoustical insulation

Metal deck

Folded profile at junction between facets

Typical section on angle

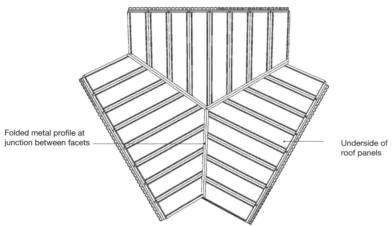

Folded metal profile at
junction between facets

Underside of
roof panels

Axonometric: principle for the underside of roof

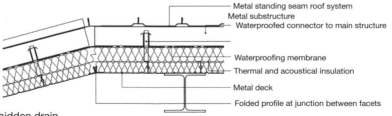

Metal standing seam roof system
Metal substructure
Waterproofed connector to main structure

Waterproofing membrane

Thermal and acoustical insulation

Metal deck

Folded profile at junction between facets

Typical section of hidden drain

Bordeaux Cahors

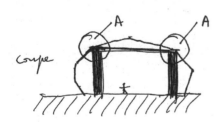

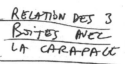

_3

_2

#1

RELATION DES 3
BOITES AVEC
LA CARAPACE.

(Laissons de côté
la galerie de verre
pour cette
question)

coupe

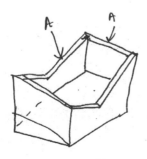

A   A

A   A

A discuter ce mercredi matin.
le point A (ou plutôt la ligne A)
est-elle une ligne "dure"
(une ligne fixe) dans le projet.
C'est à dire :
le sommet du mur
de béton fermant la salle
(chaque salle) est-il toujours
le lieu du pli de la
Carapace?
Si non, comment ferme-t-on
l'interstice entre le mur et

Merci pour les 3 planches "VUES DE HAUT"/ETUDE ENVELOPPES" 20.06.06

Remarque
l'équivalent d'une poutre agrive

① La planche "VOLUMES UTILES (et MURS PORTEURS principaux).
a encore trop de résidus de décisions subjectives sur les murs verticaux des 3 salles.
SVP: enlever le "couvecle" des salles et ne montrer que
le faîte des murs verticaux à l'endroit de la ligne
de points d'appui probables de la structure. A ce stade, cette
ligne doit correspondre exactement avec la ligne d'isolation
acoustique entre l'intérieur des salles et les foyers (ou les
                                          renflements
                                              futurs).
                                     (à revoir

Tous ces murs sont verticaux (par exemple la partie supérieure du mur por-
teur de la ligne ⑰ sur la coupe cc, en oblique, est gratuite et suspective
à ce stade du projet: remettre vertical.)
Tous ces murs sont également porteurs (béton ou métal ave placo)
jusqu'à nouvel avis. Tous ces murs sont isolants.

② LA PLANCHE "STRUCTURE" doit montrer des poutres dont la
partie supérieure est alignée sur le faîte des murs principaux:

                          ou   etc

③ LA PLANCHE "ENVELOPPES" devra sera développée par JJ
sur la base des deux planches "volumes utiles et murs porteurs" et "structure".

Excerpts from faxes regarding how the performance boxes should support the outer envelope and
not be independent, for reasons of cost and simplified acoustic insulation

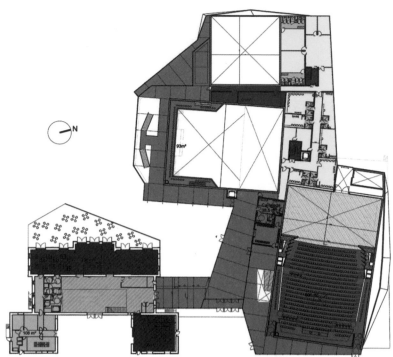

Plan, ground floor, upper level

Plan, ground floor, lower level

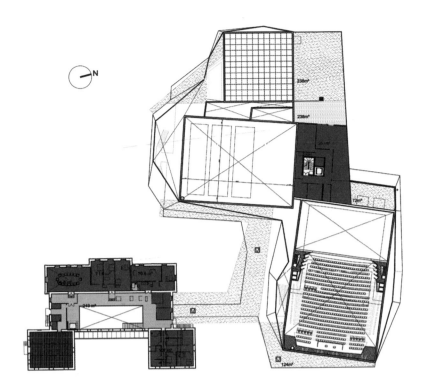

Plan L+1

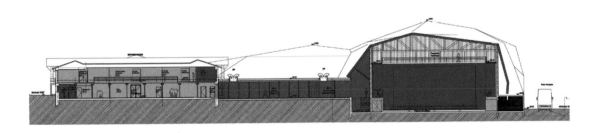

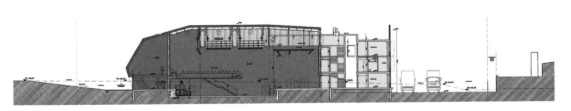

Sections

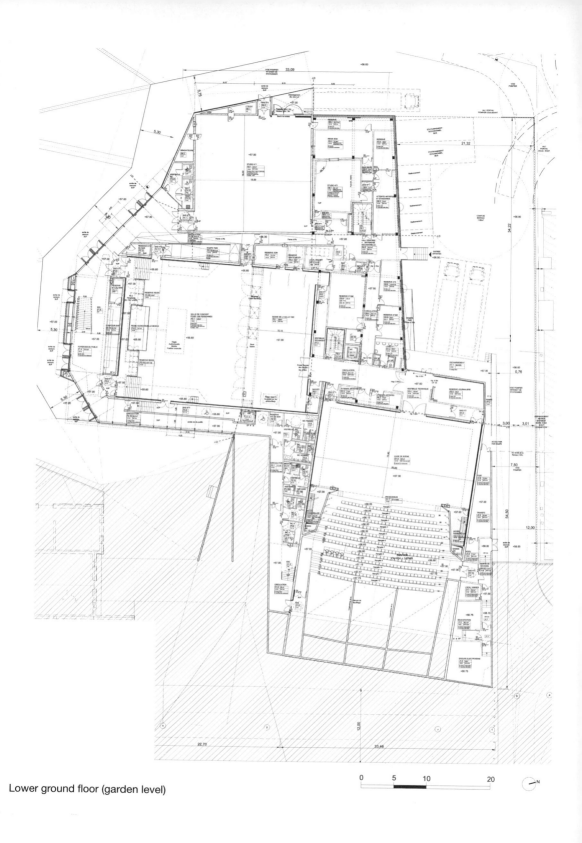

Lower ground floor (garden level)

0 5 10 20

N

Upper ground floor (entrance level)

0   5   10   20   N

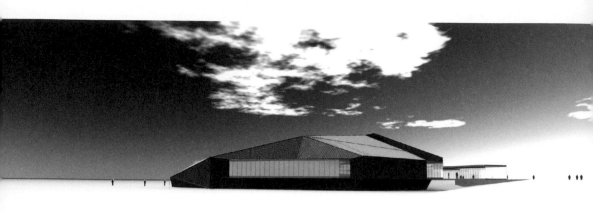

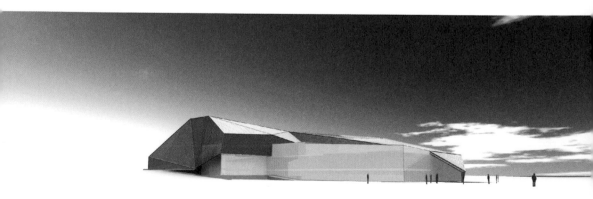

Elevations

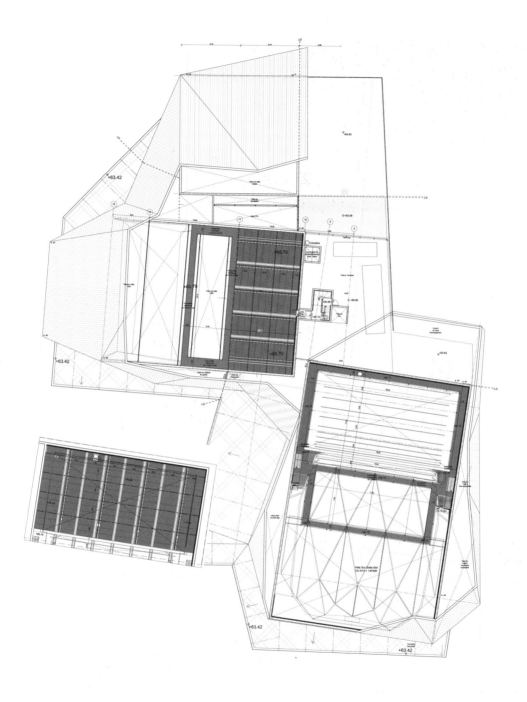

Plan R+2

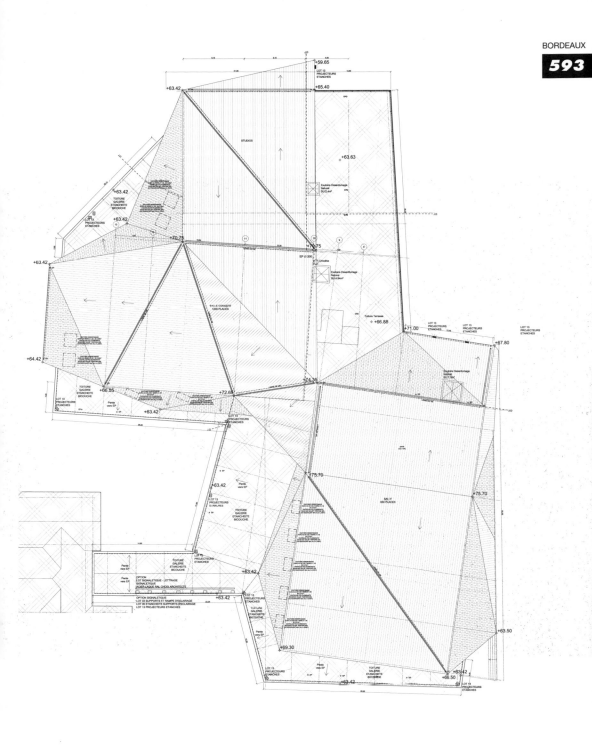

+59.65

LOT 13
PROJECTEURS
ETANCHES

+65.40

+63.42

STUDIOS

+63.63

Exutoire Desenfumage
Naturel
9U2,4m²

+63.42
TOITURE
GALERIE
ETANCHEITE
BICOUCHE

LOT 13
PROJECTEURS
ETANCHES

+63.42

+63.42

+70.75

+70.75

EP Ø 300

Grilcaline

Exutoire Desenfumage
Naturel
9U 4,94m²

+63.42

+64.42
TOITURE
GALERIE
ETANCHEITE
BICOUCHE

LOT 13
PROJECTEURS
ETANCHES

SALLE CONCERT
1200 PLACES

Toiture Terrasse
+66.88

+71.00

LOT 13
PROJECTEURS
ETANCHES

LOT 13
PROJECTEURS
ETANCHES

LOT 13
PROJECTEURS
ETANCHES

+67.80

+66.55

+74.35

Exutoire Desenfumage
Naturel
9U7,9M²

+63.42

Pente
vers EP

+75.70

+63.42

Pente
vers EP

LOT 13
PROJECTEURS
ETANCHES

+75.70

+75.70

LOT 13
PROJECTEURS
ETANCHES

TOITURE
GALERIE
ETANCHEITE
BICOUCHE

SALLE
650 PLACES

LOT 13
PROJECTEURS
ETANCHES

TOITURE
GALERIE
ETANCHEITE
BICOUCHE

+63.42

Pente
vers EP

+63.42

Pente
vers EP

OPTION
LOT SIGNALETIQUE - LETTRAGE
SIGNALETIQUE
ACIER LAQUE RAL CHOIX ARCHITECTE

OPTION SIGNALETIQUE -
LOT 03 SUPPORTS ET RAMPE D'ECLAIRAGE
LOT 05 ETANCHEITE SUPPORTS D'ECLAIRAGE
LOT 13 PROJECTEURS ETANCHES

+63.42

LOT 13
PROJECTEURS
ETANCHES

TOITURE
GALERIE
ETANCHEITE
BICOUCHE

+63.50

+69.30

Pente
vers EP

+63.42

+63.42

LOT 13
PROJECTEURS
ETANCHES

TOITURE
GALERIE
ETANCHEITE
BICOUCHE

+66.50

LOT 13
PROJECTEURS
ETANCHES

0   5   10   20   N

Roof plan

The 650-seat auditorium: The ceiling panels of the inner envelope are identical to the outer envelope, using the same perforated and folded metal planks.

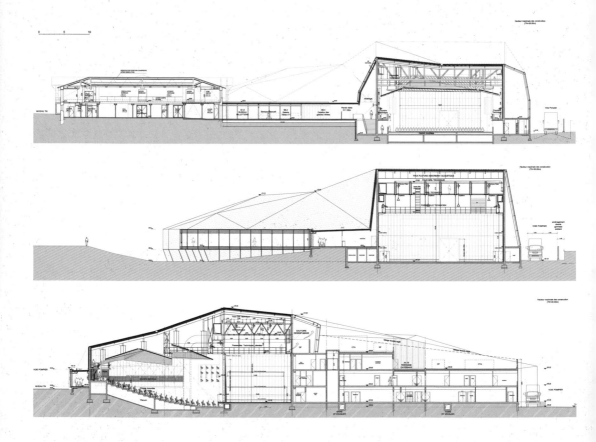

Sections

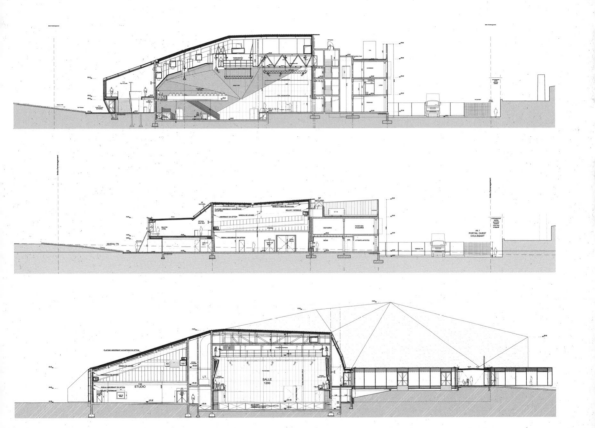

A concept-form is always a device or an empty form that awaits fulfillment. Hence it is abstract and figurative at the same time, for as soon as one fills the abstract form with the necessities of content, it inevitably becomes figurative. In other words, a concept-form is an abstract figure that precedes figuration. A concept-form begins as a dematerialized or immaterial form, but it cannot escape its subsequent materialization.

H. Filter Envelopes

The question of camouflage and envelopes has already been explored in *Event-Cities 3*. It takes on a new dimension in the renovation of the Zoo de Vincennes in Paris, since the buildings are required to serve as a near-invisible backdrop for the animals that are on display. Is this a concept-form or the ultimate dissolution of form? A formlessness of concept-form?

Paris, New Zoo de Vincennes, 2008-

Formless Filters

Toward a New Type of Zoo

As one of the oldest cage-free zoos in the world, the Paris Zoo has been a proponent of animal conservation since its opening in 1934. A majority of the more than 85 animal species housed in the zoo are considered endangered, with natural habitats that are nearing destruction. Situated in the historical Parc de Vincennes, the relatively small zoo is distinguished by nearly a century of preservation efforts aimed at safeguarding the different animals of the world in an urban environment.

Constructed mostly from artificial concrete rock (which, after 70 years, is now unsafe for habitation), the Zoo's reconstruction builds on its important conservationist inheritance in order to preserve its identity while creating a new mode of animal preservation and educational experience for the zoo's visitors.

Immersion and Camouflage

Developed by Jacqueline Osty Associates for landscape and urban design, Bernard Tschumi urbanistes Architectes (with Véronique Descharrières) for all new construction, and Synthèse Architecture (with Bernard Hemery), the project is based on a program by the National Museum of Natural History. The program is characterized by immersion and camouflage. The design concern goes beyond the decoration and mimicry of nature common to traditional zoos and moves into the requirements specific to each animal. The design priority is not to create architecture in the traditional sense of the term, but rather to engage specific mediums so as to hide, complement, or blend the buildings into a natural setting, allowing for a sense of immersion.

For each of the six "biozones," the architecture is carefully designed to achieve near-invisibility of effect. The buildings are never visible as such; they are either perceived from a distance as a singular geometry associated with the landscape, or from the interior after crossing a threshold of vegetation and nature. The new zoo will also incorporate invisibility into the barrier between the public and the animals. Enclosure will be managed as much as possible through such natural elements as cliffs, vegetation, and moats.

Several circulation paths will loop through the biozones, allowing visitors to be drawn into the natural surroundings specific to each species. Visitors will thus find themselves inside a greenhouse or an aviary, in direct contact with the animals. The circulation paths attempt to catalyze such unexpected interactions.

As a result, the zoo no longer appears as a large diorama that happens to house animals; it is intended to become an experience in itself. By placing the visitor within the realm of the animals and not the other way around, the public is called to active and attentive exploration. The experience is intended as an educational device to encourage users to learn and partake of the zoo's rich history of wildlife conservation.

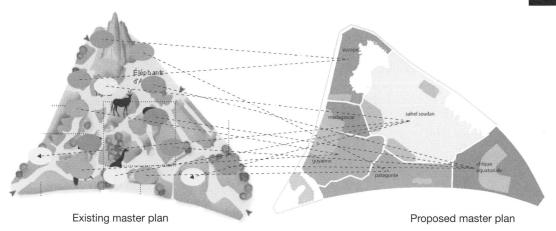

Existing master plan   Proposed master plan

Re-organization based on biozones:
The new master plan examines relocating animal habitats according to biozone as opposed to the
more dispersed, older version of zoo. (landscape by Jacqueline Osty)

Territorial textures: Europe, Guyana, Madagascar, Patagonia, Saharan Africa, Sudan

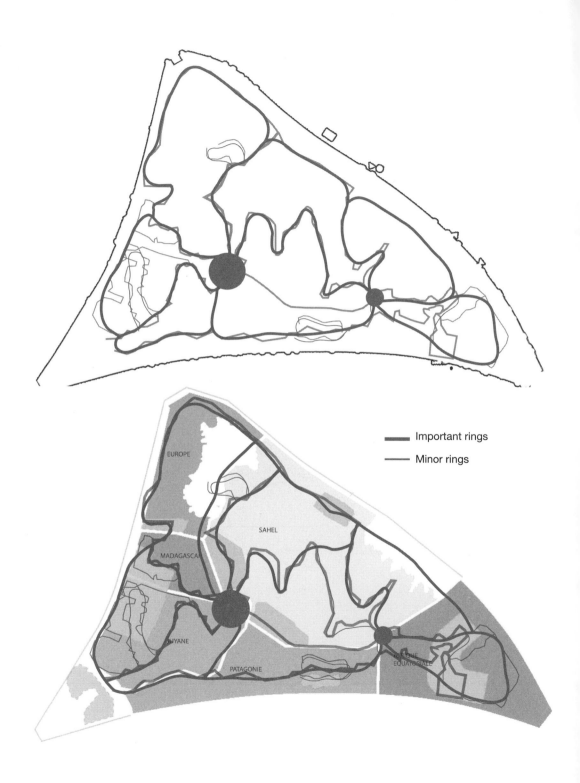

Important rings

Minor rings

EUROPE

SAHEL

MADAGASCAR

GUYANE

PATAGONIE

AFRIQUE
EQUATORIALE

Kiosks

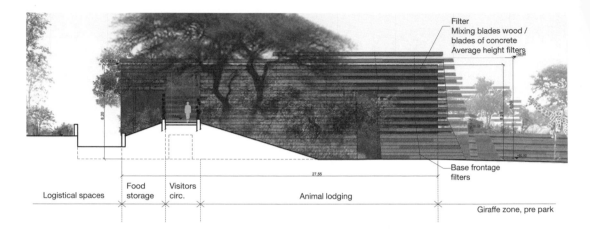

Filter
Mixing blades wood /
blades of concrete
Average height filters

27,55

Base frontage
filters

Logistical spaces	Food storage	Visitors circ.	Animal lodging

Giraffe zone, pre park

North facade, elevation

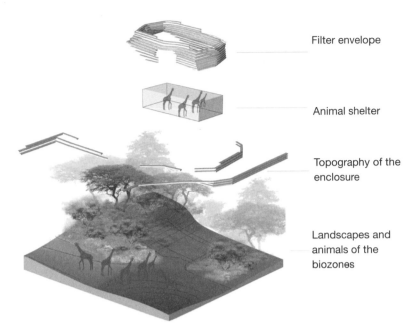

Filter envelope

Animal shelter

Topography of the enclosure

Landscapes and animals of the biozones

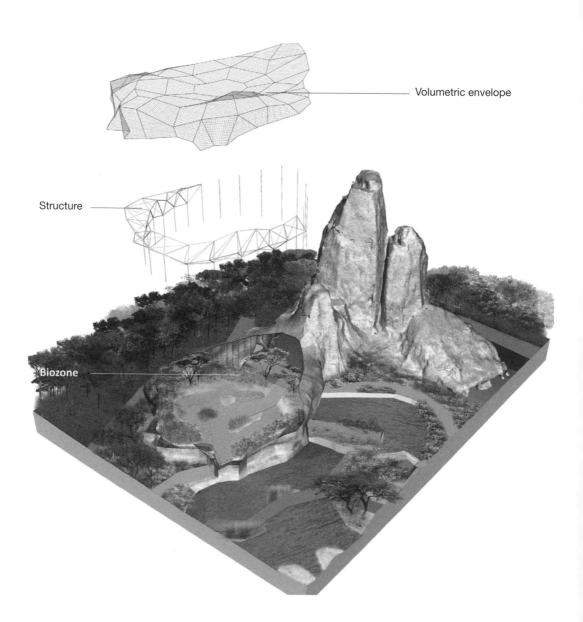

Volumetric envelope

Structure

Biozone

Installation of the envelope

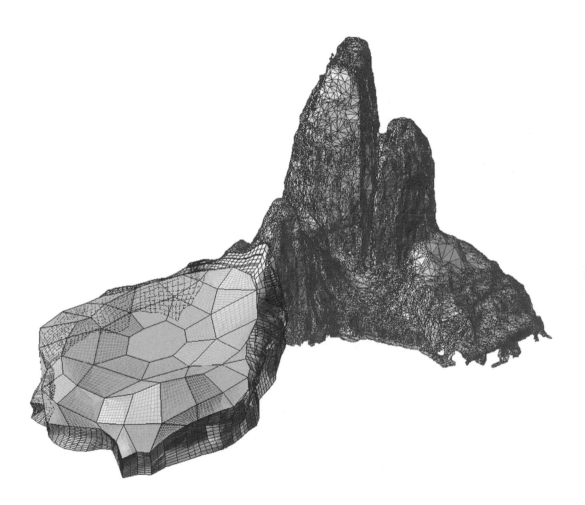

Project Teams

TypoLounger
Bernard Tschumi, Nefeli Chatzimina, Kim Starr

Dominican Republic, IFCA Master Plan (Elliptic City)
Bernard Tschumi, Kim Starr, Christopher Lee, Dominic Leong, Loren Supp, Paula Tomisaki, Angie Co, Yang Yang, Stephanie Chaltiel, Nefeli Chatzimina
Associate Architects: Carter-Burgess (Jacobs), Dallas (Cesar Vallerilla, Paul Maute, Tim Norton, Brian Adams, Emily Drake, Shea O'Kirkman)

Alésia, MuseoParc
New York: Bernard Tschumi, Joel Rutten, Kim Starr, Adam Dayem, Jane Kim, Kyungjune Min, Adrien Durrmeyer, Matthew Stofen, Paula Tomisaki, Nefeli Chatzimina
Paris: Bernard Tschumi, Véronique Descharrières, Antoine Santiard, Jean-Jacques Hubert, Rémy Cointet, Alice Dufourmantelle, Anaïs Le Brun, Sarah Gould, Agnes Winiarzska, Christina Devizzi, Adrien Del Grande
Exhibition Design: G.C. François with J.H. Manoury and Pascale Guillou; *Landscape*: Michel Desvigne with Sophie Mourthé; *Structural*: ACI; *Mechanical*: Choulet

Athens, Bank
Bernard Tschumi, Joel Rutten, Christopher Lee

Rolle, Carnal Dome
Bernard Tschumi, Kate Scott, W.Y. Frank Chen, Athanasios Manis, Ciro Miguel, Kim Starr, Colin Spoelman, John Eastridge, V. Mitch McEwen, Taylor Burgess, Alexa Tsien-Shiang

La Roche-sur-Yon, Pedestrian Bridge
Bernard Tschumi and Hugh Dutton
New York: Bernard Tschumi, Ben Edelberg, Francoise Akinosho, Kim Starr
Paris: Bernard Tschumi, Véronique Descharrières, Rémy Cointet, Vincent Prunier, Alice Dufourmantelle
Hugh Dutton Associates: Hugh Dutton, Pierluigi Bucci, Pierre Chassagne, Francesco Cingolani, Maria Angela Corsi, Pietro Demontis, Gaëtan Kohler, Cathy Shortle, Romain Stieltjes, Carla Zaccheddu
SNCF Engineering Department: Jean-Marie Garnier

Dubai, Opera Island
Bernard Tschumi, Phu Hoang, Kim Starr, Rémy Cointet, Dominic Leong, Christopher Lee, Angela Co, Yang Yang

Paris-Saclay, EDF
New York: Bernard Tschumi, Kate Scott, Joel Rutten, Christopher Lee, Nefeli Chatzimina, Paul-Arthur Heller, Colin Spoelman, Kim Starr, Taylor Burgess, V. Mitch McEwen, Ciro Miguel, W.Y. Frank Chen, Mathieu Crabouillet, John Eastridge, Alexa Tsien-Shiang
Paris: Bernard Tschumi, Véronique Descharrières, Vincent Prunier, Alice Dufourmantelle, Anaïs Le Brun
Structural and Mechanical: IOSIS (Alain Collet, Eric Pillier, Mario Figueiredo); *Environmental*: ELIOTH (Joseph Benedetti); *Landscape*: Société Forestière de la CDC

(Caroline Girardière); *Structural and Environmental*: Buro Happold (Cristobal Correa, Steven Baumgartner, Joe White); *Renderings*: Labtop

Abu Dhabi, Media Zone Master Plan and Links-Shabaka

Bernard Tschumi, Kim Starr, Kate Scott, Christopher Lee, Joel Rutten, Nefeli Chatzimina, Rémy Cointet, W.Y. Frank Chen, John Eastridge, Julien Jacquot, Athanasios Manis, Ciro Miguel, V. Mitch McEwen, Taylor Burgess, Colin Spoelman, Laurence Sarrazin, Danny Thai, Paula Tomisaki, Micheal Young, Shaikha Al Mubaraki
Structural: Buro Happold (Craig Schwitter, Cristobal Correa, Alan Harbinson, Steven Baumgartner, Dennis Burton, Robin Mosley); *Programming*: Yves Dessuant; *Renderings*: dbox

Abu Dhabi, Sheikh Zayed Museum

Bernard Tschumi, Kim Starr, Christopher Lee, Paula Tomisaki, Loren Supp, Colin Spoelman, Francoise Akinosho, Nefeli Chatzimina, Kyungjune Min, Thad Nobuhara, Sara Arfaian, Guillaume Vallotton, Micah Roufa, Sae-Hyun Kim

Busan, Cinema Complex

Bernard Tschumi, Phu Hoang, Dominic Leong, Angie Co, Yang Yang, Kim Starr, Rémy Cointet, Adam Marcus

Singapore, Master Plan

Bernard Tschumi, Kim Starr, V. Mitch McEwen, Nefeli Chatzmina, Joel Rutten, Christopher Lee, Francoise Akinosho, Taylor Burgess, Piyush Bajpai, Micheal Young, Alexa Tsien-Shiang, Rychiee Espinosa
Associate Architects: CPG Consultants PTE LTD (Kuan Chee Yung, Sora Koestoer, Lee Ping Ping)

Paris, Pavillon de l'Arsenal

Bernard Tschumi, Véronique Descharrières, Antoine Santiard, Vincent Prunier

Paris, Ile Seguin II

Bernard Tschumi, Véronique Descharrières, Antoine Pradels, Angelina Alfieri, with Hugh Dutton Associates

The Hague, Passage and Department Store

Bernard Tschumi, Joel Rutten, Christopher Lee, Athanasios Manis, Dominic Leong, Paul-Arthur Heller, Paula Tomisaki, Mathieu Crabouillet
Associate Architects: B+M Den Haag bv

Toulouse, Airbus Delivery Center

New York: Bernard Tschumi, Joel Rutten, Phu Hoang, Adam Dayem, Matthew Hufft, Kim Starr, Irene Cheng, Yang Yang, Dominic Leong, Alan Kusov
Paris: Bernard Tschumi, Véronique Descharrières, Jean-Jacques Hubert, Rémy Cointet, Antoine Santiard, Vincent Prunier

Aix, Courthouse

New York: Bernard Tschumi, Paula Tomisaki, Loren Supp, Dominic Leong, Francoise Akinosho, Thad Nobuhara

Paris: Bernard Tschumi, Véronique Descharrières, Alice Dufourmantelle, with Technip TPS

Dallas, University of Texas Student Services Center
Bernard Tschumi, Kim Starr, Joel Rutten, Christopher Lee, Francoise Akiuosho, Nefeli Chatzimina, Loren Supp, Colin Spoelman, Piyush Bajpai

Lausanne-Renens, ECAL School of Art and Design
Bernard Tschumi, Joel Rutten, Rémy Cointet, Kyungjune Min, Paula Tomisaki, Yang Yang
Associate Architects: CFSA Lausanne (Claude Fehlmann, Serge Fehlmann)

Lausanne, Interface Flon M2 Metro Station
Bernard Tschumi, Joel Rutten, Christopher Lee
Associate Architects: M + V Architectes (Luca Merlini, Emmanuel Ventura)

New York City, BLUE Residential Tower
Bernard Tschumi, Kim Starr, William Feuerman, Adam Dayem, Dominic Leong, Alan Kusov, Casey Crawmer, Shai Gross, Adam Marcus, Amy Yang, Adrien Durrmeyer
Associate Architects: SLCE (Saky Yakas, Carlos Palacios, Jerry Vanek); *Structural*: Thornton Tomasetti (Eli Gottlieb)

Beijing, West Diaoyutai Tower
Bernard Tschumi, Joel Rutten, Yang Yang, Adam Dayem, Irene Cheng, Kim Starr
Structural: Buro Happold

Abu Dhabi, Housing Study
Bernard Tschumi, Kim Starr, Adam Dayem

Bordeaux-Cenon, Cultural Center
Paris: Bernard Tschumi, Véronique Descharrières, Vincent Prunier, Antoine Santiard, Jean-Jacques Hubert, Anaïs Le Brun, Alice Dufourmantelle, Fernando Ituarte, Yann Le Drogo, Valérie Manuscan, Martial Marquet, Densi Vadakumcherry
New York: Bernard Tschumi, Loren Supp, Thad Nobuhara
Engineering: Technip TPS (Didier Delamarre); *Landscape*: Michel Desvigne with Sophie Mourthé; *Acoustics*: CIAL with J.L. Lecocq

Paris, New Zoo de Vincennes
Paris: Bernard Tschumi, Véronique Descharrières, Vincent Prunier, Rémy Cointet, Alice Dufourmantelle, Anaïs Le Brun, Yann Le Drogo, Joachim Bakary, Martial Marquet, Laurent Esmilaire, Will Fox, Pascal Lavaud, Catherine Kim, Sarah Gould
New York: Bernard Tschumi, Julien Jacquot, Micheal Young, Laurence Sarrazin, Gary He, Rychiee Espinosa, Melissa Goldman, Taylor Burgess, Nefeli Chatzimina, Francoise Akinosho, Mathieu Crabouillet, Paul-Arthur Heller, Kate Scott
Design Team: Jacqueline Osty Associates (*landscape and urbanists*); Bernard Tschumi urbanistes Architectes, with Véronique Descharrières; Synthèse Architecture with Bernard Hemery
Renderings: Labtop

Project List

2009

EDF Project, Saclay, France (*competition*)
Carnal Dome, Rolle, Switzerland (*competition: first place*)
Prince George's African American Museum, North Brentwood, Maryland
Anafolie, Paris, France (*study*)
Media Zone, Links-Shabaka, Abu Dhabi, United Arab Emirates (*competition*)

2008

Aphrodite Astir Hotel, Athens, Greece (*competition: first place*)
Parliament, Lausanne, Switzerland (*preliminary study*)
Uni-Cité, Lausanne, Switzerland (*competition*)
Media Zone, Master Plan, Abu Dhabi, United Arab Emirates
Stade Ladoumègue, Paris, France (*competition*)
Zoo Expansion, Paris, France
Student Services Center, Dallas, Texas (*study*)
TypoLounger

2007

Mediapolis, Master Plan, Singapore
MegaHall, Montpellier, France (*competition*)
Cocteau Museum, Menton, France (*competition*)
Printemps Facade, Lille, France (*study*)
Hôpital Beclère, Paris, France (*competition*)
Sheikh Zayed Museum, Abu Dhabi, United Arab Emirates (*competition*)
Courthouse, Aix, France (*competition*)
Pedestrian Bridge, La Roche-sur-Yon, France

2006

Bank, Athens, Greece (*competition: first place*)
International Architecture Biennale, Swiss Pavilion, Venice, Italy (*one-person exhibition*)
ECAL Art and Design School, Lausanne, Switzerland
Austerlitz Master Plan, Paris, France (*competition*)
Town Hall, Toulouse, France (*competition*)
Cultural Center, Bordeaux-Cenon, France (*competition: first place*)

2005

Opera Island, Dubai, United Arab Emirates (*competition*)
IFCA, Master Plan, Dominican Republic
Cinema Complex, Busan, South Korea (*competition*)
Department Store and Cultural Center, The Hague, The Netherlands
Surf City, Biarritz, France (*competition*)
Housing Study, Abu Dhabi, United Arab Emirates (*study*)
Ceramic Tiles of Italy Pavilion, Orlando, Florida

2004

Airbus Delivery Center, Toulouse, France (*study*)
Architecture Foundation Building, London, UK (*competition*)
West Diaoyutai Tower, Beijing, China (*competition: first place*)
Multi-Hall, Montbéliard, France (*competition*)
Houses, Beijing, China (*study*)
Interior, Beijing, China
Ile Seguin II, Paris, France (*competition*)
Sophia-Antipolis Campus Master Plan, Nice, France (*competition*)*
Factory 798, Beijing, China (*study*)*
BLUE Residential Tower, New York, New York
Business Center, Kansas City, Kansas (*study*)

*Project and bibliographic information prior to 2004 (and including the Sophia-Antipolis Campus Master Plan and Factory 798) are included in the first three volumes of *Event-Cities*.

Books, Catalogs, and Selected Articles by or on Bernard Tschumi

2004

Event-Cities 3: Concept vs. Context vs. Content. Cambridge, MA and London: MIT Press, 2004.

Slessor, Catherine, ed. *CA: Contemporary Architecture*. Australia: The Images Publishing Group Ltd, 2004.

2006

Tschumi on Architecture: Conversations with Enrique Walker. New York: The Monacelli Press, 2006. (With Enrique Walker)

Tschumi, Bernard. "Tschumi on Moneo." *The Architect's Newspaper* (New York), no. 9 (25 May 2005), pp. 9-10.

2008

de Bure, Gilles. *Bernard Tschumi*. Paris: Editions Norma, 2008.

2009

"Bernard Tschumi." In Jo Steffens, ed. *Unpacking My Library: Architects and Their Books*. New Haven: Yale University Press, 2009, pp. 140-159.

ECAL by Tschumi. Ecole Cantonale d'Art de Lausanne, ed. Paris: Editions Favre, 2009.

"Foreword." In Jacques Gubler, *Jean Tschumi: Architecture at Full-Scale*. New York: Skira International, 2009, p. 7.

The New Acropolis Museum. Bernard Tschumi Architects, ed. New York: Rizzoli International Publications, 2009.

Selected Criticism, Reviews, Published Interviews on Bernard Tschumi

2004

"Bernard Tschumi (Infinite Bamboo)." *CR Land* (Beijing), 31 (October 2004), p. 23.

"Cinematographic Architecture of Bernard Tschumi." *Modern House* (Moscow) no. 8 (October 2004), pp. 20-25, 220-221.

Coates, Nigel. "Wiggle Wiggle—Architecture Has a New Squiggle." *The Independent* (London), 29 February 2004, Arts Etc. section.

Fei, Qing and Gang Fu. "Interview with Bernard Tschumi." *World Architecture* (Beijing), no. 166 (April 2004), pp. 20, 36-39.

Futagawa, Yoshio. "Bernard Tschumi: Vacheron Constantin Headquarters and Watch Factory." *GA Document* (Tokyo), no. 83 (December 2004), pp. 96-107.

Hartoonian, Gevork. "Bernard Tschumi: Return of the Object." *Architecture and Ideas* (Canada), vol. IV, no. 2 (2004), pp. 24-49.

Hayes, Christa-Maria Lerm. "The City: Literary Sites as Art Spaces" in *Joyce in Art: Visual Art Inspired by James Joyce*. Dublin: The Lilliput Press, 2004, pp. 266-67.

"The New Acropolis Museum." *GA Document International* (Tokyo), no. 79 (April 2004), p. 64.

"Infinite World Architecture: Bernard Tschumi." *Archi100* (Beijing), no. 22 (July 2004), p. 56.

"Mr. Tschumi: Six Keywords." *New Real Estate* (Beijing), no. 20 (December 2003/January 2004), pp. 88-97.

Last, Nana. "Conceptualism's (Con)quests: On Reconceiving Art and Architecture." *Harvard Design Magazine* (Cambridge, MA), no.19 (Fall 2003/Winter 2004), pp. 14-21.

J.J. Barba and Spiros Papadopoulos, eds. *Metalocus* (Madrid), 15 (2004), pp. 34-37, 57.

"Tschumi in China." *Dí Magazine: Architecture and Design* (Beijing), no. 115 (December 2004), pp. 86-91.

2005

"Beijing Factory." *32BNY*, 5/6 (Winter 2005), pp. 40-43.

Bell, Jonathan. "Light Clock Works." *Wallpaper* (London), no. 77 (April 2005), p. 89.

Cabral, Nicolás. "El Concepto y el Contexto." *La Tempestad* (Mexico City), 6, no. 42 (May/June 2005), pp. 56-59.

"Derrida, allié à l'architecture." *Diagonal* (Paris), no. 167-168 (February 2005), pp. 12-13.

Futagawa, Yoshio. "Bernard Tschumi: Limoges Concert Hall." *GA Document: International 2005* (Tokyo), no. 83 (June 2005), pp. 7-10, 96-101.

Germain, Christiane. "L'homme des villes." *Maison Française* (Paris), no. 535 (April 2005), pp. 51-52.

Giordano, Maurizio. "Time that Unites Tradition and Innovation: The New Headquarters of Vacheron Constantin in Geneva." *Architettura OFX* (Milan), no. 83 (March/April 2005), pp. 94-103.

Lacayo, Richard. "Starchitecture Comes Home." *Time Style & Design*, Fall 2005, pp. 31-34.

Lefèvre, Jérôme. "Une architecture contemporaine pour Vacheron Constantin." *Archistorm* (Paris), no.12 (March/April 2005), pp. 70-77.

Maffioletti, Serena. "Contemporary Itinerary: Infrastructures." *Area* (Milan), no.79 (March/April 2005), pp. 178–91.

Magalhães, Andréa. "Architecture, Movement and Cinema." *Escala* (Buenos Aires), no.17 (March 2005), pp. 26-31.

Massarente, Alessandro. "Representation versus Participation: London Center for Architecture." *Area* (Milan), no. 79 (March/April 2005), pp. 192-93.

Molteni, Cristina. "Conventions: 'Architettura Come Evento': Bernard Tschumi." *Architettura OFX* (Milan), no. 84 (May/June 2005), pp. 44-45.

"Museum for African Art." *Architecture, Technology & Design* (Hong Kong), no. 126 (March 2005), pp. 88-91.

Orlandoni, Alessandra. "Interview with Bernard Tschumi." *The Plan* (Bologna), no. 010 (June 2005), pp. 101-06.

Paganelli, Carlo. "Double peau: In Geneva." *L'Arca International* (Paris), no. 63 (March/April 2005), pp. 20-27.

Simenc, Christian. "Un lieu, un designer: Le siège et la manufacture Vacheron Constantin par Bernard Tschumi." *Les Echos* (Paris), no. 36 (May 2005), p. 28.

Stephens, Suzanne. "Bernard Tschumi's Sleek, Curvilinear Skin Heightens the Profile of the Vacheron Constantin Headquarters and Factory Outside Geneva." *Architectural Record* (New York), 193, no. 6 (June 2005), pp. 98-105.

"Zeitzeichen: Vacheron & Constantin Zentral, Genf/CH." *DBZ Germany* (Berlin), May 2005, pp. 28-35.

2006

"Bernard Tschumi Designs Residential Tower in New York." *A+U* (Tokyo), March 2006, pp. 6-7.

de Bure, Gilles. "Le Musée de l'Acropole." *Le Journal des Arts* (Paris), no. 234 (31 March 2006).

Campbell, Katie. "Parc de la Villette." In *Icons of Twentieth-Century Landscape Design*. London: Frances Lincoln Limited Publishers, 2006, pp. 148-53.

Mack, Gerhard. "Laufstege fur den Alltag." *NZZ am Sonntag* (Zurich), 3 September 2006, p. 60.

Merkel, Jayne. "Hitting the Books: University of Cincinnati Athletics Center." *Architectural Record* (New York) Supplement (October 2006), pp. 7-14.

Ouroussoff, Nicolai. "Inside the Urban Crunch and its Global Implications: 2006 Venice Biennale." *New York Times* (New York), 14 September 2006, p. E6.

Smith, Terry. "Architecture's Unconscious: Trauma and the Contemporary Sublime at Ground Zero." In *The Architecture of Aftermath*. Chicago: University of Chicago Press, 2006, pp. 124-26, 166.

"University of Cincinnati Athletics Center." *Building Design* (Oakbrook, IL), no. 1734 (11 August 2006), p. 1

2007

Amelar, Sarah. "Lindner Athletics Center." *Architectural Record* (New York), January 2007, pp. 72-77.

"Athènes: Le nouveau museé de l'Acropole emmènage." *Archéologia* (Paris), no. 449 (November 2007), pp. 4-5.

"Bernard Tschumi Architects." *Detail IW Magazine Special Issue* (Taipei), 2008, pp. 107-12.

Bossi, Laura. "Light at the Zénith." *Domus Special Issue: Space, Light, and Architecture*, June 2007, pp. 29-31.

Brayer, Marie-Ange, Jane Alison, Frederic Migayrou, and Neil Spiller. "Bernard Tschumi." In *Future City: Experiment and Utopia in Architecture*. New York: Thames & Hudson, 2007, pp. 174-77.

Cardani, Elena. "Musica Rock Nella Foresta." *L'Arca* (Milan), no. 226 (June 2007), pp. 64-71.

Costanzo, Michele. "La Concert Hall di Limoges di Bernard Tschumi." *Metamorfosi* (Milan), no. 66 (May/June 2007), pp. 46-51.

Descombes, Mireille. "Iril: Les habits neufs de l'ECAL." *L'Hebdo* (Paris), no. 36 (5 September 2007), pp. 90-93.

"Gare Austerlitz Master Plan." *GA Document* (Tokyo), no. 97 (June 2007), pp. 66-68.

Glancey, Jonathan. "Acropolis Now." *The Guardian* (London), 3 December 2007, p. 23.

Gonchar, Joann. "A Temple to Transparency Rises in Athens." *Architectural Record* (New York), 196, no. 6 (June 2007), pp. 176-79.

Grossman, Vanessa. "Le Zénith de Limoges: Interview de Bernard Tschumi." *Archistorm* (Paris), May/June 2007, pp. 99-103.

Kennicott, Philip. "Greeks Go for All the Marbles in Effort to Get Back Artifacts." *The Washington Post* (Washington, D.C.), October 7, 2007, p. R12.

Kockelkorn, Anne. "Zénith in Limoges." *Bauwelt* (Berlin), no. 22 (June 2007), pp. 36-37.

Lacayo, Richard. "The New Acropolis Museum." *Looking Around/Time.com*, 28 October 2007. http://lookingaround.blogs.time.com/.

"Limoges Concert Hall." *Archiworld: Special 21C New Architecture, Spotlight 9 Projects* (Seoul), no. 145 (June 2007), pp. 166-75.

"Limoges Concert Hall." *Details* (South Korea), 2007, pp. 30-39.

"Limoges Concert Hall, Concept Recontextualized." *Interior Design China* (Beijing), June 2007, pp. 126-29.

"New Acropolis Museum Athens." *Blueprint* (London), no. 260 (November 2007), pp. 76-80.

Orlandoni, Alessandra. "Die 'Schule' von Miami." *Cer Magazine International* (Milan), no. 19 (Spring/Summer 2007), pp. 62-65.

Ouroussoff, Nicolai. "A Ragtag Neighborhood's Big, Blue Newcomer." *New York Times* (New York), 4 September 2007, pp. E1, E5.

Ourourssoff, Nicolai. "Where Gods Yearn for Long-Lost Treasures." *New York Times* (New York), 21 October 2007, p. AR1, pp. 32-33.

"Qu'est-ce que l'architecture aujourd'hui?" *Beaux Arts Editions*, January 2007, p. 11.

Smith Macisaac, Heather. "One for the Ages: The New Acropolis Museum Debuts Soon." *Culture+Travel* (New York), vol. 2, no. 1 (Winter 2007), pp. 26-30.

2008

Aspden, Peter. "A Manifesto for the Parthenon Marbles." *Financial Times* (London), 29 November 2008.

Beard, Mary. "Classical Comeback." *Royal Academy* (London), no. 98 (Spring 2008), p. 39.

"Blue Residential Tower." *Archiworld Korea* (Seoul), no. 152 (2008), pp. 84-93.

"Blue Residential Tower." *Details* (Seoul), no. 08 (March 2008), pp. 30-37.

Britt, Aaron. "Conversation: Bernard Tschumi." *Dwell* (San Francisco), 8, no. 7 (June 2008), pp. 128-32.

Catsaros, Christophe. "Noveau Musée de l'Acropole, Athènes." *d'Architectures* (France), no. 170 (February 2008), pp. 56-59.

Coen, Lorette. "Bernard Tschumi, Constructeur du movement." *PME Magazine/Le Temps* (Geneva) Succès! Supplement, April 2008, pp. 4-11.

Cook, Peter. "Drawing and Motive: Communicating with Clarity." In *Drawing: The Motive Force of Architecture*. Great Britain: John Wiley & Sons Ltd., 2008, pp. 23-27, 36-40.

"Elliptic City, Santo Domingo." *Bauwelt* (Berlin), 180, no. 48 (December 2008), pp. 42-45.

Gage, Eleni. "New Acropolis Museum." *Travel+Leisure* (New York), November 2008.

"Hitting a High Note." *Plan Magazine* (Dublin), June 2008, pp. 67-71.

Hodson, Mark. "The New Greek Acropolis Museum." *The Times* (London), 6 July 2008.

Jodidio, Philip. "Zenith Concert Hall: Limoges, France." *Architectural Record* (New York) 196, no. 1 (January 2008), pp. 120-24.

"Konzerthalle mit Variationen: Konzerthalle in Limoges." *DBZ Germany* (Gutensloh), May 2008, pp. 60-64.

Krohn, Carsten. "Architektur ist die Materialisierung eines Konzepts" and "Architektonische Paradoxie." *Neue Zürcher Zeitung* (Zurich), 16 August 2008.

Levine, Edward. "Urban Digs: Interview with Bernard Tschumi." *The New York Times Magazine* (New York), 8 June 2008, pp. 42-44.

McKeough, Tim. "Deconstructing Tschumi." *Azure* (Toronto), July/August 2008, pp. 82-87.

"Mekka der Meisterarchitekte." *Bilanz* (Zurich), no. 14 (2008), pp. 76-83.

Mrduljas, Maroje. "Interview with Bernard Tschumi: Architecture is Not the Knowledge of Form but the Form of Knowledge." *Oris* (Zagreb), no. 48 (2008), pp. 52-73.

"The New Acropolis Museum." *Concept* (Seoul), no. 110 (June 2008), pp. 74-77.

Orlandoni, Alessandra. "Interview with Bernard Tschumi." *Cer Magazine* (Italy), 21, no. 1784 (June 2008), pp. 22-25.

Phillips, Stephen. "Bernard Tschumi's New Acropolis Museum." *Building Design* (London), 12 December 2008. http://bdonline.co.uk/.

Puglisi, Luigi Prestinenza. "After Deconstructivism 1988-92." In *New Directions in Contemporary Architecture*. England: John Wiley & Sons Ltd., 2008, p. 12.

Stathaki, Ellie. "Bernard Tschumi Q&A Exclusive." *Wallpaper* (London), 8 August 2008.

"Superimposition of Points, Lines and Surfaces: A Park for the 21st Century." *In Landscapes of the Imagination*, Erik de Jong et al, eds. Rotterdam: NAi Uitgevers, 2008, pp. 128-35.

Timm, Tobias. "Antike im Glaskasten." *Die Zeit* (Hamburg), *KulturSommer* Supplement, April 2008.

"Two Pieces of Jade." *A+A: Architecture and Art* (Beijing), 4, no. 28 (2008), pp. 14-19.

2009

Baker, Kenneth. "In Athens, A Museum Fit for the Gods." *The San Francisco Chronicle* (San Francisco), 9 August 2009, p. Q17.

"Bernard Tschumi Architects: Blue." *A+U* (Tokyo), no. 467 (July 2009), pp. 52-57.

Bors, Chris. "New Acropolis Museum Worth the Wait." *ArtInfo*, 23 June 2009. http://www.artinfo.com/.

Callocchia, Arianna. "New Acropolis Museum: Una Promenade Attraverso il Tempo." *OfArch* (Milan), 19 May 2009, pp. 2-9.

Carassava, Anthee. "In Athens, Museum is an Olympian Feat." *New York Times* (New York), 19 June 2009, p. C1.

"Demütig und Arrogant." *Der Spiegel* (Hamburg), no. 25 (16 June 2009), p. 26.

Dillon, David. "Tschumi-Designed Acropolis Museum Opens." *Architectural Record* (New York), 197, no. 6 (June 2009).

Edelmann, Frédéric. "L'allure de Manhattan redessinée par une série d'édifices novateurs." *Le Monde* (Paris), 18 January 2009, p. 23.

Edelmann, Frédéric. "Le Musée de l'Acropole, bouleversant et maudit." *Le Monde* (Paris), 20 June 2009, p. 25.

"Elliptic City: International Financial Centre of the Americas," *GA Document* (Tokyo), 108, (June 2009), pp. 80-83.

Emerling, Susan. "Is Greece Losing its Elgin Marbles?" *Foreign Policy* (Washington D.C.), 21 August 2009. http://www.foreignpolicy.com/.

Fernández Cendón, Sara. "The New Acropolis Museum: The Parthenon Gets a Bold New Neighbor." *AIArchitect*, 15 May 2009. http://info.aia.org/.

Ferrari, Antonio. "Apre il Super Museo dell'Acropoli." *Corriere della Sera* (Milan), 20 June 2009, p. 17.

Filler, Martin. "Grading the New Acropolis." *New York Review of Books* (New York), 56, no. 14 (24 September 2009), pp. 53-56.

Gage, Eleni. "If We Ask Nicely, Can We Have Our Marbles Back?" *The Huffington Post*, 22 June 2009. http://www.huffingtonpost.com/.

Giarlis, Alexander. "Alexander Giarlis Enjoys Bernard Tschumi's New Acropolis Museum." *Architecture Today* (London), 1 July 2009, pp. 16-25.

Guislain, Margot. "Un Bâtiment en offrande au Parténon d'Athènes." *Le Moniteur* (Paris), no. 5516 (14 August 2009), pp. 32-35.

Hitchens, Christopher. "A Home for the Marbles." *New York Times* (New York), 19 June 2009, Opinion Section C1.

Hitchens, Christopher. "The Lovely Bones." *Vanity Fair* (New York), no. 587 (July 2009), pp. 44-47.

Hollenstein, Roman. "Ein Parthenon aus Stahl und Glas" *Neue Zürcher Zeitung* (Zurich), no.139 (23 June 2009), p. 13.

Hope, Kerin. "Acropolis Now." *Financial Times* (London), 18 April 2009.

Hume, Christopher. "Modernity Enhances Antiquity." *The Toronto Star* (Toronto), 11 July 2009.

Kilston, Lyra. "Modern Ruins." *Modern Painters* (New York), vol. XXI, no. 5 (Summer 2009), pp. 28-29.

Kimmelman, Michael. "Elgin Marble Argument in a New Light." *New York Times* (New York), 24 June 2009, pp. C1, C7.

Kimmelman, Michael. "Light, Air, and Old Issues at the Acropolis." *The International Herald Tribune* (Paris), 24 June 2009, p. 1.

Knapp, Gottfried. "Die Tochter des Parthenontempels." *Süddeutsche Zeitung* (Munich), 20 June 2009.

Kreykenbohm, Susanne. "Akropolis Museum: Im Historischen Kontext Gebaut." *DBZ Deutsche BauZeitschrift* (Gütersloh), July 2009, pp. 18-25.

Lüscher, Genviève. "Auf Augenhöhe mit der Antike." *Neue Zürcher Zeitung* (Zurich), 28 June 2009, p. 46.

McGuigan, Cathleen. "Romancing the Stones." *Newsweek* (New York), 15 June 2009, pp. 62-63.

"Milestones." *The Economist* (London), 391, no. 8637 (27 June 2009), Books And Arts Section, pp. 15, 89.

Moore, Rowan. "Now Let's Return the Elgin Marbles." *London Evening Standard* (London), 24 June 2009. http://www.thisislondon.co.uk/.

Morel, Guillaume. "L'Acropole s'offre un nouveau musée." *Connaissance Des Arts* (Paris), no. 674 (September 2009), pp. 106-111.

Moss, Stephen. "Our Goal is to Have the Best Museum in the World." *The Guardian* (London), 16 June 2009, G2, p. 6.

"Μουσείο Ακρόπολης." *Kathimerini* (Athens) Magazine Supplement no. 321 (July 26, 2009).

"New Acropolis Museum," *Bauwelt* (Berlin), no. 32-33 (August 2009), pp. 13-39.

"New Acropolis Museum, Athens Greece." *IW Magazine* (Taiwan), no. 68 (July 2009), pp. 52-59.

"New Acropolis Museum by Bernard Tschumi Architects." *Dezeen*, 10 April 2009. http://www.dezeen.com/.

Pearman, Hugh. "New Athens Museum Needs Parthenon Sculptures." *The Sunday Times* (London), 28 June 2009. http://entertainment.timesonline.co.uk/.

Petrakis, Maria. "Return Elgin Marbles, Says Acropolis Museum Creator: Interview." *Bloomberg*, 27 May 2009. http://www.bloomberg.com/.

Pirovolakis, Christine. "A New Way to See Ancient Athens." *The Wall Street Journal* (New York), 12 June 2009. http://online.wsj.com/.

Ryan, Raymund. "Letter From America." *The Plan* (Milan), no. 036 (September 2009), pp. 2-16.

Stephens, Suzanne. "New Acropolis Museum." *Architectural Record* (New York), 197, no. 10 (October 2009), pp. 76-83.

Stewart, Dan. "A Hard Act to Follow: The New Acropolis." *Building* (London), 12 June 2009.

Soares, Claire. "Acropolis Now! A Museum for the Elgin Marbles." *The Independent* (London), 20 June 2009, pp. 28-29.

Verdan, Nicolas. "Tschumi offre à la Gréce un écrin pour ses trésors de l'Acropole." *24 Heures* (Switzerland), 18 June 2009.

Vidal-Naquet, Maud. "Athènes belle d'été." *Le Figaro* (Paris), 20 June 2009, pp. 80-86.

Wise, Michael. "Acropolis Now." *Architect Magazine* (Washington, D.C.), 98, no. 9 (September 2009), pp. 48-51.

Photography Credits

All images are courtesy of Bernard Tschumi Architects, with the following exceptions:

p. 29 Contemporary Arts Center **p. 35** Cefinte **p. 98-99/140-141/198-199/224-225/332-333/360-361/374-375/432-433/444-445/456-457/474-475/494-495/516-517/542-543/572-573/608-609** Google Earth **p. 102** René Goguey/MuséoParc Alésia **p. 176-177/178-179/180/182-183** Hugh Dutton Associates **p. 226-227/231/234/240-241/246-247/249** Labtop **p. 258-259/329** twofour54 **p. 274/276/278/280-281/284/286-287/328** dbox **p. 382-383** CPG Consultants PTE LTD **p. 414** Your Captain Luchtfotografie/Multi Corporation **p. 480-481** Maurice Schobinger/ECAL **p. 482-483/487b** ECAL **p. 486b/490-491/508/510-511/512/514/527/535/536/538-539/540-541** Peter Mauss/ESTO **p. 526** Albert Vecerka/ESTO **p. 612-613/618-619/622-623** Artefactory